Reviews

Xavier Herbert in The National Times. [1]

The eminent Australian literary figure Xavier Herbert wrote of *Massacres to Mining*: 'She handles her history with a restraint that makes it a work deserving to be established as a classic in our history. The effect on myself was profound. I who thought I knew "all about it" was appalled ... it should be required reading.'

'In all my long literary career, I have written only one piece of this kind, and that under pressure from two strong-minded literary ladies of the past, Dymphna Cusak and Miles Franklin, authors of *Pioneers on Parade*. So why then am I acceding to this request?

'The answer is: if I squibbed it, I should be as guilty as most of the rest of my countrymen in their disregard of the monstrous wrong done, and still being done after nearly 200 years, to the people who were so ruthlessly dispossessed of this country we glibly lay claim to as our nation, our native land.

'In fact I should far more guilty than others ... I was born in the Murchison district of Western Australia, where the evil done the Aborigines was as bad as anywhere on this we dare to call The Lucky Continent, because here they fought the invaders as fiercely as anywhere, their need to resist compounded by the knowledge that existence in their desert homeland was too tenuous to allow of invasion of any sort, let alone that of the Murchison gold rush of the late 1990s...

'Despite their greed, the all-abiding primary need of the invaders was water. The Aborigines' need of the same resource was such that use of it was an essential part of the culture by which they had lived satisfactorily in that seeming waste for time beyond reckoning except in rocks, the rare sources of it, the *gnamas* regarded by them rather as shrines than the mere wells the Whiteman considered them.

'As a child I heard my elders chuckling over how the invading bravos located the *gnamas*. As no male "nigger" or "buck," so-called, could be made to betray the secrets, the prospectors captured women or children and fed them salt until they became mad with thirst. But it was probably untrue. Aboriginal women and children lacked fortitude no less than did their menfolk. Our forbearers were great liars. Most of our traditions are based on lies. - the greatest of them being that written into our Constitution, which states this continent was ownerless when annexed in the name of the English Crown...

'As a child I myself went in fear of the blacks, wretched beaten creatures as were those I had first contact with ... an uncle of mine was supposed to have been killed by them. The fear served me well when in maturity I went into remoter parts where the people were still living as of old, turning, as it did, to respect as I came to understand they were as human as myself, which was the true way of the country itself – a damned sight more intelligent...

'But I am not here to tell my own tale. I've written what foregoes because in my deep shame I could not help it. My task is to commend Massacres to Mining as the most telling exposure of the evil ever done, and still being done, to the Aboriginal natives of this so-called Australia.'

Melbourne Herald

'To get her facts Miss Roberts picked up her swag and went to see it for herself all over the most rugged parts of Australia, sitting down with the Aboriginal elders and listening to their stories. 'I have been with people who see the countryside as their Bible,' she says, 'as they showed me around, it was like walking through a medicine cabinet or a cookery book – every tree, every shrub has its use as a medicine or in cooking. It is a fascinating land.'

'And she tells of seeing the whitened bones of Aborigines slaughtered by police earlier in the 20th century so that cattlemen could take the land, the theft of sacred objects by prospectors and the bulldozing of burial grounds.'

Alice Springs Star

'Jan Roberts does not look like the sort of woman you'd find sitting in the bush having a feed of goanna or a file snake for that matter. The only indication that the British-born sociologist showed that she roughs it was a mass of mosquito bites on her legs. For the rest she was pretty much haute courture. Jan is the author of *Massacres to Mining: the Colonization of Aboriginal Australia*,' an extensively documented work on white oppression and degradation of Aborigines, and the destruction of their lands. Her book has already inspired the Granada film *Strangers in their Own Land*.'

Northern Territory News.

'A softly spoken woman of surprisingly strong character, educated at the London School of Economics, Jan Roberts says: 'Most white people remain ignorant of what was done to Aboriginal people.' She quotes Aboriginal spokesman Mr. Galarrwuy Yunupingu: "My land is my foundation. Without land we will be the lowest people in the world because you have broken down our backbone, took away my arts, history and foundation. My people don't want to be like you.' She nevertheless insisted: 'This is not an anti-mining book. There is I am convinced, a way forward based on mutual respect and justice.'

---

[1] Xavier Herbert is the Australian equivalent to Tolstoy. His epic novel 'Poor Fellow My Country' depicted life in the Outback brilliantly – at least in my poor opinion. That is why I dared to ask him for a review. It appeared in *The National Times* of May 2nd, 1982

Other Works of Janine Roberts

Jack of Cape Grim   (New edition 2008)

'The book is an extensively researched account of five Tasmanian Aborigines who declared war on settlers on the outskirts of Melbourne in 1841. ... The story of Jack is dramatic ... well researched'. Guy Parsons.. 'The story of a 'natural leader of the Aborigines' based on a "treasure trove" of material – letters, journals and official records.' The Age; a review entitled 'Barbarous spectacles that Melbourne forgot.'

'There is not much we don't know about Truganini, that comely and diminutive Tasmanian. Historians have found delight in her. Most artists of the early colony painted her portrait. Less well known ... is that she and four other Tasmanians went on a lawless campaign that would rival Ned Kelly's... they took off to join their fellows who were at constant warfare with the white invaders.' 'Jan Roberts has written probably the fullest account of this.' Noel Shaw.

The Mapoon Books, a trilogy edited and co-authored by Jan Roberts, about an Aboriginal community, the attitudes of the church and state towards them and the community's hard-fought campaign to regain their much loved hunting lands from which they had been removed in chains in the 1960s, with their lands given to mining companies. The publication of these books helped finance the successful Aboriginal return to their land. This work was reviewed by an eminent Australian historian, Humphrey McQueen, as 'the finest, best researched and through study to appear in the Whitlam era.' The authors had full access to the records of the Presbyterian Church mission and its first name correspondence with mining company executives and state government officials, and were greatly helped by the memories of the Mapoon Aborigines.

Munda Nyuringu: he has taken our land, he believes it is his, he won't give it back, a film the author co-produced with Aboriginal spokesman Robert Bropho. It tells in Aboriginal words the story of the West Australian Gold Rush and its devastation of the local Aboriginal peoples. It won an unanimous AFI Best Documentary Nomination. Bropho said: 'What happened to the Aborigines here was a microcosm of what happened all over Australia.' The author's role was reviewed in The Age under the headline 'Irish eyes bring Australia's dispossessed into sharp focus.' It was the film of the week in the Sydney Morning Herald – and is now available again.

Glitter and Greed: *The Secret World of the Diamond Cartel*   This investigative work is the result of years spent travelling the world, working with Canadian First Nations, with Indians and with Africans, in Israel, Russia, Japan, Namibia and South Africa, researching the international diamond cartel's operations, including by obtaining formerly secret USA government papers that detailed how Hitler was supplied with vital industrial diamonds that prolonged the war and how the USA was rationed, how the dictator Mobutu was funded secretly, and how uranium was hidden in diamond shipments. It also reveals how the cartel tried to manipulate the ANC South African government and the role played by diamonds in many secret service operations. The literary editor of *The Independent* in the UK reported called this resulting book 'the product of hair-raising research,' 'enthralling', 'formidably well-researched' and a 'gripping book for once merits that tarnished plaudit "brilliant." He concluded: 'One of the most damning exposes of a near-monopolistic industry to appear in years. The wonder is that it appeared at all.'

The Diamond Empire   Written and produced by the author, this film was shot in six continents and is perhaps the most international investigative films ever made. It reveals many human rights violations in the diamond trade and inspired the Conflict Diamond campaign. It was made for the BBC, WGBH Boston and the ABC (Australia). US Congresswoman Cynthia McKinney invited her to testify and show this at Congress, saying of her: *'Janine Roberts is that rare individual who unflinchingly speaks truth to power. She battles her way through all obstacles and provides us with a glimpse of those who are in the innermost circles of global power. ... I count myself among the privileged of this world to know Janine and her work.'*

The Seven Days of my Creation   She has also written, under her family name of 'Farrell-Roberts,' an entertaining and honest memoire that describes, among other things, how her life was enriched by the 15 years she working with Aborigines, and a spiritual journey that took her to explore the foundations of Western spirituality.' 'Robust scholarship runs throughout this passionate and honest autobiography... Hers is a strong voice that both challenges and touches the heart.' 'Fascinating, and inspirational – and a must read.'
\

Fear of the Invisible   Coming out in 2008– this is a major investigation of the pharmaceutical industry that draws on inside-industry sources to reveal the carelessness and poor science that undermines the safety of vaccines and anti-viral medications, including those given against AIDS. It looks at the nature of the poliovirus, the measles virus and considers just how did HIV come to exist. It raises major questions about many famous virology experiments. Finally she shows how cutting-edge modern biology is revolutionising our view of the relationship between the cell and the virus, challenging many established views in virology, (This book developed out of a Channel 4 Dispatches program '*Monkey Business'* that she co-produced with Rosie Thomas.)

For information on how to obtain copies of her works, please contact the author on jan@janineroberts.com or go to www.janineroberts.com

MASSACRES To MINING

The Colonisation of Aboriginal Australia

Jan Roberts

IMPACT INVESTIGATIVE MEDIA PRODUCTIONS

Designed by Brian Seddon
Original Typesetting by Dove Communications

This edition is published by
Impact Investigative Media Productions
Leonid, Bristol Marina,
Hanover Place, Bristol BS1 6UH
UK.

Acknowledgements. We are gratefully for the financial assistance of the
World Council of Churches in putting out this new edition on the
recommendation of Mick Dodson, Aboriginal Spokesman and Professor.

We have attempted to trace the source of all copyright material used and
credit it accordingly. We thank the following cartoonists and publishers:
Akwesasne Notes, Mohawk Nation Newspaper USA (p 142); Cook and the
National Times (pp 14, 84); Homer and the Age (p152); Kimberley Land
Council News (pp. 58, 59, 66); Mitchell and the North Queensland Message
Stick (p 108) Nicholson and the Age (pp.57, 79, 168); Parker & Hard and Field
Enterprises Inc. (p 161); Petty and the Age (pp. 11, 77, 138, 184); Tandberg
and the Age (pp. 135, 191); Tanner and the Age (p 49).

Contact: investigate@janineroberts.plus.com

Website: www.janineroberts.com

ISBN 978-0-9559177-1-4

Cataloguing-in-Publication entry:

Roberts J. Pl (Janine Patricia)
          Massacres to Mining: The Colonisation of Aboriginal Australia.
          International Edition

          Previous editions
          Dove Communications, Blackburn, Vic. Australia, 1981
          (Former ISBN 0 85924 171 8.)
          London Edition: CIMRA and War on Want, 1978.
          Includes index.

                    1.   Aborigines, Australian – Treatment
                    2.   History, Australia
                    3.   History, mining industry

Foreword for the 2008 Edition

This book grew out of the author's involvement in the continuing Aboriginal fight for their lands, with its first edition launched in the UK and Holland in 1979 by an Aboriginal delegation from Northern Queensland that came to ask RTZ and Shell to respect their rights to the lands that their people still occupied and used.

They came with the story of how they defeated the Dutch when they first arrived – an oral history that is still recounted in detail by Aboriginal 'bards' yet it happened in 1606. They also announced that they intended to defeat Shell. Their campaign in Holland was so successful that, astonishingly, Shell promised the delegation before TV cameras to leave the 580 square miles of monsoon forest they had planned to strip mine for bauxite at Aurukun in northern Queensland, not far from the remains of the houses and well of the old Dutch settlement.

But RTZ responded very differently. Lord Shackleton, its Deputy Chairman, insisted during a three-hour meeting at their headquarters that the morality of Australian laws was solely a matter for Australians. He insisted that RTZ had an obligation to use the law as it stood to benefit their shareholders, no matter if it robbed Aboriginal people. The Queensland Government had given his company a 1,000 square mile mining lease over much of the largest Aboriginal Reserve in Eastern Australia, despite this forested land still being hunted and gathered by Aboriginal people.

The first Australian edition of this book was launched in 1981 in front of RTZ's Melbourne skyscraper, but the doors were barred to the publisher, the author and an Aboriginal delegation when they jointly tried to present the book to the company. The journalists present were given a note by RTZ warning that, if they covered the book launch, legal action might result. We could not have paid for the resulting publicity. Full-page favourable reviews appeared in major papers as well as major pieces on the ABC – and no legal action ensued.

Following this, the author worked on films on Aboriginal issues for the BBC and ABC, and co-produced with Aboriginal Elder Robert Bropho the 1985 AFI Best Documentary Nominated film *'Munda Nyuringu: they have taken our land, they believe it is theirs, they won't give it back,'* probably the first film to tell of 'the stolen generation, the issue for which an Australian Prime Minister would apologize in 2008. We interviewed Aboriginal people seized from their parents since, 'as they had some white blood they were capable of education.' The 'Full-Bloods' were abandoned without government provision of education.

In 1989 the author began work on her film *"The Diamond Empire'* on how the diamond industry was engaged in world-wide exploitation. This project had its genesis in the Kimberly of NW Australia after RTZ declared it intended to take over the ancient 'Barramundi' sacred ritual site of Aboriginal women at Argyle, since the company wanted the diamonds that lay underneath. The author was smuggled into this by Aboriginal elders to show her the beauty of what was about to be destroyed. She was, in the mid-1980s, the mining officer of the National Federation of Aboriginal Land Councils.

But at that time she was optimistic that things were about to improve. Anthropologists supported the claims of the Aborigines at the Argyle diamond site. The Pitjantjatjara regained several thousand square miles in Central Australia and it felt as if the Aboriginal people were starting to walk taller and with more confidence. Many communities were leaving mission stations to live in the bush in 'outstations' to teach their children their traditional survival knowledge. However poverty persisted for most. They still lived on average twenty years less than Whites. (A 2008 survey of 4,000 Aboriginal houses found only one third had the facilities needed to wash a child.)

In 1990 the author began work on blood diamond issues. She travelled to the Canadian Arctic to work with communities threatened by diamond mining on their caribou rutting grounds. In South Africa and Namibia De Beers banned her from diamond mines, but the African workers smuggled her into them – and showed her film within them. In New York the top diamond cutter William Goldberg told how he was pressured not to be in her film. 'They phoned me and said you worked with Australian Aborigines and made life difficult for mining companies.' He still agreed to an interview, but afterwards found his diamond supplies severely restricted.

Meanwhile resentment built up in Australia against Aboriginal victories in the courts. Professor Larissa Behrendt of the University of Technology in Sydney reported: 'Prime Minister John Howard won power in 1996 in part on a platform to claw back the native title rights recognized by the Australian High Court in 1992; in part on a platform that was xenophobic and anti-immigrant.' She added: 'Howard had a very personal passion for reclaiming the national story to one that celebrated the white settler past and rejected what he called a "black armband" view of history, one that paid too much attention, in his view, to the atrocities committed against Indigenous people in the past.'

Thus books such as this became disregarded, despite being solidly based on historical documents, despite having outstanding reviews. When its publisher was taken over, the new company allowed it to go out of print, saying the public had moved on, despite sales never dropping. Australia refused to sign the Declaration on the Rights of Indigenous Peoples in the United Nations General Assembly. The Federal Government seized control over Aboriginal townships and enterprises in the Northern territory.

But in 2008 the Howard Government fell and a new Labour government led by Kevin Rudd swore it would right these wrongs, beginning with an overdue apology in Parliament. He stated: 'I MOVE that today we honour the Indigenous peoples of this land, the oldest continuing cultures in human history. We reflect on their past mistreatment. We reflect in particular on the mistreatment of those who were Stolen Generation … We apologise for the laws and policies of successive Parliaments and governments that have inflicted profound grief, suffering and loss on these our fellow Australians. We apologise especially for the removal of Aboriginal and Torres Strait Islander children from their families, their communities and their country.'[1]

So why are we putting this book back into print in 2008? Because only with a good understanding of history can we put things right for the future. We must understand why things went wrong in the past if we are to make sure these things can never happen again.

This book documents how mining companies went onto Aboriginal lands and tried to either fool their elders or to overrule or manipulate them. This has not stopped. In May 2007 Yvonne Margarula, Elder of the Mirarr people, made clear her people would not agree to the development of the Jabiluka uranium deposit, despite RTZ comments to the contrary. This is reportedly the world's largest unmined deposit. She pointed out that the nearby RTZ Ranger uranium mine had led to despair and ills among those dispossessed.

A council of senior Aboriginal women is currently leading the fight to stop the building of a national nuclear waste dump on Aboriginal land near Woomera. Many years ago I went to visit these people. They took me to a settlement set up some two days journey into the desert where they taught their children how to live in and care for their lands, a vital enterprise if they are to

---

[1] The Age, March 29, 2008

survive as a people. The only white people present were the teachers they had hired to ensure their children learnt what they must to survive outside these lands.

I learnt from local Aboriginal health workers that some 400 Aborigines died as a consequence of the British atomic bomb tests in the 1950s on unfenced tribal lands near Woomera – these people know the danger of radioactivity far better than most of us.

Sadly a similar Aboriginal project is now threatened by RTZ's plans for yet another uranium mine, at Kintyre in Western Australia, near the world-renowned desert Rudall River National Park, with its beautiful permanent water holes and rare vegetation. Here other Aboriginal people, the Martu, use their land as a sanctuary.

Today politicians are arguing that we need nuclear power stations to counter global warming – and thus that we need the uranium on Aboriginal lands. This strengthens the hands of RTZ. It seems it is hard luck to Aborigines if this spoils their cultural survival plans!

A recent Wilderness Society report recorded: 'At a meeting in Alice Springs, the Martu people made public their feelings on the possibility of uranium mining on their land. "We don't want uranium from our country to hurt other peoples. The Aboriginal experience with uranium mining continues to result in the genocide of our community and the destruction of our homelands and country. Rock shelters in the region illustrate continuous human occupation from at least 5000 years ago. In the 1950s and '60s the Martu were rounded up and removed by the state so the area could be used for government Blue Streak Missile tests.'

I hope this new edition will serve them in their long struggle to protect their land, children and culture. I feel most privileged to have been for some 15 years a very small part of their fight.

Jan Roberts   June 21st 2008

Dedication

To the Aboriginal People of Australia

May you long celebrate the beauty and power

Of your most ancient of continents,

May your wisdom inspire the rest of us

To care for our world

With respect, strength and determination.

FOREWORD

This book is written by a white person about the behaviour of whites in a stolen land. It is the Australian updated edition of a book first published in 1978. It will be as valuable as that 1978 London edition, maybe more so, as I hope that white Australians, ignorant of what is going on around them, may be educated. Once you have read this book I hope you will want to know more. As Gary Foley points out in the 1978 foreword, there are many black writers with this story, their own story, told with bitter experience.

Gary Foley wrote: 'This book is a beginning'. A beginning it has been, that has triggered off a film and much support from overseas. Now the world will sit back and watch the reaction of all Australians with this edition of *Massacres to Mining*.

The sweet scent of eucalypt and earth. The sounds of life, love and laughter. All this and peace, borne on the winds that kiss this land. A land with gifts beyond man's wildest dreams and with beauty such as has never been seen. Populated with a people who have learned to live within the beauty, harmonising with and becoming a part of it. A people possessing all the beauty, within themselves, that the land around them has — no more, no less — for they are a part of the land and all things are a part of the people. All things — tangible and intangible, animate and inanimate.

Then, for some unknown reason and in the most sadistic way imaginable, this all ends when fools come to the shores of this Utopia to rape and destroy. Steered by greed, lust and many more concepts as totally alien to this land as the aliens themselves.

The horror is far more horrendous than the world has ever and will ever see for in this land all the evil that could ever be perpetrated has been perpetrated in excess on the land and her people.

May the God, in whose name these aliens acted, have mercy on their damned souls.

The massacres have not ended. People are not being rounded up and killed, but far more subtle methods are being used. If you take the people from their land and homes they will die. The mining, pastoral, forestry and tourism bodies are doing this every day of the year in Australia. But more importantly, as this land, its animals, fish, birds and insects, its plants, the water and sea, the rocks, the sky and in fact all things are a part of us as we are a part of them both physically and spiritually, then to destroy all this — the environment — is to destroy the people. Massacre!

Remember, you are not responsible for the actions of your ancestors but you are responsible for the perpetuation of the monstrous acts perpetrated on the Aborigines and their land.

Boolidt boolidtba. Ya-idthma-dthang Warrallba Kinninneemoonkoong, Pert—boolok Tjappwoorrong.
Chairman Aboriginal Mining Information Centre

FOREWORD TO THE BRITISH EDITION

The true history and ultimate fate of Australian Aborigines has long been distorted and ignored by the white Australian population. Innumerable people, from all levels of white society, have participated in a long-term, deliberate and carefully planned 'cover up' designed to conceal from Australians and the world the enormous crimes that were perpetrated against my people. This conspiracy began in the earliest days of the occupation of Australia by British colonialists and continues as I write these words. It has meant that generations of white Australians have grown up in blissful ignorance of the terrible criminal acts that have been inflicted upon large numbers of their fellow Australians. Furthermore, this conspiracy of silence has allowed whites to justify the current oppression of Aborigines and enable a new enemy to slip easily into Aboriginal lands to continue the exploitation and destruction of black society. I speak, of course, of the capitalist multi-national mining corporations who, motivated by greed, sit poised, waiting for government permission to move in and plunder Aborigines of the last vestiges of their land, culture and dignity.

This book has been written by a white person who is appalled that her fellow countrymen know virtually nothing of the true history of Australia. Appalled that this ignorance is now leading white Australians into condoning what could well be the ultimate destruction of black Australia.

The book is an attempt to set the record straight. As such it is a lucid and vivid documentation of the appalling treatment my people have suffered and continue to suffer.

Because it is being published internationally, it can only assist us by creating awareness among those most likely to provide support for us in our continuing struggle against oppression and injustice.

Equally as important is the fact that it will provide an inspiration for the growing number of black Australian writers who are beginning to tell the world their own story. I hope that readers of this book will obtain the books of black writers and read our version of this appalling story. After all, it is black Australians themselves who can best relate their own experiences and propose constructive ideas for the future. This book is a beginning.

Gary Foley
London, May 1978

CONTENTS

Dawn breaks over the land of the Jigalong Aborigines, central Western Australia (Jan Roberts).

PREFACE

Nipper Tabagee, a wise old man living on Noonkanbah Station in the Kimberleys, with deep eyes and an agility belying his years, took me when I visited Noonkanbah on a jolting ride across the sands of Fitzroy River to a nearby low rocky hill concealed among trees. This, he told me, was Djada Hill, joined by Dreamtime stories to Pea Hill across the river, where miners were to drill for oil.

Djada Hill is a place where his people used to gather to celebrate their law and their understanding of their land. It was here that they used to keep their most sacred ceremonial objects.

He took me up to caves in the hill and there showed me what had happened to his people. In the caves were the whitened bones of people slaughtered by police earlier this century so that cattlemen could safely take Aboriginal land. He told me how his people had been massacred, had spilt their blood for their land, right along the Fitzroy River.

Then, without the appearance of bitterness, he gently told me that, not long ago, a party of mineral prospectors had taken from this hill the sacred objects treasured by his people from generation to generation and had smashed some and stolen others. He told me that mining companies had driven bulldozers through their nearby burial grounds. Djada Hill, with its caves, had itself already been pegged as a mining prospect. Despite legal actions and many protests, the Noonkanbah people had been denied the right to protect the land they loved and died for.

I had heard, and was to hear, the same story in many other parts of Australia. Even in long-colonised Victoria, Aboriginal people remember the massacres. And in all parts of Australia, the first Australians dread the current mining boom, fearing that it will destroy the lives of the communities that still have use of their tribal lands.

This book came out of my experiences with these Australians, it is formed by what I learned from them. It is my attempt to tell the story that lies behind so much of the current news of Aboriginal protest and impoverishment, so that all Australians may better understand what is happening in their country. It starts from the beginning of the invasion, the arrival of the first Europeans, and goes up until the most recent developments as this book goes to press.

This book has also, uniquely, been part of the Aboriginal international campaign to gain support as a people in their own right, and to gain justice from the multi-national mining companies. Its first edition was launched by a North Queensland Land Council delegation in London on the first Aboriginal speaking tour of Europe. The next, in German, was launched by a delegation from the Aboriginal Health Service. I have now extensively rewritten, expanded and updated the book for its first Australian edition.

It is not an anti-mining book. It finishes with suggestions from Aboriginal organisations on how mining can be carried out without clashing with Aboriginal culture and rights. There is, I am convinced, a way forward based on mutual respect and justice. I hope this book contributes to this.

But it is hard to be hopeful. Right now the Northern Territory government is preparing proposals for mining the Aboriginal lands restored in the Territory by the 1976 Land Rights Act. They are whittling away the little protection that these people have achieved. Yet these, and the Pitjantjatjara in the remote deserts of South Australia, remain the only Aboriginal people in Australia to have their right to their ancestral lands recognised in white man's law. The Queensland and West Australian Governments remain totally opposed to land rights. Other State Governments, such as the Victorian, have simply ignored all Aboriginal demands for land. All this I have documented in this book.

It will continue to be a hard struggle for Aboriginal people to achieve justice. A whole shameful history of oppression and racial discrimination has to be reversed. Most white Australians

Nipper Tabagee, an Elder at Noonkanbah, shows where his massacred people were buried (Jan Roberts).

remain ignorant of what white people have done to the people from whom they took this continent. Yet what happened, and what continues to happen, to Aboriginal Australians is a frightening endictment of our so-called 'civilisation' and its values. Until this history is understood, most Australians will not be able to fully comprehend or respond to the desperate Aboriginal cry for justice that is today reaching around the world.

The Chairman of the Aboriginal Mining Information Centre, Boolidt-boolidtba, recently returned from a speaking tour in England, said in September 1981: 'We are not a mob of political activists requesting political and legal relief, but instead a nation of people *demanding* our rights.'

I hope that the voice of Aboriginal people is being listened to in Australia. They have now their own representative organisations, such as the land councils, the health and legal services, which articulate the demands of their people.

The bicentennial of the invasion of Australia is approaching. I hope, above all, that legislation is passed before then to give due recognition to the Aboriginal people's right to live free in their own land.

Jan Roberts
September 3rd, 1981

The word 'conquer' is a very hard word, but it is also a very true one ... Why is it that Aborigines always have to bow down and accept with their eyes shut what the white man tells them is good for them, even now when we are supposed to be equal? Because, in one way or another, the word 'conquer' is still there.
Burramarra, M.B.E.,
Chairman of the Mala Leaders' Council
at Galiwin'ku, Elcho Island, Arnhemland, N.T.
(From My Mother, the Land, *ed. Ian Yule,*
Galiwin'ku Parish, 1980)

1 AUSTRALIA BEFORE THE EUROPEANS

Aboriginal people had lived in Australia for over 40,000 years before the first Europeans reached the continent. Some now say for over 100,000 years.[1]

Their culture thus predates by tens of thousands of years the building of the Pyramids a mere 4,500 years ago. The Bunggunditj tribe of around Mt Gambier in South Australia has in its oral history how Mt Muirhead erupted (20,000 years ago) and then Mt Gambier (5,000 years ago). At Keilor, near Melbourne, an Aboriginal camp has been found 31,000 years old. People then hunted wombat-like creatures as big as rhinoceroses and ten foot tall kangaroos. These became extinct about 15,000 years ago, but they are still remembered in the history told from generation to generation by the descendants of those who hunted them—so too is the flooding of Bass Strait between 12,000 and 20,000 years ago which cut off the Australians who lived in Tasmania.

Along the northern coast they had frequent contact with Indonesian and other Asian fishermen and explorers, but they held the continent, as far as we know, without serious challenge. They lived in the harshest parts of the continent as well as the fertile well-watered plains. They evolved many complex and peaceful regional cultures by which they lived with the land without destroying it. They found ways of cooking and preparing many of the natural plants. Their hunting was under the control of the Elders who made certain that killing was only for need. They hunted and fished by canoe in the rivers and sea. By using birth control, they preserved their population at a level that did not exceed the capacity of the land to supply their needs. They reserved easily digested food for the elderly. They lived well.

In some forested regions they used burning to maintain an open forest with good grazing so that grazing animals were plentiful and it was easier to hunt. They used fire in the dry regions to improve the yield of plants.

Before the British came, there were some 500 Australian nations (many of which have now been wiped out) and as many languages.

In this book we will use the term 'Aborigine' to mean the people who descend from, and identify with, the Australian race that inhabited Australia before the arrival of the Europeans. We will not attempt to divide them according to the percentage of European blood individuals may have—such distinctions have been deplored by many Aboriginal leaders as a tactic to divide their people.

The Aboriginal tribes have many names for themselves. Some of the names mean 'the People' or 'Man'—sometimes qualified by a description of their place or language or food. Thus 'Mara' of S.W. Victoria means 'People'. 'Koorie' and 'Murri' (the most commonly used terms today on the East coast—the first in Victoria and NSW and the second in Queensland) both mean 'Man'. The tribe on whose stolen land Melbourne is built is the Wurundjeri. This means 'The people who live in the land where the manna-gum grows and who eat the grub living in that tree.'

A Western District Aborigine, his sons watching, prepares to cook a kangaroo (R. Tonkinson).

The indigenous peoples of the Americas have similar names for themselves. Thus the Eskimo call themselves 'Inuit', meaning 'the People'. The Mohawks are the Ganienkehaga—'the People of the flint stone', the Senacas are 'the People of the Great Hills' and the Six Nations or 'Hau de no sau nee' are the 'People who build'. North American Indians today often say 'the Native Americans' for themselves.

We do not know the number of people in Australia when the British first arrived. The figure that used to be given—200,000—'conveniently saved explaining the massacres', according to the Australian Commissioner for Community Relations in 1977.[2] More recent estimates have been around 315,000. By 1945, however, there were estimated to be under 90,000—a number that doubled by 1977 to around 180,000 according to government estimates. However, some Aboriginal organisations give a figure of around 320,000 for the Aboriginal population today.

Each nation or tribe, was made up of a number of clans. Each clan held their own land, and they invited others to use their lands at proper times. Marriage interlocked the clans of a nation and set up links between nations, for marriage could not take place between a man and a woman of the same clan.

People lived within a vastly extended family. A person could travel from one nation to another and immediately be assigned his own proper place within the new community. The people traded between themselves along trade routes that stretched the length and breadth of the continent.

Their societies were so organised that they had no families holding hereditary rights of government over the rest of the population. There were no special castes of priests or centralised systems of authority. Since they believed that territorial responsibilities had been laid down for all time, there could be no wars of conquest, despite the punitive expeditions that might, from time to time, extract revenge and punishment for the crimes of sacrilege and other violations of the law.

Aborigines and their land

It is very hard for a European Australian to explain just what land means to Aborigines. We have a totally different way of looking at land. For most of us, land is 'property' over which we or the relevant authorities are absolute dictators. We can chop it up, destroy it, transform it.

But all this would be for the Aborigines a terrible atrocity, a rape of the land—violating all the law, violating all that should be held sacred. It would be destroying them. Many have sickened and died when these things have happened to their lands.

But these things are best explained in the words of the Aborigines themselves. First, the words of the first Chairman of the Aboriginal Northern Land Council, Silas Roberts, speaking out in 1976 on the possible uranium mining of their land:

Aborigines have a special connection with everything that is natural. Aborigines see themselves as part of nature. We see all things natural as part of us. All things on earth we see as part human. This is told through the idea of dreaming. By dreaming we mean the belief that long ago, these creatures started human society; they made all natural things

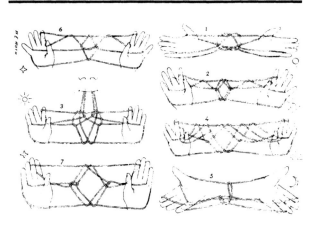

String games played in North Queensland before the invasion. 1. Sun clouded over. 2. Sun, full rays. 3. Sun, full rays. 4. Sun setting. 5. Moon. 6. Star. 7. Star.

and put them in a special place. These dreaming creatures were connected to special places and special roads or tracks or paths. In many cases the great creatures changed themselves into sites where their spirits stayed.

My people believe this and I believe this. Nothing anybody says to me will change my belief in this. This is my story as it is the story of every true Aborigine.

These creatures, these great creatures, are just as much alive today as they were in the beginning. They are everlasting and will never die. They are always part of the land and nature as we are. We cannot change nor can they. Our connection to all things natural is spiritual. We worship spiritual sites today. We have songs and dances for those sites and we never approach without preparing ourselves properly. When the great creatures moved across the land, they made small groups of people like me in each area. These people were given jobs to do but I cannot go any further than that here.

It is true that people who belong to a particular area are really part of that area and if that area is destroyed they are also destroyed. In my travels throughout Australia, I have met many Aborigines from other parts who have lost their culture. They have always lost their land and by losing their land they have lost part of themselves.[3]

Another Elder, Albert Chevathen, spoke out in 1975 against aluminium companies taking his people's land for strip-mining bauxite:

My dear people, all my brothers and sisters and cousins and grannies. I am talking for my land, not only my land but your land too. We have to stand up for it. We don't want any enemy coming to destroy our land . . . we've any amount of plants, any amount of food. We don't go short of nothing at all. We don't buy. No, we get free what God gives us . . . The land we have is our forefathers' land . . . we cannot give away our land. We don't want jobs. We don't want money. We don't want the companies to take our land.[4]

Galarrwuy Yunupingu, who became the second Chairman of the Northern Land Council in 1976, explained in a letter to white people how he felt about his land:

When I was 16 years old, my father taught me to sing some of the songs that talk about the land. He told me . . . (they) are the history of the Gumatj people, which talks about us being one with nature.

In all these ceremonies, I learnt things that only tell about the tribal land–how it is talked about, sung, dance, paint and, most of all feel as though the land is another you.

One day, I went fishing with Dad. As I was walking along behind him I was dragging my spear on the beach which was leaving a long line behind me. He told me to stop doing that.

He continued telling me that if I made a mark, or dig, with no reason at all, I've been hurting the bones of the traditional people of that land. We must only dig and make marks on the ground when we perform or gather food.

The land is my backbone . . . I only stand straight, happy, proud and not ashamed about my colour because I still have land. I can dance, paint, create and sing as my ancestors did before me.

I think of land as the history of my nation. It tells of how we came into being and what system we must live. My great ancestors who lived in the times of history planned everything that we practise now. The law of history says that we must not take land, fight over land, steal land, give land and so on. My land is mine only because I came in spirit from that land, and so did my ancestors of the same land . . .

My land is my foundation. I stand, live and perform as long as I have something firm and hard to stand on. Without land . . . we will be the lowest people in the world, because you have broken down our backbone, took away my arts, history and foundation. You have left me with nothing. Only a black feller who doesn't care about anything in the world. My people don't want to be like you![5]

Some myths about Aboriginal life

Australian school children often learn that Aborigines were a primitive and stone-age nomadic people, without fixed lands or houses or clothes, who simply wandered about at random without any fixed territories, hunting and gathering. A handout on 'Australia' from the London Australian High Commission in 1978 states: 'The only inhabitants were primitive nomadic Aborigines. Early explorers opened the way for settlement.'

But they were nomadic only in the sense that they had circuits of hunting and ceremonial ground around which they moved—always within defined territories.

The picture painted to modern school children is based on a distorted image of the fugitive Aborigine, and on the desert Aborigine of the centre of Australia.

These desert Aborigines still have many of their traditions intact. Their foraging for food has to cover a very much wider area than that of the Aborigines of the better watered parts of Australia, thus their territories are often much larger and traditionally they travel greater distances. Their shelters are built out of sparse desert vegetation, and cannot be used for long before they have to leave to find more food. But these shelters are not, as so often described, the only form of traditional Aboriginal housing.

The possession of clothes, fixed housing and territorial limits are not in any case real standards against which a culture can be judged. All human cultures have their achievements—not least the Aboriginal culture. This culture embodies the experience of thousands of years. Through it, the Aboriginal race lived in harmony with their world, stayed clear of the craving for material possessions that dominated the lives of many another people. They put the preservation of their natural world first.

As for their style of life at the time of the invasion, historical accounts paint a very different picture from that commonly taught in schools. When the Dutch first arrived in 1606, they wrote of Aboriginal houses on the beaches. Captain Cook spoke of huts. Others gave very

much more detail. Grey, exploring Western Australia in 1841:

. . . followed it (the Hutt River) for two miles and in this distance passed two villages, or as the men termed them, towns, the huts of which they were composed differed from those in the southern districts, in being much larger and more strongly built, and very nicely plastered over on the outside . . . so that, although now uninhabited, they were evidently intended for fixed places of residence . . . these superior huts, well marked roads, deeply sunk wells and extensive warran (yam) grounds all speak of a large and comparatively stable population.[6]

In 1845, Eyre in S.E. Australia:

At other times, large long huts are constructed in which five to ten families reside, each having their own separate fires . . . (huts) formed of thick logs of wood.[7]

George Robinson, the Melbourne-based Chief Protector of Aborigines, visited an Aboriginal settlement in May 1841. His official report stated:

Tapoc, the Mount Napier of Mitchell, is an isolated hill of volcanic formation. The natives are still the undisputed occupants (of this area) —no white man having been there to dispossess them. The people who occupy the country have fixed residences. At one village were thirteen huts. They are warm and well constructed, in the shape of a cupola or 'kraal' . . . (some) sufficiently strong for a man on horseback to ride over.[8]

At Bathurst Island in the north, Stokes found:

Several native habitations . . . stout poles, fourteen to sixteen feet high were brought together at the top: a stout thatching . . . completely excluded the wind.[9]

Recent archaeological research in Victoria has discovered the remains of houses built of low circular stone walls and wooden roofs with internal fireplaces, also elaborate and extensive canal systems with stone dykes and weirs—the canal dykes being some four foot high and stone weirs up to 400 yards in length.

Aboriginal people of the Mara 'confederacy' of tribes in coastal Western Victoria recall today the settlements they once had. They explain that one way they had of supporting a residential population was by their fish-farming techniques. These were reported on by Robinson in 1841. He saw near Mt William swamp in Western Victoria 'one continuous treble line' of trenches some 500 yards in length and covering over ten acres, excavated as one vast eel fishery. On the Moyne River near Port Fairy, families had built a 200 foot weir five feet high with nets placed in gaps from which great numbers of fish were secured. The Gunditj-mara (recently in the news because of their efforts to stop Alcoa's smelter being built on tribal land near Portland) had a similar eel-fishery near Lake Condah. The Jaadwa and Mukdjarawaite had dug a canal-fishery three-quarters of a mile long and twelve feet wide.

This was south of the Victorian Little Desert.

Not all lived by hunting and fishing. William Thomas reported in 1843 that Aborigines had told him:

there are in the Australian Alps a race of Blacks who live in stone houses made by themselves (not caves) and that some of these Blacks never go out to seek their food like other Blacks but eat herbs and what Blacks give them . . . that these Blacks are very good . . . and they teach other Blacks dancing and singing.[10]

William Thomas was, however, wrong in reporting that these Aborigines were a 'race'. They were Aboriginal Elders chosen for their spiritual gifts and trained to be spiritual guides for the Ya-idthma-dthang tribe and neighbouring tribes to the west and north.

Arnhemland Aborigines in a dry season camp (Nicolas Peterson).

What happened to those more settled Aborigines is today practically erased from the history books as if they and their cultures never existed. However, there are today, among the 17,000–22,000 Aborigines in Victoria, some 3,000 descendants of the Mara Aborigines. These and the other Aborigines of Victoria are still living and fighting for recognition of their rights. Although their rich, well watered and open lands were the first to be taken, they still remember and value their culture. But the Europeans who have taken their lands still remain in shameful ignorance of what their race destroyed.

Legally, the most dangerous of all the myths is that Aborigines passively and weakly, without resistance, ceded their land to white people as if they did not see it as their land and as if they did not value it. It is on this myth that the legal justification for the dispossession of Aboriginal people is based.

One example of this distortion in Australian history is in a letter published in the Brisbane *Telegraph* on 11th March 1977:

In many other countries, the lands belonged to the original inhabitants who were over-run by force, whereas Australia merely was occupied by exploration. Our Aborigines can thank their lucky stars their ancestors were not put into chains and sent away as slaves like African negroes were.

'Our white forefathers built this country into what it is today through courageous expeditions, hardships, sacrifices and sheer hard work. Through it all, the Aborigines continued with their lazy life, walkabouts and what have you.

However, Judge Willis in Port Phillip in 1841 stated that the frequent conflicts made it

sufficiently clear that the Aboriginal tribes are neither a conquered race nor have they tacitly acquiesced in the supremacy of the settlers.[12]

Because of the current importance of this myth, it will be investigated at some length in the early chapters of this book.

Author's note

In the first edition of this book, written in England, I wrote:

What happened to the more settled Aborigines is practically erased from the history books, and one is left to presume that they, or at least their cultures, were totally destroyed by the invasion of the Europeans. Certainly their richer, better watered and cleared lands were the first to be taken.[13]

I am happy to say that since returning to Australia I have learnt that my presumption was wrong. Many of them survived. I have been privileged to work with them at the Aboriginal Mining Information Centre and to learn from them that they still retain their culture.

Footnotes

1. Statement by two scientists attached to Western Australian museum, May 1978.
2. Some, quoted in the 1977 report of the Australian Commissioner for Community Relations, have estimated the pre-invasion population as high as 1.2 million. Other estimates of the current Aboriginal population vary from 165,000 to 500,000. Aborigines were not counted in national censuses, nor were birth certificates necessary, until around 1967.
3. Evidence to Ranger Uranium Enquiry, June 1977, quoted in *Land Rights News*, the Northern Land Council, Darwin.
4. Jan Roberts (ed.),, M. Parsons, B. Russell, D. McLean, *The Mapoon* Books (International Development Action, 1975), Book One, p. 37.
5. *Black News Service*, Black Resource Centre, Brisbane, December 1976.
6. George Crichton, 'Housing in pre-white Australia', in *Victorian Naturalist*, vol. 94, March/April 1976.
7. *ibid.*
8. *Victorian Historical Magazine*, 12, 3(1928), pp. 149-150.
9. *ibid.*
10. W. Thomas, *Report* 1st December 1843 to 1st March 1844, Box 12 APR, ProVic.
11. Oral tradition from Les Russell, 1981.
12. *Port Phillip Patriot*, 20 September 1841.
13. Jan Roberts, *From Massacres to Mining*, CIMRA and War on Want, (London, 1978), p. 8.

2 THE DUTCH DEFEATED AND BRITISH THEFT

The Duyfken in the Gulf of Carpentaria, 1606.

The Dutch defeated

In 1606, the Dutch ship *Duyfken*, helping to establish the Dutch Empire in the East Indies, ventured south to see what spoils could be won, and reached the Australian coast. It was a smallish ship, two masted with eight cannon. The first Australians, or Aborigines, to sight Europeans were the people of Mapoon on the west coast of Cape York in north-west Australia.

The *Duyfken* first stood off the Mapoon territory 'but every attempt to land was opposed by hostile Aborigines with spears in their hands.'[1]

They then moved about 200 km south along the coast until they reached Cape Keer-weer. The ship's diary remained silent on what happened here, apart from recording that they had a clash with the inhabitants. But the Aborigines from that Cape remember precisely what happened. In 1975, the descendants of those who met the Dutch heard that the leading mining company in the consortium planning a major mine for their land was Dutch. One of them then said, 'We defeated the Dutch before. We will defeat them again.' (The company is the Shell-owned Billiton.)[2]

They told the author that the Mapoon people had tried to deflect the bullets with spears. The Dutch then came to near Aurukun. Wallamby, one of the descendents of the people on whose land the Dutch entered, told the story in 1975.

The Europeans sailed along from overseas and put up a building at Cape Keerweer. A crowd of Keerweer people saw their boat sail in and went to talk with them. They said they wanted to put up a city. Well, the Keerweer people said that was all right. They allowed them to sink a well and put up huts.[3]

Then the Europeans started to take the Aboriginal women. Wallamby recounts

Then one European woman took away from my cousin-brother his wife and lived with her. They forced them to work for them. They just work, work, work, work.[4]

Eventually these abuses of hospitality provoked hostility. Many Aborigines were shot down but several of the Dutch were also killed. When the Aborigines in their canoes got among the European boats on the beach and started setting fire to them, the Dutch broke and ran. Naming the headland 'Cape Keerweer', Dutch for 'Turn-around', the captain of the *Duyfken*, with half his crew dead, was forced to leave Australia.

Several other Dutch ships came and explored other parts of the coast. They found no precious spices, and the inhabitants hard to subdue, so they withdrew.

Aboriginal Elders at Noonkanbah remember the story of another landing:

They been landing along at Derby. You know that pub, right down that way? Soon as he been landing at Derby? All the gudia (whiteman) been coming along. This is a long, long time ago.

Soak water been there, like a spring, near the pub now. There's a soak water there. They been coming along, all the gudia, not that Captain Cook, different one. They been shoot them all with their long long rifles, and they had those pointed hats. (William Dampier landed at Derby at the site of the hotel, in 1688.)[5]

... and British theft

In 1770, Captain Cook landed on the southeast coast of Australia at what is now part of Sydney. Two Australians who happened to be on the beach tried to prevent the landing. It took several shots before they retreated from the beach.

Cook's secret instructions from the Admiralty were:

*'You are **with the consent of the natives** to take possession of convenient situations in the country in the name of the King of England; or, if you find the country uninhabited, take possession for His Majesty by setting up Proper Marks and Inscriptions, as first discoverers and possessors.'*[6]

But, after many encounters with Aborigines, some of these friendly, he chose strangely to act as if the country were 'uninhabited' and, on August 22nd, he wrote in his diary:

I now once more hoisted English Colours, and in the name of His Majesty King George the Third, took possession of the whole Eastern coast.[7]

Perhaps he felt such an action would please his superiors. At least no complaint or reprimand is recorded.[8]

Yet Cook described the Australians as people to be admired. He wrote that they were:

'in no way inclined to cruelty, as appeared from their treatment of one of our people ... they may appear to some to be the most wretched People on Earth; but in reality they are far happier than we Europeans, ... They live in a tranquility which is not disturbed by the inequality of condition [i.e. the distinction between rich and poor]. *The earth and sea of their own accord furnished them with all things necessary for life ... they have very little need for clothing ... many to whom we gave cloth, etc, left it carelessly upon the sea beach and in the woods as a thing they had no manner of use for; in short they seemed to set no value upon anything we gave them, nor would they part ever with anything of their own for any one article we could offer them. This, in my opinion, argues that they think themselves provided with all the necessaries of life, and that they have no superfluities.'*

'Their features are far from disagreeable, and their voices soft and tunable.'[10]

Although Captain Cook looked on the Aborigines with admiration in his diary, he still did not hesitate to treat them as a people without legal rights to their own country, in seeming defiance of his own instructions from the British authorities.

No other invaders are known to have landed on the southern coast of Australia. The inhabitants were mostly prepared to treat the new arrivals with respect and friendship. Perhaps if he had been met by standing armies, the explorer's decision would have been different.

Cook would have known that the British authorities, losing control over most of their North American colonies, urgently needed him to discover countries which could be alternative suppliers of raw materials for British industry — places where they could safely use the jailed English and Irish workers to further their commercial interests—and preferably countries where the inhabitants were not organised to withstand modern European weaponry.

The eastern coast of Australia must have seemed nearly ideal—it was described by Cook as having in parts a soil 'capable of producing any kind of grain,' and having as fine meadows 'as ever was seen.'[11]

Cook, in ignoring the indigenous people and declaring their country the possession of the British Crown, set the foundations of Australian law up until today. His action, fully supported by the British authorities, was seemingly in sharp contrast to British policy in Canada—for, in Canada, the British had to compete with the French for the loyalty of the native people. Thus, just seven years earlier, the King had declared the rights of the Indians of Canada to the undisturbed use of their land. (This declaration was soon to be set aside once it became inexpedient to the invaders.)

Generally speaking, the colonising countries of Europe equated civilisation with the possession of a centralised executive. They normally made no legal provision for the recognition of the rights of the people, other than sovereigns or dictators, to land or minerals. European law was based on the interests of an entrenched *elite* who were only prepared, it seems, to recognise the interests of similar *elites*. Aboriginal society had no ruling *elite* they could favour to gain favours in exchange.

In Australia, there was to be, by high policy, no declaration of war. The invaded Australians, or Aborigines, were declared the King's subjects before they were conquered. Henceforth, their resistance was 'rebellion', a criminal act, deserving punishment. If war on the Aborigines had been declared, then there would have been need to respect the conventions of warfare: the proper treatment of prisoners and the signing of treaties.

Some of the first whites to go to what is now Melbourne drew up a treaty (Batman's Deed) with the inhabitants, by which they leased land for a small annual payment. But this was declared illegal by the Colonial authorities, located 600 miles away in Sydney, when they heard of it. They announced that any of His Majesty's subjects who claimed title by treaty or bargain with the natives would be regarded as trespassers on Crown land.[12]

Two heroes of the Gwiyagal people resist Cook's armed party on their landing at Botany Bay, April 1770. A sketch by one of Cook's party, Sydney Parkinson.

Batman's deed was an effort by a man who had previously killed many Tasmanian Aborigines to so impress the British authorities that they would recognise his acquisition of the choice 600,000 acres he had selected. (He gave the Aborigines two hundred pounds worth of trinkets in return. At that time, a group of humanitarians led by Wilberforce had succeeded in having slavery outlawed by the British Parliament and, horrified by the massacres in Tasmania and Southern Africa, had formed in London the 'Aborigines Protection Society'. This group had particular influence at the Colonial Office.

However, the deed was a confidence trick of Batman. He knew that it had not been properly negotiated with the Aborigines. They had searched for some days for some Aboriginal people—and eventually contacted a hunting party and had them sign the deed. Later, they claimed that the appropriate Aboriginal chieftains had signed the deed, but Wedge, one of the party, wrote:

there is no such thing as chieftainship (among the Aborigines), but this is a secret that must be kept to ourselves, or else it may affect the deed of conveyance. [13]

It was nevertheless highly embarrassing to the Colonial authorities who saw through it but could not say it was unjust to the Aborigines since they themselves were taking Aboriginal land without Aboriginal consent. Nor could they recognise the Deed without invalidating their own seizure of Aboriginal land without Aboriginal consent.

Again in 1834 when the British colony in South Australia was begun, the preamble of the Act of Parliament authorising the colony stated that the area to be colonised consisted of 'waste and unoccupied lands'. But the official report on the site had referred to 'great numbers of natives' on this very land. This contradiction was pointed out by a Select Committee of Parliament in 1837.

Their report stated:

It might be presumed that the native inhabitants of any land have an incontrovertible right
to their own soil; a plain and sacred right, however, which seems not to have been understood. Europeans have entered their borders uninvited, and when there have not only acted as if they were the undoubted lords of the soil, but have punished the natives as aggressors if they have evinced a disposition to live in their own country. They have been treated as thieves and robbers. They are driven back into the interior as if they were dogs or kangaroos. [14]

This committee's protests led to instructions to the new colonisers from the government that land

now actually occupied or enjoyed by ... (natives) should not be taken from them. [15]

However, these instructions were ignored. Once more the Aborigines were driven from all the best lands. In practice, the British authorities had no compunction about using military force, and even declaring martial law, to ensure the removal of the Aborigines.

Footnotes

1. Recorded in the captain's diary.
2. Jan Roberts; oral tradition recorded by the author at Aurukum 1975.
3. *ibid.*
4. *ibid.*
5. Oral tradition related by Ginger Ngunwilla to Steve Hawke , 1978.
6. Quoted in Barrie Pittock, *Aboriginal Land Rights*, IWGIA, (Copenhagen, 1972), p. 71.
7. A. Reed (ed.), *Captain Cook in Australia — his diaries*, (A. Reed, publ.) 1969, p. 123.
8. An attempt was made by three Australian Aborigines to show just how ridiculous this was. In 1977 they landed on Dover Beach, planted an Aboriginal flag and claimed all of England. Since then they have also claimed the British Embassy in Canberra. No matter how ridiculous this seems, the identical act by Captain Cook remains the near-sacrosanct foundation of Australian land ownership law.
9. A. Reed (ed.), *Captain Cook*, p. 136.
10. *ibid*, p. 95.
11. *ibid*, p. 45.
12. C.M.H. Clarke, *Selected Documents in Australian History*, pp. 225-227.
13. Letter to Simpson dated 9 August 1935, *Port Phillip Assoc. Papers*, (La Trobe Collection).
14. *Report from Select Committee on Aborigines*, Commons Papers, 1834, vol. 7, pp. 212 ff. See Pittock, p. 9.
15 Pittock, p. 10.

3 GENOCIDAL ATTITUDES

The settlers coming on to the Aboriginal lands killed the Aborigines 'as if they were dogs or kangaroos'. If they recognised the Aborigines as Australians, as people with rights, this would have stood in the way of their plans to get rich quick by seizing vast areas for their sheep or cattle stations. Australia was (and is) *par excellence* the land of the 'get-rich-quick' mentality. So the settlers started to construct myths to justify their treatment of the Aborigine. They were helped in this by the development in England and other parts of Europe of a very racist evolutionary theory. The ideas of Darwin were opportune and could easily be made to justify the massacres that followed the arrival of the British. The theory of the 'survival of the fittest' made the dying out of the Aborigines something inevitable—since it was obvious to the settlers that they themselves were the superior species!

Racist theories, evolved to justify slavery in the West Indies and southern United States, were imported into Australia and the same sterotypes applied to 'blacks' in the Americas were applied to 'blacks' in Australia. However, in Australia these same arguments were used not to justify slavery but extermination!

Thus Oldfield in 1865 was uncertain, from the appearance of the Aborigines,

whether we have to do with intelligent monkeys or with very much degraded men.[1]

Max Muller in 1870, in the *Anthropological Review*, London, classified the human race into seven categories on an ascending scale— with the Aborigines on the lowest rung and the 'Indo-German' or 'Aryan' type supreme.[2] (These theories, of course, were later used by Hitler.)

The Social Evolutionist, H. K. Rusden, explained in 1876:

The survival of the fittest means that might is right. And thus we invoke and remorselessly fulfil the inexorable law of natural selection when exterminating the inferior Australian and Maori races . . . and we appropriate their patrimony cooly.[3]

Thus a writer in *The Queenslander* newspaper explained on 4th September, 1880:

Nothing we can do will alter the inscrutable and withal immutable laws which direct our progress on this globe. By these laws the native races of Australia were doomed on the advent of the white man and the only thing left for us to do is to assist in carrying them out with as little cruelty as possible.

He then wonders if reserves for Aborigines would be any use, concluding:

We must rule the Blacks by fear, teaching them the uselessness of waging war on the settlers.

In 1883, the *Normanton Herald* argued *that even half-civilised niggers were no more than wretches whom it were more of a mercy than a crime to wipe off the face of the earth.*[4]

James Barnard, the Vice-President of the Royal Society of Tasmania, wrote in 1890: *that the process of extermination is an axiom . . . (of) the law of evolution and survival of the fittest'.* There was, he continued, no reason to *'suppose there had been any culpable neglect on the part of the white settlers.*[5]

Vincent Lesina told the Australian Parliament in 1901:
The law of evolution says that the nigger shall disappear in the onward march of the white man.[6]

A well-known explorer and historian of northern Australia, Logan Jack, reflected these theories when he wrote in 1922:

This northern land is thinly peopled by a feeble folk inevitably doomed to vanish from the face of the earth within the current century . . . the more the native blood is diluted the better. To any stud-master, or student of eugenics, the idea of leaving the future of the North to a breed tainted at its foundation-head is in the last degree repugnant, and politically it is full of danger.[7]

In April 1883, the British High Commissioner, Arthur Gordon, wrote candidly and privately to his close friend, Prime Minister Gladstone:

*The habit of regarding the natives as vermin, to be cleared off the face of the earth, has given to the average Queenslander a tone of brutality and cruelty . . . I have heard men of culture and refinement, of the greatest humanity and kindness to their fellow whites . . . talk, not only of the **wholesale** butchery . . . but of the individual murder of natives, exactly as they would talk of a day's sport, or of having to kill some troublesome animal.*[8]

Footnotes

1.   Evans, Saunders and Cronin, *Exclusion, Exploitation and Extermination: Race Relation in Colonial Queensland* (ANZ, 1975), p. 75.
2.   Evans, p. 15.
3.   Evans, p. 81.
4.   Evans, p. 67.
5.   Evans, p. 80.
6.   Evans, p. 82.
7.   Jack Logan, *Northernmost Australia*, 1922.
8.   Evans, p. 78.

4 ABORIGINAL RESISTANCE – AND THE MASSACRES

The Australians, now known as Aborigines, resisted the invasion (although today most 'Australian' school books scarcely mention this). As the whites attempted to take their lands, the inhabitants banded together to fight guerrilla campaigns. Often the Aborigines' first target was the cattle and sheep of the encroaching settlers. Despite having usually only spears to fight guns, this warfare lasted some 160 years from the first clashes around Sydney to the last massacres reported in the 1940s in the Kimberleys.

Sydney and New South Wales

When the British Government lost control over the American colonies in 1776, they also lost a dumping ground and convenient use for British convicts and Irish prisoners. These had been used as forced labour to enrich both settlers and Government.

In 1784, the British authorities decided to find another suitable colony, and in 1786, decided on the evidence brought by Cook and the botanist who travelled with him, Joseph Banks, that Botany Bay was the place. Here, in January 1788, the first shipment of convicts arrived under the authority of Governor Phillip and his troops.

For the Aboriginal people, the new arrivals were utterly strange. Many speculated that they were the re-incarnated spirits of their dead. Some thought they were devils.[1]

Lieutenant (later Governor) King realised just how their clothes made them look to the Aborigines. The natives 'seemed quite astonished at the figure we cut in being clothed. I think it is very easy to conceive the ridiculous figure we must appear.'[2]

The Aborigines wondered what sex these strange creatures were under their clothes. Lieutenant King reported:

they took us for women, not having our beards grown. I ordered one of the people to undeceive them in this particular, when they made a great shout of admiration.[3]

They fared better than another landing party under Captain Tench of the Marines, who also had to prove their masculinity when they met with a group of 'Indians':

'These people seemed at a loss to know . . . of what sex we were, which having understood they burst into the most immoderate fits of laughter, talking to each other at the same time with such rapidity and vociferation as I had never before heard.'[4]

Initially, the Aborigines assisted by showing where they could find good water. But the British soon overstayed their welcome. On January 21st, the British started clearing land.

Louis Ngulgure, of the Ngarrindjeri whose land is beside the River Murray's mouth, with a deadly *kaike* or reed-spear, c. 1860 (S.A. Museum).

Lieutenant Bradley reported:

The Natives were well pleas'd with our People until they began clearing the ground at which they were displeased and wanted them to be gone. [5]

The Aborigines were also upset by the large amounts of fish the British were taking out of their waters. By October 1780, Bradley reported:

'Latterly they have attack'd almost every person who has met with them who has not had a musquet [gun] *'.* [6]

Already the British had started over-running the Australian land with scant regard for the rights of the Australian owners.

In December 1788, Phillip ordered the kidnapping of two Aborigines so as to learn from them if the Aborigines could threaten the settlement and to see if they could be 'civilised'.

In April next year, a plague of small-pox struck the Aborigines. Aborigines had no natural immunity to this disease brought to them from Europe. Bradley reported:

'From the great number of dead natives found in every part of the Harbour, it appears that the smallpox had made dreadful havoc among them; we . . . were told that scarce any had been seen lately except laying dead in and about their miserable habitations.' [7]

At least half of the Aboriginal population died. The disease from Sydney spread right over the continent.

In 1790, Phillip sent out fifty soldiers, after his gamekeeper was speared. One of the party reported:

'We were to cut off and bring in the heads of the slain, for which purpose hatchets and bags were furnished.' [8]

However, they failed to find a single Aborigine.

In 1791, the next plague struck the Aborigines—venereal disease. Collins wrote:

'At one time, about the year 1791, there was not one of the natives, man, woman or child, that came near us, but was covered with it. It raged violently among them, and some became very loathsome objects.' [8]

Despite all this, Aboriginal resistance to the British was growing. In 1795, open warfare was reported along the river previously known to the Aborigines as Deerubbun, now renamed the Hawkesbury. The Aborigines were resisting being driven off their land. They were attempting with spears and clubs to protect their lands, stripping the crops out of fields the settlers planted, taking off the grain and corn in blankets and nets.

Troops were sent out,

with instructions to destroy as many as they could meet with of the wood tribe . . . and, in hope of striking terror, to erect gibbets in different places, whereupon the bodies of all they might kill were to be hung. [9]

However, although they did kill some Aborigines, they did not capture any bodies to string up as the Aborigines took off their dead.

In 1799, an Aboriginal leader and hero, Pemulway, was captured after a long and daring guerrilla campaign in what is now the inner Sydney suburb of Parramatta. His pickled head was sent to Sir Joseph Banks in London. (Sir Joseph Banks was the very able naturalist who accompanied and advised Captain Cook.)

In 1805, the colonial authorities ordered:

'No natives are to be suffered to approach the ground or dwellings of any settler . . . If any settler harbours any natives he will be prosecuted.' [10]

In 1804, after renewed fighting on the Hawkesbury, the tribes were promised that they could keep their lands on the lower river—a promise that was no sooner made than broken.[11]

In 1816, Governor Macquarie resolved to break Aboriginal resistance once and for all. The Aborigines had forced some settlers to abandon attempts to establish farms on their tribal lands. He sent out a military expedition lasting 23 days to Aboriginal-held areas on the Hawkesbury, Nepean and Grose Rivers with orders to seize all Aborigines including children and to hang all that resisted. Many were killed. At Appin, women and children threw themselves in despair over a cliff. The Governor expressed his hope in a proclamation issued on May 2 1816 that his actions would terrorize the Aborigines.

'it will eventually strike terror amongst the tribes.' [12]

Governor Macquarie, in this proclamation, ordered that any unarmed group of Aborigines of more than six in number could be shot, and that any armed Aborigine within a mile of any white habitation could also be killed.

Finally, he stated that Aborigines who wished protection would be issued with passports provided they did not carry weapons.

A few months later, on 20th July 1816, he outlawed ten Aboriginal warriors and declared that if they could not be captured, they were to be killed.

The initial settlement would scarcely have impressed the Aborigines with its level of spiritual and moral civilisation. The Aborigines, who knew no slavery, saw established a British colony of slaves and masters. The convicts were the slaves, the government officials and army officers the masters. For the first fifty years, N.S.W. was ruled by a few rich 'gentlemen settlers' who used convict labour to establish their estates and enrich themselves. They were very much opposed to freeing the convicts.

Until 1838, all settlers could obtain convict labour for the price of their keep. Some in the Hunter Valley had up to 150 convict-slaves although in 1835 a limit of 70 was imposed. Aborigines were thus not wanted even as labourers by those who had taken their lands.[13] Instead, military outposts were established to control the Aborigines and kill them when they resisted the invaders. A few missionaries were also sent to 'civilise' them—although many doubted that Aborigines were capable of having spiritual values! In the Hunter Valley, escaped convicts joined with the Aborigines in opposing the settlers.

In the 1830s, free labourers started coming, brought out by the Government on the proceeds of selling stolen tribal lands to the settlers. These were initially mostly mechanics and women, both in short supply among the convicts.

At this time too the wealthy settlers, often with their convict-slaves, realised that fortunes could be made from wool—and started to rush out to 'squat' the lands of previously undisturbed tribes. This was illegal in the eyes of the colonial authorities—who claimed all the lands belonged to the crown and had to be purchased from them. However the 'squatters' were rich and powerful and forced the government eventually to recognise their claims. Both government and squatters ignored the rights of the Aborigines.

An 1840 report by Governor Gipps stated: *Among the squatters of N.S.W. are the wealthiest of the land, occupying, with the permission of the Government (since 1836) thousands or tens of thousands of acres. Young men of good families and connections in England, officers of the army and navy, graduates of Oxford and Cambridge, are also in no small number among them.*

It was these men who were to be responsible for invading vast areas of N.S.W. and Victoria, massacring the tribes, because of the fortunes to be made from wool.

The lawlessness of this frontier, where settlers guarded their vast claims one from another and formed united militia against the Aborigines, prompted Governor Gipps to form a paramilitary 'Border Police'—and to make an example of some shepherd-convicts who had massacred Aborigines at Myall Creek.

Although these Border Police were used more to protect settlers in their occupation of tribal lands against Aborigines, the squatters who had to pay for their services, resented the interference of the Governor. They declared that his protection of Aborigines had encouraged the general insurrection of the tribes that occurred throughout N.S.W. and Victoria in the 1830s and 1840s. They did not see that it was their own invasion of tribal lands that sparked this insurrection.

In 1824 martial law was declared around Bathurst to give the army full rein to squash the Aborigines. Soon after this an armed party of police drove Aborigines into a swamp and rode around them shooting till all were dead.

One missionary, Rev. Thelkeld, reported:

Forty-five heads were collected and boiled down for the sake of the skulls. My informant, a Magistrate, saw the skulls packed for exportation in a case at Bathurst ready for shipment to accompany the commanding officer on his voyage to England. [14]

Few records have been kept of the slaughter —but one rare court record of 1838 speaks of 28 Aborigines taken from the hut of a friendly stockman, tied up and slaughtered. A newspaper, the *Monitor*, explained on 14th December 1838:

'In order that their cattle might never more be 'rushed', it was resolved to exterminate the whole race of blacks in that quarter.' ('Rushing' or chasing, reduces the yield of beef.) By 1855 New South Wales was 'pacified'.

Tasmania

Tasmania, like New South Wales, was a convict settlement. The elimination of most of the Aborigine inhabitants took place between 1804 and 1834. The massacres began on 3rd May at Risdon when the 102 Regiment of the British Army shot dead 50 Oyster Bay people, including women and children. The Tasmanians had approached without spears and with green boughs in their hands (the universal sign of peace). The commanding officer said afterwards that he did not 'apprehend' that the Aborigines would be 'any use' to the British. [15]

Many similar massacres followed. Sometimes the testicles of male Tasmanians were cut off to give the settlers 'exclusive rights' to the women. Tobacco pouches were made out of the testicles and sold. Poisoned food was distributed to the Tasmanians.

The Aboriginal resistance for a while barred the expansion of the European settlement. In 1831 they began to use captured firearms against the colonialists. This caused alarm. The *Colonial Times* stated:

'They are now becoming dangerous and, if not checked, in time will become as formidable in their descents on the settlers, as those of the Caffres at the Cape of Good Hope.' [16]

In 1828 Tasmanians were forbidden to enter European settlements. The colonialists' Executive Council concluded in the same year:

'to inspire them with terror . . . will be found the only effectual means of security for the future.' [17]

In 1829 all the settled areas were put under martial law. The Governor offered a reward for every adult and child captured. Under this prominent Australians, such as Batman, made a useful income for themselves. Batman's efforts resulted in his killing of at least thirty blacks and capturing eleven. [18]

Finally, late in 1830, the whole island was put under martial law and 5,000 whites mobilised to march in a 'black line' nine feet apart to drive the Tasmanians into a narrow peninsula in the South-East. This drive lasted two months and was a total failure with the only Aborigines captured—a boy and an old man—escaping and five whites dying from misadventure.

The fate of those who survived is further described in Chapter Six. Some were taken to Victoria as mistresses of white men. Many Victorian Aborigines have Tasmanian blood from this. Some who were brought to Victoria joined the Victorian Aborigines in their fight against the colonialists and were killed. Others were herded onto islands in the Bass Strait from whence eventually some returned to Tasmania.

Victoria

Victoria was first officially settled by the 'gentlemen-squatters' coming from New South Wales and Tasmania in the 'wool-rush' some forty-six years after the arrival of the First Fleet in Sydney Harbour. However from 1790 the coastal tribes were raided by sealers who established their mostly seasonal camps along the shore. They were often fought off by the Aborigines. Many Aborigines died and many Aboriginal women taken prisoner and raped. Some sealers camps were reportedly more permanent, with timber cutting between seal-hunting seasons.

The first offical attempt at a settlement was by Lt Col David Collins, who was sent by the British authorities in 1803 to exercise authority over the sealers and to raise the British flag. They were particularly concerned to show the French that the British had already claimed Victoria. He established his camp at Portsea and raised the flag. But he lasted less than a year. After several clashes with the Aborigines around Corio Bay he packed up and left. He noted before he left that one legacy of the invasion had arrived before him—many of the Aborigines were marked by small-pox. Thousands had in fact died, making the task of the later invaders much easier.

In 1834 the Hentys came with thousands of sheep to the land of the Gunditj-Mara at what is now Portland. It was a private venture, unauth-

orised by the British authorities, but the Hentys notified the authorities in London that they were willing to pay the Crown for the land they were taking. There was no talk of compensating the Gunditj-Mara. The Gunditj-mara resisted, and for six years held them to the Portland town site under siege.

A year later Batman arrived at the site of Melbourne. He was after 600,000 acres, thirty times as much land as Henty, and he attempted to lease this from the Wurundjeri nation. But his 'treaty' was broken almost as soon as it was made. Affluent squatters poured their sheep in. Within a year over 25,000 sheep had arrived in Melbourne and the squatters moved out to take tribal lands. Others cam down overland from Sydney.

The initial traditional hospitality of the Aborigines was soon ended. One squatter, Neil Black who came out in 1839, wrote that the most profitable runs were to be established well out of Melbourne where the land was cheapest:

'provided the conscience of the party was sufficiently seared to enable him to, without remorse, slaughter natives right and left.' (N. Black, Journal, La Trobe Collection.)

Wherever the squatters went, the native animals on which the Aborigines depended were driven out and sacred places desecrated. The people were given the choice of fighting and being killed, or reduced to destitution and beggary. Many fought.

In 1836, one year after Batman's arrival, the war was started. Warriors from the Kurung tribe overran the Mt Cottrell Station on the Werribee River. They were joined by the Wathaurung tribe as they attempted to stop the invasion of their lands. Bands of up to 200 warriors gave such fierce resistance that in 1837 the settlers of the Geelong area appealed to the Government for protection. In July 1838 the army was ordered to establish outposts across Victoria to protect the road to Sydney. The military became more actively involved in the Victorian wars and in 1840 were permitted to take hostages from the Goulburn Valley tribes. In 1839 the authorities formed the mounted para-military Border Police, convicts with military experience, for use against the Aborigines. They also recruited Aborigines into a 'Native Police' force to use them against their own people. They were usually employed against distant tribes that were effectively 'foreigners', or traditional enemies to the recruits. This force, under white officers, carried out many atrocities throughout Australia.

In 1838, three hundred warriors from the Pangerang Tribe drove out, with a series of attacks, the squatters attempting to take their lands near Wangaratta. The Aboriginal tribes united to co-ordinate attacks across Victoria and into New South Wales after soldiers broke up their Kulin 'Confederacy' Yarra Camp. The Aborigines were cruelly out-weaponed, but soon they acquired guns and learnt to use them. In 1840, twenty armed with guns attacked stations near King River.

In 1841 the *Port Phillip Herald* reported,

numerous attacks have been committed in the Westernport direction by a party of Aborigines . . . accompanied by two male Van Diemen's Land [Tasmanian] blacks and three women, who are as well skilled in the use of firearms as the males . . . (extending) to Dandenong and its vicinity. (29th October 1841)

In the Western District from the 1830s through the 1840s the Mara 'confederacy' of tribes, the Gunditj-Mara, the Tjapwurong, the Bungaditj, plus the neighbouring Kirrae and other tribes, fought a sustained guerilla war. They had their base camps in rocky areas such as the Stoney Rises and the Grampians which were impenetrable to troopers. In 1840 they drove off 1,300 sheep from the Grange Station. In January and February 1842 the war reached its height. Over 4,000 sheep were driven off. The thousands of stolen sheep were held by the Aborigines on their own vast sheep runs. Guns were stolen and used. The Portland *Mercury* in August 1842 reported:

the region may just as well be in a state of War.

In the 1840s the Aboriginal tribes were co-ordinating and arranging simultaneous attacks throughout Eastern Australia from Queensland to Portland.

The Mara concentrated their attacks on colonialists who had taken land around traditional meeting areas and sacred sites near Port Fairy, Mt Rouse, Mt Napier and Lake Condah. The Gunditj-Mara in 1842 with a series of raids forced the Eumeralla Station near Lake Condah to be evacuated. The Gunditj-Mara almost forced the evacuation of the district between 1844–5. Appeals went out for mounted police and troopers. The Wedge Brothers at the Grange and the Campbells at Flooding Creek stations installed swivel guns. Aborigines tried to right the balance by obtaining guns, so in 1840 it was made illegal to sell guns to Aborigines. All around Victoria fighting was severe. In August 1843 six hundred Aborigines attacked a station established near present-day Echuca. The defence of the Goulbourn valley was well planned. Whites blamed this on Winnaberrie, a warrior-leader of the Wurundjeri. During 1841 there were nearly daily raids between Melbourne and the Goulburn and Loddon Rivers.

The defence of the Wimmera was also well planned. The Jaardwa had one major guerrilla base at Mt Arapiles near Horsham. They even established a sheep station there. A squatter wrote:

they drove off a considerable number of my sheep and formed a station north of mine . . . where they made a bush-yard and shepherded the sheep during the day and yarded them in the usual way at night. [19]

Gippsland was equally well defended. Armed Aborigines held out there into the 1850s.

But by 1850, thirteen years of guerrilla warfare had exhausted the Tribes. They had been decimated by disease, by outright massacring by gun and poison, and overwhelmed by a never ending flood of fresh invaders. By 1841 Melbourne's population had risen to 20,000.

The invasion of the Aboriginal lands escalates — thousands join in the Victorian gold rush in the 1850s.
(Latrobe Collection)

By 1851 Victoria's white population was 77,000 — and then the gold rush started and by 1861 there were 540,000! The Aboriginal population has been estimated at 15,500 at the start of the invasion. In 1861 the Board for the Protection of Aborigines estimated the surviving population at 2,341.

It was not just loss of their ancestral lands that drove the Aborigines to war against the invaders. Most of the squatters despised the Aborigines. Most had no comprehension of Aboriginal culture and no wish to learn. Rather the native people were a pest to be exterminated. One squatter, Alexander Majoribanks, wrote:

The Aborigines are universally allowed to be the lowest race of savages in the known world . . . their extirpation would be of great benefit to the whole of the country.[20]

The Whyte Brothers who took up the Konong-wootong Run in the Western District immediately shot down and wiped out all but one of the local tribe.[21] At Murdering Hills in the Wando valley, for taking fifty sheep, fifty-one Aborigines were killed and their bones left to bleach in the sun.

Henry Meyrick described what was happening in Gippsland:

men, women and children are shot whenever they can be met with.[22]

The following story is recalled by Aborigines today. It comes from the high country in north-east Victoria. Old Mr Birt would tell it. He had heard it from his mother who was of the Ya-idthma-dthang Tribe whose land lies from the centre of the high country north to the plains, including Benambra and Mt Buffalo.

My mother would sit and cry and tell me this: they buried our babies in the ground with only their heads above the ground. All in a row they were. Then they had a test to see who could kick the babies' heads off the furtherst. One man clubbed a baby's head off from horse-back. They then spent most of the day raping the women, most of them were then tortured to death by sticking sharp things like spears up their vaginas until they died. They tied the men's hands behind their backs, then cut off their penis and testes and watched them run around screaming until they died. They killed in other bad ways too.

'I lived because I was young and pretty and one of the men kept me for himself, but I was always tied up until I escaped into another land to the west.

Mr Birt said of himself:

In my life, I spent all my younger years keeping away from the Board of Protection for Aboriginals and the law (police) and trying to live the way I was brought up–the traditional way–but the white man wouldn't let me and he wouldn't let me have my own beliefs. Even these he wished to change.[23]

Similar events occurred at the same time in the interior of New South Wales.

The British authorities proclaimed while this was happening that they had accorded to the Aborigines the great privilege of British citizenship, and that the Aborigines were free to seek justice in the courts. However, any Aboriginal who tried this found that he was not allowed to give evidence. The only acceptable evidence in law was that of the whites. Thus if the only witnesses to a massacre were Aborigines and the white killers, only the killers' evidence could be heard! Also, if an Aborigine were accused–he or she was not allowed to give evidence in his or her defence, call other Aborigines as witnesses or give an alibi.

William Charles Wentworth, the so-called 'Father of Australian Democracy' said,

that it would be quite as indefensible to receive as evidence in a court of justice the chatterings of the ourang outang as of this savage race.[24]

South Australia

South Australia was settled without the use of convicts and under stricter governmental control. In 1836 Adelaide was established without initial conflict, it seems, on the lands of the Kauna Tribe. But by 1842 troopers were being called in to suppress the Kauna, who, according to Police-Commissioner O'Hallern, were showing, 'great courage and resolution' in defence of their lands in the Wakefield district.

The Whalers settled on Kangaroo Island were notorious for their raids on mainland tribes for women.

At Rufus River, the 'Protector of Aborigines' led an armed party in a massacre of

A Lake Tyers family in the 1860s (Latrobe Collection).

over 30 Aborigines. At Rivoli Bay, poisoned food was given out. The Police Commissioner's report of 1840 stated that:

damper poisoned with corrosive sublimate was given them. [25]

Queensland

Since Queensland was invaded later, the resistance was carried on into this century. The first colonialists to enter this State were brutal in the extreme. Groups of well-armed whites would go out to avenge any killing of a settler, a cow or a sheep. A witness wrote:

the white man's revenge is pure terrorism, in the waterholes in some parts of the north may be seen the ghastly remains of the dead blacks, skulls, ribs and thigh bones strewn out. [26]

A government report estimated that 50 Aborigines were killed for every white killed. [27]

One report in 1885 stated:

The niggers (were given) . . . something really startling to keep them quiet . . . the rations contained about as much strychnine as anything else and not one of the mob escaped . . . more than a hundred blacks were stretched out by this ruse of the owner of Long Lagoon. [28]

Another recalled 'hundreds of blacks shot and left to rot like cattle where they fell.' [29] The present author has been told by Aboriginal Elders of the far north of how a well-known European explorer, Jardine, used to pick up Aboriginal children by the ankles and kill them by swinging their heads hard against trees. [30]

In 1857 a 'squatters' crusade waged for six months in the Dawson and Burnett region of Queensland, incorporating small armies of settlers and police patrols, against *all* Aborigines in the region—in the course of which hundreds of Aborigines were captured, chained up and killed. [31] In 1875 Aborigines attacked and killed a settler-couple. The revenge extracted was horrific:

'*Scores of skeletons lie bleaching in the noonday sun in the scrubby coast ranges adjoining the scene of that awful murder.*' [32]

Such incidents were commonplace.

Despite the massacres, Aboriginal bands continued to try to stop whites taking more and more of their lands. The cattle stations had to be built with loop-holes for rifles in their thick walls. When gold was discovered at Palmer River the Aboriginal people tried to stop the gold-rush on to their lands. Several hundred whites died. The Cooktown *Courier* reported in 1873 that the road to the gold field was

'*almost milestoned by the corpses of white men.*' [33]

A long campaign was fought by one tribe known as the Kalkadoons during the 1880s stopping all settlement in some parts near Cloncurry. They numbered about two thousand fully trained warriors. [34]

One of the descendants of the Kalkadoons, Mr Shorty O'Neill (in 1980, editor of the North Queensland Land Council newspaper *Messagestick*') told the author of how in 1884 nearly all his people were massacred. First most of the women, children and old people were surprised and shot down in Skull Gorge. Then, not long after, the men were cornered on Battle Hill. They did not have the choice of continuing their well tried and successful guerrilla tactics. The place where they were was very sacred and they felt they could not leave it undefended. They all died in its defence.

The Mapoon people told the author that they stopped the first cattle station being built on their lands. [35] The strength of the tribes in the north was never finally broken. The Cooktown *Courier* reported:

'*The struggle has been obstinate and fierce. Although an unusually large and costly body of police has for years engaged in exterminating the Aborigines, and few whites miss a chance of shooting any they may encounter, the strength of the tribes has not been broken. No doubt their numbers have been greatly thinned but they have not been cowed. Consequently there is no part of Queensland in which more European lives have been lost . . . Prospecting for minerals can only be carried out by well-armed and equipped parties. Evidently, settlement*

*must be delayed until the work of extermin-
ating is complete—a consumption of which
there is no present prospect—or until some
more rational and humane methods of dealing
with the blacks are adopted.'* [36]

It was not that there was no protest against
the massacres. By this time the liberal press
was full of outraged horror. There were out-
cries against the police: 'The barbarous corps of
exterminators,' 'a system of native slaughter . . .
merciless and complete,' 'our trained murderers
. . . saturated with innocent blood.' But the
government coolly answered that 'no illegal
acts were occurring'—at the worse, there were
only 'indiscretions'. Genocide was, it seems,
official government policy. [37]

The same stories are repeated throughout
Australia. The last areas to be colonised were
north west Australia (the Kimberleys), central
Australia and central northern Australia (Arnhemland). Central northern Australia with
part of central Australia, now constitutes the
Northern Territory.

Western Australia

The colonisation of Western Australia pro-
ceeded in the same fashion as in the Eastern
States, excepting that before the introduction
of convicts in 1850 Aborigines were sometimes
utilised as a labour force for the stations. Even
after that date, as the convicts were not permitted north of the Murchison River, Aborigines were invaluable in the north as a labour
force. They were forced to live in labour
camps near the station homesteads.

Many who settled the Kimberleys brought
both their cattle overland from Queensland and
their attitudes towards Aborigines. Killings
were frequent.

The Rev. J. Gibble, an Anglican Missionary
at Forrest River, reported in 1886;

*'Many natives were shot in the back for no
other reason than they were running away from
their slave masters.'* [38]

However, Aboriginal resistance had one
success in the Kimberleys when in 1909 Aborig-

inal killing of cattle induced the government to
resume over one million acres at Moola Bulla
on the upper Margaret River for the Aborigines
to run as their own cattle station.

The move to set up cattle stations across
northern Australia was the first serious threat
to the tribes of the north. To quell their resistance punitive police expeditions would massacre whole tribes.

One of the last documented massacres in
the northwest took place in 1928. In that year
a missionary took it upon himself to investigate
the reports of continual massacres given to him
by Aborigines. He tracked a police party that
had come on to the Forrest River Aboriginal
Reserve. He discovered that these policemen
had arrested a tribe, chained them up by the
neck, and then killed all but three women.
They then burnt the bodies and took the three
women to their camp. Before leaving the
camp, they killed and burned these women too.

The evidence of the missionary eventually
resulted in an enquiry entitled *'The Royal
Commission into the Killing and Burning of the
Bodies of Aborigines in East Kimberley and
into police methods when effecting arrest'*
(1928 West Australian Parliamentary papers
vol. 1, page 10).[39] Despite this, the police responsible were never brought to trial.

Nipper Tabagee, Elder of the Yungngora
community on Noonkanbah, told the author
in 1979 of how Sandmara, known to the
harassed settlers and police as Pigeon, had led
a band of about fifty warriors for three years.
He struck fear into the colonists of the region,
striking again and again from their hideouts in
the caves of Wyndjina Gorge and elsewhere.
On one occasion they burnt down the local
strongly constructed police station (the remains
of which I have seen). Eventually he was killed
in a long drawn out gun-battle, in 1897. His
lieutenant, Captain, was sent to the Aboriginal
prison on Rottnest Island two thousand miles
to the South. The Aborigine who persuaded
him to take up arms, Ellamara, was hung at
Derby.

The author was also shown buried in caves
the bones of Aborigines who were killed by the

Nipper Tabagee shows a cave where the dead, killed by the police, are buried at Djada Hill, Noonkanbah (Jan Roberts).

'Now one day they been killing a bullock, you know, bush boys. Big mob of bush boys been there when that manager come mustering around. See bones of bullock and they following the tracks, follow them up, just round them up and shoot them like a kangaroo.

'Same feller chaining them up . . . tie them up longa tree . . . start a fire . . . one Gudia [European] finish them off. They take kerosene along in backpack, chain them up, when they been getting along the camp, take the chain off and start all the fire. Put them right around the tree . . . put them right around, right . . . go in there and tie them up inside and put the kerosene . . . chuck him right around . . . and chuck it on the boys too. Right, get a match.' (Ginger Ngunwilla lights a match and throws it to the ground, raises his eyebrows and shrugs.)[40]

police when they came along the Fitzroy River to 'pacify' the tribes. Noonkanbah Station is on land that Aborigines died to defend. Skeleton Hill on Noonkanbah is named after the bones left around it after the visit by police.

Ginger Ngunwilla, a very senior Elder at Noonkanbah, told in 1978 of one incident. The son of one white man on Quanbun Station (adjacent to Noonkanbah Station) died when he was out working bullocks because he could not find water. His father, however, blamed the Aborigines. So he got out his gun and called in the police.

He been shooting all along this river (the Fitzroy River on Noonkanbah). We can show you any time you know—bones laying just like rubbish. Right along he go shooting . . . From here must be down to Jubilee, must be from Fitzroy to Fossil Downs. After that one they been going shooting in George Ranges, gone back, killing whole lot, nothing left.

Ginger Ngunwilla also recalls that when he was young—about four foot tall—a terrible massacre occurred between Christmas Creek and Bohemia Downs Station east of Noonkanbah.

The Northern Territory

The first Europeans to arrive on the Northern Territory coast were the Dutch. They found gold and planned a settlement, but were sent on their way by the coastal tribes. The next to arrive were the British who set up Fort Dundas on Melville Island in 1823.

The local Aborigines laid siege to the fort making a misery of the lives of the garrison, so in 1829 it was abandoned.

Giles, 'exploring' the Musgrove Ranges around 1873, spoke of the way the people tried to throw his party of well-armed men out. In what he called 'The Battle of the Officer', two hundred attacked with the cry, in pidgin, 'Walk, whitefeller, walk'. At Ularring he described the attack:

'At a first glance this force was most imposing; the coup d'oeil was really magnificent; they looked like what I should imagine a band of Comanche Indians would appear when ranged in battle line. The men were closely packed in serried ranks and it was evident they formed a drilled and perfectly organised force . . . approached in a solid phalanx of five or six rows, each row consisting of eighteen or twenty warriors.'[41]

The role of Giles and the other 'explorers' was to map out a path by which Europeans could take over the better parts of the land. The first substantial white settlement in the Territory was not begun until 1869 when surveyors arrived to plan the port of Darwin (then called Palmerston). About the same time they also started surveying the route for the overland telegraph to the South. Because the Aborigines resisted this invasion of their lands, the telegraph stations were built like forts with stone walls and narrow slit windows. Although the first cattle station was started in 1860, it was not until the late 1870s that any cattle stations were successfully founded. The others were abandoned because of Aboriginal resistance.

Some officials did attempt to see events from an Aboriginal point of view. An outstanding example of this was the Government-Resident's Report on the Northern Territory in 1889:

'After careful inquiry, I am of opinion that this is the attitude of the aborigines towards Europeans. Entrance into their country is an act of invasion. It is a declaration of war, and they will halt at no opportunity for attacking the white invaders.

'. . . occupation of the country for pastoral purposes and peaceable relations with the native tribes are hopelessly irreconcilable.'

He went on to recommend the establishment of reserves in which the tribes would retain 'absolute rights and full control'–i.e.–sovereignty.

But the lands given to the cattle stations by the British authorities were huge. Some were (and are) the size of Belgium or Wales. The cattlemen ruled (and rule) like barons over thousands of square miles of former Aboriginal land.

What happened to the Aborigines whose land was given to the cattle barons? Some still live in squalid labour camps on the cattle stations, but many were simply massacred. This was the instinctive response of the white settlers to any resistance by the tribes. Up until the Second World War, whole tribes would be exterminated if Aborigines tried to resist by killing cattle, or by killing white people who had invaded their land, desecrated sacred places and polluted precious and vital springs.

Just one example of the many such massacres in the Northern Territory would be the slaughter of at least 51 Aborigines by a revenge party of police and cattlemen in 1928 near Coniston. Some Aborigines, in trying to protect their land by deterring the colonialists, had killed one white man and some cattle. A Board of Inquiry into the atrocity said that the police had killed in 'self-defence' 34 Aborigines. One policeman said that he had to shoot to kill as he wouldn't have known what to do with wounded prisoners so far from 'civilisation'. Reports from Aborigines suggest that over 60 were, in fact, killed.[42]

A picture of the way in which Aborigines were treated on the cattle stations in the 1930s can be obtained from a letter in the *Northern Territory Standard* in 1938. The writer said he used a summary justice on his station and that:

'I had a letter from a man who was attacked by niggers in the Gulf Country: "I shot at sight. Have killed 37 to date." Another man boasted that he had inflicted his punishment with a stock whip and wirecracker. To be particularly severe he sharpened a piece of sapling and drove it through both hands of the offender. He assured me that he was ceasing to have trouble with niggers.'[43]

In belated conscience, under pressure from concerned humanitarians and churchmen, the various State governments decided to create reserves for the 'dying-out' desert Aborigines in central Australia on land unwanted by the cattle men and to put on these reserves church missions to protect, control and confine the Aborigines. The central Australian desert reserves were instituted between 1920 and 1954.

The hills and plateaus of Arnhemland, east of Darwin, were held by the tribes as their sovereign territory up until the 1930s. In 1930 and 1932 several white men who entered the territory were killed. After the killing of a constable in 1933, it was announced that a punitive police expedition would be sent in. But some missionaries met with the leader of the Aborigines, Tuckiar, and persuaded him to go to Darwin for negotiations with the authorities. Instead he was gaoled. He was eventually found not guilty—but in the meantime the authorities had decided to make Arnhemland into a major Aboriginal reserve and to authorise the Yirrkala Methodist missionary station on the reserve to pacify and 'civilise' the Aborigines.

This was, in a way, a partial victory for the Arnhemland tribes. They had won their fight to preserve most of their lands even though they had to accept government and missionary settlements and coercive regulations. They were to keep these lands up until the 1960s when international mining companies would start to covet and take their land.

Footnotes

1. Keith Willey, *When the Sky Fell Down*, 1979, p. 52.
2. Willey, p. 43.
3. Willey, p. 45.
4. Willey, p. 45.
5. Willey, p. 46.
6. Willey, p. 69.
7. Willey, p. 72.
8. Willey, p. 85.
9. Willey, p. 173.
10. Robinson and York, *The Black Resistance* (Widescope, 1977).
11. Willey, p. 175.
12. Willey, p. 196.
13. Some stations did employ Aborigines, particularly after the start of the gold rush when they lost their employees to the gold-fields. Some stations owed their survival to Aboriginal labour. By this time (the 1850s) many Aborigines had lost their lands and were starving.
14. Willey, p. 214.
15. Robinson & York.
16. Robinson & York.
17. Robinson & York.
18. J. Blackhouse, *A Narrative of a Visit to the Australian Colonies* (London, 1843).
19. Bride, quoted in Christie, *Aborigines in Colonial Victoria* (1980), p. 166.
20. A. Marjoribanks, *Travels in N.S.W.* (London, 1843), p. 82.
21. Sievewright to Earl Grey, 8 May 1847, Box 14 APR, ProVic.
22. H. Merick, 30 April 1846, letter to family in England. La Trobe Collection, SLV, quoted in Christie, p. 51.

23. Account given anonymously to author.
24. *Sydney Morning Herald*, 21 June 1844.
25. South Australian history was similar to Victorian in its treatment of Aborigines.
26. Evans, Saunders and Cronin, *Exclusion, Exploitation and Extermination: Race Relations in Colonial Queensland* (ANZ 1975), p. 49.
27. Archibald Meston, Report 1889, in Evans, p. 51.
28. Evans, p. 49.
29. *ibid.*
30. Jan Roberts, *The Mapoon Books* (International Development Action 1975) Book One, p. 6.
31. Evans, pp. 51-2.
32. Evans, p. 53.
33. Evans, p. 44.
34. Robinson & York, p. 53.
35. Jan Roberts, *Mapoon Book One*, p. 6.
36. Quoted in S. Stone, *Aborigines in White Australia* (Heinemann 1974), p. 93.
37. Evans, pp. 62-3.
38. J. Gribble, *Dark Deeds in a Sunny Land*.
39. 1928 West Australian Parliamentary papers, Vol. 1, p. 10, in Sharmon Stone, *Aborigines in White Australia, documentary history* (Heinemann Educational, Australia, 1974).
40. As told to Steve Hawke by Ginger Ngunwilla in 1978 – unpublished manuscript.
41. Stone, p. 149.
42. *The Coniston Killings*, unpublished manuscript, S. Nugent, Anthropology Dept, University College, London. Geoff Eames, 'Aborigines, law and land rights' in *Legal Service Bulletin*, Dec. 1976, p. 103.
43. *Northern Territories Standard*, 1938.

5 WOMEN ENSLAVED

In the early days of settlement, white women were few and far between, so white men took to abducting Aboriginal women and keeping them in virtual slavery. Squatters like Robertson of Wando Vale on the Glenelg River in the Victorian Western District

'kept a harem for himself and for his men' [1]

much to the bitter hostility of the Aborigines. The same person reported that the vicious treatment of Aboriginal women was the cause of

'nearly every Aboriginal outrage that has happened in my district.' [2]

This happened right from the first. The shepherds abducted Aboriginal women and enslaved them to such an extent that Burke in 1837 issued an ineffective proclamation forbidding the forceful detention of Aboriginal women by squatters and their men.

In Tasmania, captured Aboriginal men were castrated and their women taken from them.

When the reserves and missions were established, the women on them were protected from this abuse and became the particular targets of the missionaries. From 1874, in Victoria, they were sent out to 'Christian' families as domestics on the lowest of pay. As they received more education than the men, they became the scribes of the protest movements on the reserves. In 1880, the dormitory girls of Coranderrk Reserve shocked the manager by going on strike for wages.

On the cattle stations, 'the Aboriginal woman is usually at the mercy of anybody' from among the white staff and 'locked up at night to keep the women from their own people'. [3]

In 1900, a station owned by the Queensland National Bank had 'eight or nine gins fenced in with rabbit-proof netting next to the house'. [4] One man 'sent a gin away with the mailman to Burketown to be sent south to some of his friends as a slave'. [5] Parties of men used to go out to capture 'gins'. These women were traded between stations.

A government report in 1900 stated that women were 'handed around from station to station, until discarded to rot away with venereal disease.[6]

The Aborigines fiercely resisted this slave trade. A magistrate reported: 'Every murder that occurred on the coast was due to the carrying off of gins',[7] and a select committee was told 'in the matter of kidnapping gins, you cannot control white men . . . and it is the cause of half the murders committed by the blacks upon them.'[8]

The government, however, frowned on this. They considered marriage between white men and blacks as 'degrading to the man although in nearly all cases the man is of a very low type'.[9] But especially they were against such unions as 'it means the breeding of half-castes'. The women must be put 'in absolute isolation from contacts with whites'[10] in order to prevent this calamity. These opinions were lent scientific respectability by such writings as the 1907 *Science of Man* which propounded: 'The hybrid and mongrel mixtures of mankind are as unsatisfactory as those of the lower animals and they usually degenerate and become extinct'.[11]

A more recent account of the conditions under which Aboriginal women had to live was given by Vi Stanton and Elizabeth Pearce in the book *Living Black* by Kevin Gilbert.

Elizabeth Pearce comes from an Aboriginal Reserve in the Northern Territory. Her mother was forcibly taken there from a cattle station because she had a white father and an Aboriginal mother. Elizabeth Pearce described it thus:

'There was a round-up period every so often when all the part-Aboriginal kids were gathered up from the camps and taken to various missions when the missions first started. The children had no choice. The parents didn't want them taken but they also had no choice . . . ' [12]

To this Vi Stanton added:

'The thing was, it wasn't good to see these little part or half breeds running around the blacks' camp because you didn't know who to blame. Station manager? Storeman? Policeman?'[13]

The Aboriginal mother thus was seen as having no rights to her own children. Instead she was looked on as a degrading influence on the children. The authorities thought, as Vi put it, 'there's some hope for them because they've got white blood in their veins'.

Elizabeth's mother was sent to the isolated island mission on Groote Eylandt, 'because the growing part-Aboriginal girls were running away'.

Elizabeth continued. 'Any girl causing trouble was put into stocks and leg-irons . . . the girls were allowed no contact with the tribal people.'[14]

Vi Stanton herself found that she was not allowed to get married without the Government's permission. Her white husband was warned that he had broken the law and could have been jailed for a year's hard labour for marrying her without an exemption certificate. This certificate removed her from the laws controlling Aborigines but also legally meant that she could no longer claim to be an Aboriginal.

Note: As author, I would like to apologise for the shortness of this chapter. The experiences of other Aboriginal women are described elsewhere in this book—but rather as the experiences of Aborigines than specifically as women. There are indications, some of which are given above, that women were particularly singled out by the colonists for exploitation, rape and forced labour while the Aboriginal men were killed (e.g., see section on the colonialisation of Tasmania). The lust for 'black velvet', as the white men crudely put it, caused many a massacre.

However, much more research needs to be done on this, and I do not have the materials. Up until now few Australian books on women in Australia have even mentioned Aborigines. The recently published Australian bestseller, *The Real Matilda: Women and Identity in*

A woman of New South Wales (Augustus Earle).

Australia 1778 to 1965 by Miriam Dixson, is a very good example of this blind-spot in Australia. It only mentions Aboriginal women in so far as they affected white sexual guilt feelings!

Footnotes

1. E. Parker, *Report*, 1st April to 31st June 1840, Box 5, APR, ProVic.
2. *ibid.*
3. Evans, Saunders and Cronin, *Exclusion, Exploitation and Extermination: Race Relations in Colonial Queensland* (ANZ, 1975), p. 103.
4. *ibid*, p. 107.
5. *ibid*, p. 107.
6. *ibid*, p. 116.
7. *ibid*, p. 106.
8. *ibid*, p. 104.
9. *ibid*, p. 108.
10. *ibid*, p. 108.
11. *ibid*, p. 109.
12. Kevin Gilbert, *Living Black* (Allen Lane, 1977), p. 7.
13. *ibid*, p. 7.
14. *ibid*, p. 8.

6 'LET'S CIVILISE THEM' – GOVERNMENT RESERVES

The larger reserves of the north and centre have a very different history from the smaller earlier established reserves in the south.

The larger reserves were created to help end the undeclared war against the indigenous peoples of Australia. The colonial authorities decided in the late 1890s to allow some of the remaining undefeated tribes to retain the use of their lands. Thus, in the 1890s the Weipa and Mapoon Aboriginal Reserves were established in Northern Queensland, and during the next forty years, the other major reserves of the Kimberleys and the Northern Territory.

By Government policy, these were all established on lands not then wanted by white settlers. They were considered a temporary expediant as the Aborigines would sooner or later die out. These lands were to be policed and controlled by either Government or mission settlements. It was hoped that by removing from these tribes the necessity of fighting for their lands, nearby white settlers would be made more secure. Title to these lands, however, remained with the Government.

The smaller, older reserves of the south on the other hand, have a very different history. They were initially established as a concession to the humanitarians who believed Aborigines to be capable of being 'civilised'. They were also to serve as a form of concentration camp to remove an eyesore (the Aborigines) from areas of white settlement. There was no question of allowing Aborigines to have large reserves in those areas sought after by white settlers. Normally they were located on areas of poor soil, of no use for agriculture or grazing. When the areas were wanted by whites, the reserves were soon closed.

Sydney and New South Wales

Governor Phillip, by the end of the first year of the settlement, had decided that he should make an effort at civilising some of the Aborigines. He decided that the only way to do this was to take them captive. So in December 1788, he ordered Lieutenant Ball to seize two Aborigines at Manly Cove.[1]

He only succeeded in capturing one, who was named 'Manly' and immediately given clothes to wear. The prisoner's real name was Arabanoo. He only lived five months before dying of small-pox.

In November 1789, Phillip ordered two more Aborigines to be captured and this time Bennelong and Colby were seized. Colby escaped after two weeks. Bennelong escaped in May 1790 but returned a few months later. For most of the rest of his life he attempted to fill the role of a go-between. He learnt English; none of the settlers learnt any Aboriginal language. Eventually he died, a figure of ridicule to many of the whites, and an alcoholic.

The first more systematic attempt to 'civilise' the Aborigines was an initiative in 1814 of a Congregationalist trader named William Shelley. This was adopted by Governor Macquarie as a public counter-balance to his attempts to terrorise the tribes with mass hangings and military expeditions. (See page 15)

Shelley, and then his wife, received official

support for a school for Aboriginal children in Parramatta. He set out to prove that Aborigines were capable of 'civilisation', i.e. that they could learn to live as the British. In 1819, one of their pupils came first in the Sydney *Anniversary School Examination* in which 21 Aborigines and over 100 white children took part.

In 1823, the school was moved to a reserve outside the town to 'protect' the students. The school's site became known as Blacktown. According to Rev. Leigh, many ridiculed the school's efforts, saying 'the missionary may as well attempt to teach the kangaroos and opossums.' In 1826, the school finally closed. In 1838, Mrs Shelley said that the students had afterwards 'relapsed into all the bad habits of the untaught natives.'[2]

Governor Macquarie also tried to 'civilise' the Aborigines by establishing 16 Aboriginal families on farmlets on George's Head. They were given supplies and told to support themselves by farming, and to live in the huts built for them.

The Aborigines regarded the houses as useless and did not use them. They saw no need to support themselves by farming, and instead used a boat provided to support themselves in a more traditional way by fishing. They traded surplus fish with the whites.

This attempt was the first Aboriginal reserve. The Lower Hawkesbury River was supposed to be a reserve for unconquered tribes in 1795 – but was never respected by the settlers.

The reserves were also a concession to the rise, in the 1830s, of the Wilberforce lobby in London, first against the slave trade, and then against the slaughter of the Aboriginal peoples of Tasmania.

Tasmania

In Tasmania, just over two hundred Aborigines were persuaded by a missionary to lay down their arms in return for a cease-fire and a small island Reserve. A press release to the local paper reported that large tracts of pasture previously under Aboriginal control would now be available. The Aborigines were taken to Flinders Island which, alongside Cape Barren

Island, lies off the northern Tasmanian coast.

Here the Aborigines were confined. Some of the men were castrated and the women raped by the guards, but the missionary in charge, the Rev. Robinson, concentrated on civilising not the guards but the Aboriginal children, separating them from their parents. It was also here that they became known as 'Cape Islanders' rather than Tasmanians.

Robinson had picked the site for his 'Aboriginal establishment' knowing the islands were already occupied by a mixed Aboriginal and white community. This had been formed by white sealers and local Aborigines, at first on a friendly basis but later by the abduction of Aboriginal women. Robinson thought these women would add strength to his establishment so he seized them from the sealers. However he was forced to return one wife to each sealer. In 1835 the sealers raided the Victorian coastline for more women.

Robinson found the women he had seized on the islands a constant source of trouble and left for Victoria in 1839. In 1847 the Government decided to remove some of the 'full-bloods' to Oyster Cove near Hobart. This was done because it feared that the sealing community was 'contaminating' the 'full-bloods' and this would lead to an increase in numbers, and expense. 'Half-caste' children were deplored as combining the worst features of both races.

However they left behind an increasingly thriving and independent island community that united whites and blacks in the same families. There were still at least seven 'full-bloods' among them, but they saw themselves strongly as one community. They fused elements of both cultures. They moved from island to island hunting mutton birds and seals and threaded the traditional Aboriginal shell necklaces. They also grew wheat and potatoes and reared pigs and goats.

However when they applied in 1850 for a teacher to be paid for out of the Land Fund used to support the Aborigines at Oyster Cove, they were refused by the Lieutenant-Governor on the grounds that they 'could not fairly be termed Aborigines. (Thus began the myth of their extinction.) He sent instead Anglican missionaries to the islands. Bishop Bromby in 1876 said that their Aboriginal ancestry had made them a godless community, for they continued strong and independent. Eventually some moved back to the Tasmanian mainland while others remained on the islands.

They continued to fight for recognition as Aborigines and for recognition of their right to own the islands. But most Australian history books still say they are extinct because the people at the 'official' Aboriginal settlement at Oyster Cove did not survive. Truganini was not the last of the Tasmanian Aborigines, but the last of the Oyster Cove people.

Victoria

Victoria developed the Tasmanian experiments, recruiting the Rev. Robinson from Tasmania. Its experiments with native boards of protection and native police influenced official policies throughout Australia.

The first 'reserve' in Victoria was a traditionally important Aboriginal camping place which has since been made into Melbourne's Botanical Gardens. It took only three years (1836–39) for the settlers to have this Aboriginal reserve closed and the Aborigines evicted. Captain Lonsdale had been told to 'train the infant Aboriginal so that he may merge into the ranks of colonial labourers.' But many whites saw such efforts as a waste of time because of the 'inferiority' of the Aboriginal race. Thus, when a school was established for Aboriginal children in 1846 near another traditional Aboriginal camping ground on the Merri Creek in what is now the Yarra Bend Park, the *Geelong Advertiser* was furious. It stated:

'all measures taken to the eventual civilisation of future generations are founded upon illusion . . . the perpetration of the Aboriginal race is not to be desired . . . it is no more desirable that any inferior race should be perpetuated than that the transmission of an hereditary disease such as scrofula or insanity should be encouraged.' [3]

Against such opposition, Government support for other Aboriginal stations and schools was luke-warm. Much more effort went into the war against the tribes.

By 1856, the war had died down, at least in terms of armed resistance. The Aborigines were swamped by the gold rush, and were no longer seen as a great threat. The *Argus* could write on 28th October 1856 of the Aborigines as if they were harmless children rather than wild animals. In an editorial, it stated that the Aborigine was in a position like

'to that of an infant, as yet incapable of self-control, innocent of the knowledge of good or evil and destitute alike of foresight and experience—therefore he requires protection.'

Although this reeked of paternalism, Aborigines wisely were quick to take advantage of this change of mood.

In 1859, a delegation from the Kulin tribes of the Yarra and Goulburn River valleys went to the State Government to request a tract of land unused by white man by the Acheron River and Little River junction. They were granted this and started to build their settlement, but a year later the squatters started to use their land for themselves, and the people were shifted from the land they had chosen.

Again, in 1863, Aborigines through their spokesmen, Wonga and Barak, attempted to set up their own settlement near Healesville. Sixty of them chose the land they wanted and it was granted to them by the State Government. This time some of the land chosen was fertile and could be planted. The Aborigines named this land Coranderrk and built on it a flourishing self-supporting, initially Aboriginal-controlled community.

One other reserve was set up under direct government control—Framlingham. Others were set up by church missions.

The history of the next twenty years until 1886 was dominated by government efforts to squash any sign of independence in the Aboriginal settlements and to bring the Aboriginal population directly under the paternalistic control of the 'Board for the Protection of Aborigines'.

First, the Board was concerned because many Aborigines remained on their tribal lands outside the settlements. They were also worried because the Aborigines persisted in keeping their children under their own control and in teaching them Aboriginal culture. They wanted to 'civilise' the Aborigines, i.e., give them the great gift of British culture.

The cultural arrogance of the British prevented them from seeing that the Aborigines had a culture, a law and an educational system of their own which they preferred to the British. Aboriginal people could not regard too highly a culture that used convict labour, had brutal public floggings, murdered Aboriginal children and adults and stripped the land of its native bush, animal and bird life.

Instead, many of the colonialists believed that the Aborigines did not learn white ways because of the degradation of human nature caused by Aboriginal customs. They resolved that the Aborigines should be stripped of these pagan customs. If the Aborigines would not come voluntarily to the reserves, then they must be forced.

As early as 1848, La Trobe had advocated that Aboriginal men should be subjected 'to a strict military discipline' and put to work, and that for Aboriginal children,

'nothing short of an actual and total separation from their parents and natural associates, and Education, at a distance from the parents and beyond the influence of . . . their tribe would hold out a reasonable hope of their ultimate civilisation and Christianisation.' [4]

(His strategy was to be that of most missions up until at least the 1960s.)

So, in 1869, an Act was passed in Victoria under which Aborigines could be told where they could live. Children could also be removed from their parents, and all monies earned by Aborigines were put under government control.

Aboriginal people then began a state-wide campaign. Letters were sent to the press and to the Government, summonses for assault were taken out by Aborigines against missionaries who physically punished Aborigines, delegations were sent to the Government.

Plans of the Government to shift the Coranderrk Aborigines further from Melbourne were leaked. The Aboriginal campaign under Barak intensified. The press was skilfully used with notices of deputations, letters and interviews.

Deputation of Aborigines at Parliament House, Melbourne, 1882 (Latrobe Collection).

Coranderrk,
Oct 23. 1893.

To Mr. Officer
Sir,

Dear Friend,
We have much pleasure in writing these few lines to you. We heard little
about our land going to be taken from us. There is not many of us blacks here.
They ought to leave us alone and not take the land from us it is not much. We
are dying away by degree. There is plenty more land around the country with-
out troubling about Coranderrk. We Aboriginals from Coranderrk wish to
know if it's true about the land. Please we wish to know. We got plenty from
our own cattle and we want the run for them and if the white people take it
from us there will be no place to put them. We mean cattle for the use of the
station. We never forgot Mr. Berry said to us in the town Hall when we passed
the native weapons to him. He told us we can go away and come to our home
here again any time to our station.
We don't forget Mr. Berry's word and also when we go into any of the white
people's paddock to hunt or fish, they soon clear us out of their private
premises very quickly and yet they are craving for Coranderrk we only got
enough run for to have our sports and games.

SIGNED:
Lizzy Davis,   *Peter Hunter*
Sarah Barrack   *June Donnelly*
Alfred Davis   *Alice Login*
Maggie Purcell   *Alexander Login*
Bill Russell   *Ellen Wandin*
Louise Russell

The Government suspected that Aborigines could not be doing all this by themselves. They hired a detective to find the 'white stirrer' behind the letters, but he had to report that the people were indeed writing their own letters. Government administrators and missionaries fumed about the 'insubordination', but in 1882, the Coranderrk Aborigines won the 'permanent' right to stay on the land they had chosen. Framlingham used similar tactics to prevent closure.

While this was going on, the Board for the Protection of Aborigines was evolving other strategies to silence the Aborigines. They decided first to greatly increase the managers' powers so 'insubordinate' Aborigines could be banished, and access to town and work controlled by permit.

But even more insidiously, they decided to introduce a distinction between 'Aborigines' and 'half-castes'. Such a distinction did not exist in law before. But in 1886, a law was passed banning all 'half-castes' under 35 years of age from the reserves. This law tore families apart. The Board justified it by saying that the 'half-castes' could be assimilated since they would be more acceptable to the colour-conscious whites. The Parliamentary Draftsman, Edward Guiness, wrote in a memo that the object is

'to get the half-castes off the reserves and make it possible to prosecute them under the vagrancy laws, otherwise they might refuse to work and might continue to loaf around with Aboriginals.' [5]

They also stated that this would mean that fewer reserves would be needed, so reserves could be closed and handed over to settlers; and, as the full-bloods became fewer, eventually there would be no reserves for Aborigines in Victoria.

By this Act, they attempted to strip the name 'Aboriginal' from people who lived, thought and identified as Aborigine. They believed that the 'half-castes' were the trouble-makers behind the 'full-bloods'. A prevalent idea was that the full-bloods were 'noble savages' who would not by themselves make trouble for the whites. Barak indeed had appointed two 'half-castes' who had been to school and could read and write (as he could himself) to be his assistants.

This policy of denying the Aboriginality of all who had any white blood enabled the Victorian Premier to say in 1951 that 'the problem of the Aborigines has (virtually) disappeared.' However the only problem that had been solved was that of how to dispossess the Aborigines of the last lands they had.

Only the small reserves at Lake Tyers and Framlingham were to survive due to strong Aboriginal protest and campaigns by supporters. But on these, coercive and repressive regulations remained in force. Up until 1957, compulsory work, or expulsion, could be imposed on the able-bodied; the manager had to be obeyed and all had to have residency permits. The manager's permission was needed before Aborigines could get outside work or visit towns.

Barak, Thomas Dunolly and eight other Aborigines wrote to the newspaper in protest;

'It seems that we are going to be treated like slaves . . . are we prisoners or convict(s)? We should think we are all free as any white man of the colony.' [6]

Under this law, the reserve at Coranderrk was eventually closed and the residents moved to distant Lake Tyers, far from their tribal lands.

South Australia

Initial efforts of the colonial authorities were for assimilation and a few Aborigines were initially 'given' plots of land. However, this alarmed the white settlers and the practice was soon declared illegal.

Segregated missions were established in the 1850s. Archdeacon Hale of Adelaide established a settlement at Poonindie both to isolate the younger Aborigines from the Elders of the tribes, and from the evil influence of the European settlers. The Government compelled Aborigines into these reserves.

After the gold rush began in neighbouring Victoria, many of the sheep stations started to utilise Aborigines as labour; over 150,000 sheep were cared for by Aborigines in the 1950s in South Australia.

In 1911, a still more coercive system was established by the State Government. This was to last until the 1950s. The 1911 *Aborigines Act* stated:

'Section 10: The Chief Protector shall be the legal guardian of every Aborigine and half-caste child, notwithstanding that any such child has a parent or other relative living, until such child attains the age of 21 years.

Section 17: The Chief Protector may cause any Aborigine or half-caste to be kept within the boundaries of any reserve or Aboriginal institution, or be removed from one reserve or institution and kept herein.'

(The only other people treated like this were criminals and the insane.)

The Protector was also given the right to inflict up to fourteen days prison on any Aboriginal or half-caste who in the judgement of the Protector was guilty of neglect of duty, gross insubordination or wilful preaching of disobedience.

This Legislation gave the police power to confine Aborigines on these reserves to save them from 'corruption'. (The same reasons were given by Comalco, an R. T. Z. controlled company, in 1957 to justify the removal of Weipa Aborigines.)

In Western Australia and New South Wales, unemployed Aborigines were sent to reserves 'to remove the Aborigines from temptation.'[7] These reserves were usually some eight to ten miles from the country towns.

Queensland

In Queensland, the state with the largest surviving Aboriginal population, the town reserves were 'calculated to provide both a local labour reservoir and a place where native remnants "an eyesore to everyone" could be kept.'[8] The Aborigines were not allowed to set up their own camps. 'Aboriginal camps were removed by being razed to the ground and the inhabitants driven off by mounted men wielding stockwhips or firing carbines over their heads.'[9]

However, the Queensland system did not so much segregate the white from the black as the 'useless native from the useful' one. Those in household service were not forced to go and live on the reserves, but they were subject to a curfew often 'imposed after sunset when Aboriginal labour services were no longer required.'[10] Mixed blood children were nearly always torn away by the police from their Aboriginal mothers and sent to reformatories run by missionaries on the reserves.[11] Thus the mothers could continue to serve their masters, the masters were saved any possible embarrassment, and the children's souls were cared for.

The larger Queensland reserves in the north were established at the close of the nineteenth century. A report in 1896 from the Special Aboriginal Commissioner, Meston, strongly recommended these reserves as places to which Aborigines could be removed and where

'they would present the most favourable field for a display of missionary zeal and the operation of any species of philanthropy or benevolence. To keep our aboriginals away from contact with the whites . . . is the only possible method of saving any part of the race from extinction.'[12]

By the end of 1902, 410 Aborigines had been shifted from their tribal lands in 53 different parts of the State to Fraser Island alone.

This policy was not without its opponents. Mr Lesina stated in the Queensland Parliament:

'I do not think there is any necessity why we should step out of our way to preserve the Aboriginal population. We have taken possession of this country, and, according to all laws, human and divine . . . the aboriginal population of this country must eventually disappear entirely . . . (some) say we ought

GUIDE

PHILOSOPHER
AND
FRIEND

Archibald Meston takes the fate of the 'derelict' Aboriginal in hand *(The Boomerang,* May 1891).

to step in and preserve them, and coddle them and assist them, and we should put them on reserves and assist them in a battle against evolution. The law of evolution says that the nigger shall disappear in the onward progress of the white man. There is really no hope at all. Legislation of this kind (for Aboriginal reserves) is absolutely unnecessary and its passage will entail an expenditure which is absolutely unnecessary.'[13]

The atrocious treatment of Aborigines in Queensland was described by an old Aboriginal woman:

'I was born in Mitchell in the 1920s, and my mother and father were sent to ... Purga Mission. The police just went around to pick up all the Aborigines they could to make into a reserve, they were just treated like a mob of sheep or cattle ... they threatened that if they didn't go they would shoot them or put them in gaol.

'My first job was in Lalor, housemaid for a school teacher. Then when I was older, about 15 or 16, I started work on stations. We had to sign an agreement to go out working that we would stay there for twelve months. They could just take you away from your family and put you on another settlement and you would have to stay there for one or two years. I've seen it done.

'The law just took all the black fellers away to put them on the reserve so they can't mix with the whites. To keep them all out of sight. When we wanted to go into Muroon to do our shopping we had to get a permit to leave the reserve ... the superintendent would write out a permit for so many hours we were going shopping. The boys or girls in the dormitory were only allowed to go to see their families for a couple of hours on a Sunday, and for that they needed a permit too. The parents would come down and ask the matron if the children could go out and she would write a permit for a certain number of hours. If they were not back at the right time a black tracker would go up and get them and they would not be allowed to go out again.

'If any of the children misbehaved, they could be put in gaol, locked up in a little room for a fortnight or so ... for a very small thing, like giving a white person a back-answer. The Administrator ... gave all the orders ... he had the power to send anyone off the mission or into gaol.

'The dormitories had wire over the windows and the doors were locked at night so no one could get out. And there was a fence all around the dormitory with barbed wire along the top. Just like a prison. No black kids were allowed to play in the white people's area ... no black was to be seen there after 5 o'clock.

'Whenever we went down to the mission butcher shop to get our weekly ration of meat, we just had to line up at the window and they just gave us whatever they liked . . . the white official could come along and get the best cut.'[14]

Nearly identical conditions are shown on a Queensland reserve in the one hour colour film *Protected* directed by Alessandro Cavadini available from Sydney Filmmakers Co-operative. This film tells, in the words of the still exiled Aboriginal leaders, the story of a strike on the reserve in 1957. The film was shot on the reserve in some secrecy in 1974.

Up until 1965 in Queensland, the reserve superintendent had to authorise all native dancing 'or other practices' in writing—but even so everything had to cease at midnight. Speaking Aboriginal languages was often outlawed. No Aborigine could leave the reserve without his permission. All must give up to 36 hours of work a week without pay on his demand.

Aborigines could not enter the reserve without his permission unless sent there by the police.

A former policeman who served in Darwin from 1929 to 1943 graphically described the official apartheid in the north that lasted until the change to an 'assimilationist' policy in the mid-1950s:

'Aborigines in Darwin were shut up every night after eight in a compound, except for those with written permission to sleep on their employer's premises. And these were required to be indoors by 8 pm.

'Two nights a week the curfew was extended until 11.30 pm to enable the dark people to attend the local cinema.

'Anyone with the slightest Aboriginal ancestry came under the control of the white chief protector of Aboriginals. Part-Aboriginal girls were locked up in an institution and could not marry without permission of this official.

'Some part-Aboriginals were issued with a certificate exempting them from the Aboriginals' ordinance which was termed the 'dog-collar'! The non-exempted could be ordered about by
the chief protector who controlled their whole life.

'Under the consenting clauses of the ordinance, white men were fined and often gaoled for relationships with females classed as 'Aboriginals'. Similar laws existed in all States, which were not as drastic as the Northern Territory ordinances.'

Aborigines were commonly chained together by the neck when arrested, men and women alike. This practice continued to about 1960. Aborigines in the north still commonly call the police 'neck-chainers'. They were thus often expelled from their tribal land to other reserves. Bob Holroyd, from Holroyd River, recalled in 1977:

'In 1936, Aborigines were chained by the neck and walked from Edward River to Coen and were shipped to Palm Island for standing up for their rights.'[15]

Since the reserves were intended to isolate the unwanted Aborigines, strict laws governed their involuntary incarceration. They were prosecuted for escaping from reserves in some States up until the middle of the Second World War.

All these reserves, then, functioned as detention centres for those of Aboriginal appearance, as a dumping ground for the unwanted and diseased, and centres of casual labour for the towns. It was apartheid. How-

Aborigines in chains being taken by police to Roeburn. W.A., for trial on an alleged arson charge.

ever, for many Aborigines these often pitiful small areas were the only lands they had the use of—and many came to be attached to them even though these were not their traditional territories. But for the whites, the blacks were out of sight and out of mind.

Little had changed on these reserves by the 1970s—except that many have now been closed and their populations dispersed in order to promote 'assimilation'—and to give their lands to whites.

One recent change for the worse was the introduction in 1979 of a new ordinance for West Australian reserves by which only the State Minister for Community Welfare can make out an Entry Permit for a reserve. He can thus allow whom he wants onto the reserve —and ban whom he wants. This was introduced because Oombulgurri Reserve said 'no' to two mining companies. (See Chapter 22, page 149, and Chapter 25, page 175, for more on this.)

Northern Territory

Reserves in the Northern Territory were recommended by various official reports in the 19th century. In 1889, the Government Resident reported:

'I state most confidently that the first duty of the State is to declare reserves, and within these reserves to give the native tribes absolute rights and sole control. There are on the north coast of Australia strong tribes of natives, who, as far as I can learn, live in amicable relations with each other, who have distinct tribal boundaries which are never passed except by notice. They do not wish to enter upon one another's country, and they feel that they have sufficient for themselves in their own territory . . . '

Yet, despite this report, before the Arnhemland Reserve was established, official recommendations saw the reserve as not under Aboriginal control, but for the supervision of the Aborigines:

'The large number of primitive natives in Arnhemland calls for effective measures for

their protection and supervision . . . There should be no obstacle to this (proposed reserve), as the country is very poor, no one requires it, and those who previously have taken up some of it have abandoned it.' [16]

The final impetus for the establishment of the Arnhemland Reserve was the killing of some white men who had invaded Aboriginal tribal lands in this region. Thus Northern Territory reserves were set up to control the tribes and make the region safe for white settlement.

Footnotes

1. Manly Cove was so named by Phillip because he admired the local Aboriginal 'confidence and manly behaviour' (*Dispatch to Lord Sydney*, 15 May 1788).
2. Keith Willey, *When the Sky Fell Down*, 1979, p. 175.
3. 2 May 1846.
4. Quoted in Christie, *The Colonization of Aboriginal Victoria*, 1980.
5. *Parliamentary Draftsman's papers*, Bundle 211 (*Aboriginals Bill* 1886) ProVic.
6. The *Argus*, 31 August 1882. The Healesville Nature Sanctuary is on part of Corranderrk.
7. C.D. Rowley, *Outcasts in White Australia* (Penguin Australia, 1970), p. 91.
8. Evans, Saunders and Cronin, *Exclusion, Exploitation and Extermination: Race Relations in Colonial Queensland* (ANZ, 1975), chapter 8. See also C.D. Rowley, *The Destruction of Aboriginal Society* (Penguin Australia, 1970), pp. 182-185, and Rowley, *Outcasts*, pp. 109-110.
9. *ibid.*
10. *ibid.*
11. Jan Roberts, *Mapoon Book Two* (International Development Action, 1975), pp. 50-52.
12. *ibid*, p. 32.
13. *Queensland Parliamentary Debates*, Vol. LXXXVI (1901) p. 212.
14. Jane Arnold interviewed in 'The Beach Issue, *Rabelais*, 1976 (La Trobe University).
15. *Messagestick*, North Queensland Land Council Newspaper, 1977-8. In 1978, Bob Holroyd was refused access to his people's tribal land on the Aboriginal Reserve by being barred from the Reserve itself by the Queensland Government. This was intended to stop him setting up an independent Aboriginal settlement away from the state government-controlled settlement.
16. *Report to Commonwealth Government* by J.W. Bleakley, Chief Protector, 1928.

7 'DESTROYING PAGANISM' – MISSION RESERVES

Most, if not all, the larger Aboriginal reserves were mission reserves, supervised by white clergy. Many still are.

Initially, the Christian clergy were not much interested in converting the Aborigines. Some of the Protestant clergy were influenced by theories based on the tribalism of the Old Testament and thought Aborigines descended from tribes cursed in that Testament.

The first official chaplain to the colony was Rev. Johnson who sailed with Phillip. He adopted an Aboriginal girl and tried to teach her to be Christian—but she, and her successor, returned to her own people. He then gave up on Aborigines.

The colony's Assistant Chaplain was Rev. Samuel Marsden, who arrived in 1794. He adopted two Aboriginal boys whom he taught English. They were taken as babies and therefore never learnt their own language. Both ran away—one was recaptured, but died shortly after.

Rev. Marsden had the lowest opinion of Aborigines.

'They are the most degraded of the human race, and never seem to wish to alter their habits and manner of life ... as they increase in years, they increase in vice.' [1]

The first to start work among the Aborigines was Shelley in 1814 (see page 28). He started a Christian school.

The first missionary sent from England to convert the Aborigines was a Wesleyan, the Rev. William Walker. He arrived in 1821. He wrote that they were:

'the progeny of him who was cursed to be a servant of servants to his brethren' [2]

... but he thought they would become Christians as well as servants to the settlers.

While many of the colonialists denied the very human nature of the Aborigines, some of the more devout Christians saw the Aborigines as souls to be saved from the corruption of 'paganism'. They therefore helped establish missions to preach what they saw as the 'gospel'. These missionaries were sometimes vilified by the colonialists for associating themselves with Aborigines.

Thus the first to work in an Aboriginal school in Victoria, Rev. Langhorne, found the settlers trying to discredit him by saying he was only interested in sex with his pupils.

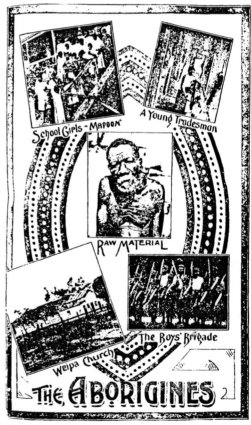

Illustration from Rev. Hey's *A Brief History of the Presbyterian Church's Mission Enterprise Among the Australian Aborigine*, (1931). He saw Aborigines as 'raw material' without any culture of their own.

Much later, in 1884, the *Cooktown Independent Record* attacked the clergy involved as 'those vile caretakers who revel in black lewdness.'

Similar racist attitudes were shared by many church authorities. Many believed Aborigines to be incapable of religious feelings and this view became widespread in church councils.[3]

When missions were established, they did help stop the massacres.

One such was the Yirrkala Mission-Reserve created in Arnhemland after a church intervention to stop a police punitive expedition. But sadly, they replaced genocide with ethnocide—with the deliberate attempt to eradicate a people's culture. Nearly all the missions saw Aboriginal culture as something vile that needed to be speedily destroyed in favour of European 'Christian' culture. Most saw their mission of spreading Christianity as identical with spreading the European 'Protestant ethic'. Practically none of the missionaries treated Aboriginal culture with respect, still fewer tried to learn from it. Rather they outlawed Aboriginal languages on the missions.

Destroying Aboriginal Law and Culture

The settlers coveted the lands of the Aborigines. The missionaries coveted their souls. Success for the missionary was to be measured by a 'captured soul-count'. Many of the missionaries could be ruthless in the methods they employed.

The settlers soon realised that they could use the missionaries as cheap guardians, custodians and pacifiers of the blacks.

The missionaries did bring medical help and some useful education in skills needed since the invasion—such as reading and writing English and growing foods to replace bush food. These skills were valued by many Aborigines.

The first reserve set up in Victoria, in what is now the Botanical Gardens, was a Mission under an Anglican minister, Rev. Langhorne. Many colonists sought to discredit his efforts to establish a school for Aborigines so they might acquire the valuable land on which the mission was established. (See reference on page 30.)

The authorities established a 'protectorate' system of mission stations under Government authority to use voluntary means of 'civilising and christianising' the Aborigines. Not much effort went into this. Rather it was an attempt to establish a good official face, while the wars and massacres continued.

The efforts of the few individuals who did try to carry out the aims of this program were in any case doomed to failure because of the attitudes of the Aborigines who refused to be 'civilised and christianised'.

In 1848 La Trobe reported his frustration to the Colonial Secretary, '[the blacks] although quite competent to form notions of the civilised life, seem utterly indifferent about availing themselves of them'.[4] A Mt Macedon Justice of the Peace, William Mitchell, reported that he had 'neither seen nor heard of any instance in which a native has voluntarily and permanently abandoned his own and adopted the habits of the European.'[5]

All this amazed the churches and authorities, and confirmed the prejudices of those who were more racist. How could the Aborigines reject a culture and religion so patently superior? The cultural arrogance of the British was such that they couldn't see that the Aborigines had a religion, culture and law of their own which they might prefer. Instead they thought that they were filling a cultural vacuum.

There were a few who did understand this. Rev. William Schmidt was in 1845 giving evidence to the Select Committee on Aborigines when he spoke of this Aboriginal preference. He was met with an incredulous:

'Do you mean they consider themselves superior to the whole of the white race, or those they see in the condition of convicts?'

He answered,

'To the whole—they preferred their mode of living to ours . . . they pitied us that we troubled ourselves with so many things.'[6]

The colonialists could not believe that this was a free choice of the Aborigines. Some opted for the solution that Aborigines were

GINX'S BABY
(Who shall decide when doctors disagree?)

DR HALE: 'No reason for breaking off the consultation, my dear colleagues. I have no intention of interfering with the exhibition of your patent medicines, and merely insist on the importance of regimen.'
DR M'NAB: 'our views differ radically, I fear. There's no salvation for the infant outside the land office.'
DR O'CONNOR: 'Bet you 28 to 2 my blue pill is the only certain cure. Warranted to disperse all dangerous symptoms.'

Solutions to the Aboriginal 'problem'. Bishop Hale recommends the feeding bottle of reserves, Rev. McNab supports granting freehold land while Sergeant O'Connor of the Native Police cheerfully prepares his gun (Queensland *Punch*, April 1879).

not yet fully developed. Bishop Frocksham said 'The Aborigines are undoubtedly the child people of the human race.' This justified the enforcing of a parental discipline over the Aborigines.

The failure of the Merri Creek School in Melbourne in 1851 reinforced the popular view that Aborigines were incapable of education and a lower breed of man. (Rather it failed because the Aborigines decided to withdraw their children to follow their traditional culture.) This was one of the first schools established for Aborigines by the colonialists.

Many of those who did believe Aborigines capable of being 'educated', despaired of ever 'civilising' the Aboriginal children unless they could be removed from all contact with their parents. This was, as earlier quoted, the opinion of La Trobe in 1848. It was earlier advocated by the Port Phillip Gazette in 1841.

Again it escaped their attention that this would be in effect cultural genocide—for they

did not believe that the Aboriginal people had any worthwhile culture to pass on to their children. This failure of the first missions was to be repeated as colonisation reached further parts of Australia. The Catholic mission at Kalumburu, established in 1908, reported in 1944:

'We have not won the full confidence of a single man . . . the uncivilised are more courteous, the civilised showing that they are such only by the dress they wear, by giving expression to much nonsense in English and by smoking and swearing. All this on top of their bush legacy of which they have not abandoned one bit.' [7]

Again at Jigalong in the Pilbara, the Aborigines welcomed with joy the abandonment of the mission in 1969 as a sign their law was stronger than the Christians. [8]

However, as the invasion continued, Aborigines had to adopt at least some aspects of European culture in order to survive. Many too became strong Christians—often fusing aspects of traditional culture with Christian beliefs. Others remained strongly anti-Christian, seeing Christianity as part of a system of oppression.

Enticement

Many missionaries attempted a very materialistic way of getting the Aborigines to come to their missions. In 1841 La Trobe authorised the distribution of flour to Aborigines on Sundays if they attended worship. This method was used by many missions from then on.

When Kalumburu was founded in 1908, Bishop Torres suggested hanging presents out on trees to entice people in. Tobacco was distributed at Lake Condah Mission in Victoria in the mid-eighteen hundreds. Obviously it was hoped that inducing dependence on tobacco would induce dependence on the mission. When Aurukun was founded in 1908 tobacco was given out. One Aboriginal elder recalled that the first missionary 'sent out people to the walk-about people with ten pound plugs of tobacco to show them.' This tactic was still used at Aurukun in the 1950s. Tobacco was similarly used by missions all around Australia.

Missions were made food distribution centres—thus the Government forced Aborigines to return to Jigalong mission by threatening to cut off their rations when they walked off the mission in 1962. The Kalumburu Mission diary records in 1935:

'This is how civilisation is accepted in this country . . . as work will be denied them here at Pago (and with it rations and tobacco); until they go where they are told, they have no option but to submit.'[9]

Coercion

The common failure of these methods of persuasion and enticement meant that coercive methods had to be adopted to get the aborigines into the missions.

In Victoria an Act was passed in 1869 which forced Aborigines to live on missions and authorised the separation of children from their parents. The missions established dormitories for the children under the strictest supervision.

On the Victorian missions whipping and other physical punishments were used. Husbands were permanently separated from their wives for such crimes as non-attendance at Sunday services. In Queensland, Aborigines were forced onto reserves from their inception . . . the voluntary stage evident in the south-east was omitted. Many of the missions were in effect prisons—some were located on islands off the coast. Aborigines were sent to these from all over Queensland so that they might be 'protected'.

Fraser Island was one of these—over 260 Aborigines were sent there at its foundation. So poorly were they 'protected' that many died from starvation.'[10] Meston reported:

'It appears that Dr Roth regards Fraser Island as a sort of penal settlement to which all the worst blacks are to be consigned indiscriminately.'[11]

This island was from 1901 an Anglican mission.

Similarly the Anglican Mission at Yarrabah employed Fitzroy Island as a 'penal reserve'. Eventually the Anglicans removed the survivors of the Fraser Island Mission to this island.

When Palm Island was being considered for a mission during the First World War years, Chief Protector Bleakley wrote to the Under Home Secretary:

'A reserve is needed for use as a penitentiary for troublesome cases and to which aboriginals from the Northern districts can be removed.'

Mapoon Presbyterian Mission was similarly used as a reformatory to which half-caste children could be sent.

In the more isolated parts of Australia, the missionaries were made by the Government into Government officers, arming them with coercive power. The missionaries were able to imprison, to exile, and to use Aboriginal land as they wished. They became the middlemen between Government and Aborigines and, as such, powerful. They doled out government

services, food and medicine, to the Aborigines—
forcing the Aborigines into the role of clients.

Invaders

The missionaries arrived as agents of colonisation
in the war against the survival of an independent
Aboriginal people. Three examples of this from
different parts of Australia would be Mapoon,
Yirrkala in Arnhemland and Kalumburu in the
Kimberleys. Mapoon in northern Queensland
was a mission of the Presbyterians. The site of
the mission was picked by the Government.
It expressed a wish that the mission might make
the area safe for white visitors. The mission
was founded in 1891. The missionaries went in
with a police escort and guns and the first
thing they did was to build a fort.

The Arnhemland missions also were seen by
Government officials as agents of colonisation:

*'The present missions are admirably situated for
fitting in with a scheme for a chain of institutions
around this area (Arnhemland), to ensure the
necessary supervision.'*

The Catholic Benedictine mission at Kalumburu was established in 1908 by armed missionaries. In an initial clash one young Aboriginal
woman was killed. By 1910 'the monastery
building was quaintly perched up on poles to
give greater safety against Aborigines.'[13]

In 1915, the Benedictine mission diary
records, 'We are in the chapel saying our prayers,
with the Rosary in one hand and the revolver
in the other.'[14]

Whilst the missions were establishing their
armed supervisory role over the Aborigines,
much greater violence was being inflicted on
the Aborigines by other invaders.

When the missionary Mr Fuller first arrived
on Hinchinbrook Island, Rev. McNabb reported
he found 'only women and children, all the
men having been shot by the Native Police a
few weeks before his arrival.' (Rev. McNabb
was one of the few missionaries who spent himself in a vain struggle to have Aboriginal land
rights recognised.)[15]

The Kalumburu Mission diary records an
Aborigine dying of deliberately poisoned flour

in 1935. The white man responsible also
vanished. In 1944 nineteen lepers had been
rounded up by the police and chained together
to prevent them escaping. However some got
away. The police shot dead one escapee and
wounded three others. At that time the police
were also inquiring about a reported massacre
of twenty Aborigines by nearby stationed
police.

Economic role

The missionaries were given an economic role,
too. They were to make Aborigines available as
cheap casual labour. Thus some of the northern
missions were responsible for supplying Aborigines to the pearling boats—despite the horrific
death-rate among the Aborigines so exploited.
The earnings of the workers were, in at least
one case, kept by the missionary and used to
expand the mission. Aborigines from many
missions were used as seasonal labour on the
cattle stations (as they still are).

The first step in getting the Aborigines
into the labouring force was seen as getting
them settled on missions and reserves.

Thus the Protector Dredge said in Geelong
in 1845:

*'No sooner does the Gospel begin to operate
on the mind of the heathen than it leads to
the first step in civilisation—the necessity of a
decent covering . . . It next induces a settled
way of life and tends to produce industry.'*[16]

Dr Thomson of Geelong wrote:

*'I highly approve of putting shoes on the feet
of the children. This would make their feet
tender and as they grow up would be useful
in restraining their erratic habits.'*[17]

It was seen as necessary at first to get them
settled down in supervised camps—and then to
immediately get them working for the Europeans. *Port Phillip Gazette's* editor, George
Arden, in 1841 advocated the gathering of all
Aborigines onto reserves by use of the vagrancy
laws and the giving of compulsory work to them.

Mapoon mission sought to inculcate all the

Protestant values, to change the whole Aboriginal way of life, to change it to that of the individualistic, property-centred Westerner.

The Mapoon missionary wrote in 1901:

'The Aborigines being a nation without recognised chiefs or constitution, order has to be maintained . . . It is Christianity that has given these moral lepers at and near Mapoon new regulations as well as a common-sense law.' [18]

And he wrote in 1907:

'Their system of socialism is as great a bar to progress as their superstition, as it hinders any improvement or rightful ownership. The healthy competition so essential to the progress of any nation is conspicuous by its absence.' [19]

In 1912 Rev. Hey of Mapoon described his methods to the Heathen Missions Committee:

'We are now at a crisis in the natives development. In their natural state they are communists of the crudest sort. Now an attempt is being made to evoke their sense of individuality. The young couples are being planted out in homesteads . . . There is a new spirit of competition, but it is a competition which has the spirit of Jesus in it.' [20]

In 1934 attitudes had not changed. The Royal Commissioner Mosely in his *Report on the State of the Aboriginal Population* of that year asked concerning the Catholic Kalumburu Mission:

'Is there not some preliminary work to be done before the christianising process begins? . . . Is it not necessary that he (the Aborigine) should at first, and for some considerable time, be trained in habits of civilisation more universal than the habit of going to church—and foremost in the habit of work?' [21]

Mission Attitudes

Missionary attitudes towards the Aborigines justified their attempted ethnocide, the attempted destruction of Aboriginal culture—and the replacement of it with the missionaries' versions of 'Christianity.'

Many of the missionaries, especially because they believed Aborigines to be a dying race, were not as much concerned about the full-blood adults, whom they saw as enslaved by Satan, as they were concerned to obtain the children—especially half-caste children, whom they believed to be more intelligent. They took the children from their parents at as early an age as possible and brought them up very much enclosed within the mission boarding school. In these schools the Aboriginal children were forbidden to speak their own languages or to learn their own culture. The missionaries believed that this culture was a creation of Satan and best totally destroyed. To be 'christianised', the Aborigines had to be trained in European ways.

At Mapoon, they despised Aboriginal culture and tribal Aborigines, and they punished any child who used their language in school. The official church historian for Mapoon declared in 1908 that Aborigines were 'cruel and treacherous, gliding like serpents through the grass,' and their women 'looked the picture of stupidity and degradation.' [22]

In spite of such attitudes and behaviour, they did not think the Aborigines were animals. As such they would have not had any 'souls' to save. Rather, Aborigines were the slaves of Satan, in mental status not above children, fit subjects for their preaching and their assumption of parental authority. 'The raw Aborigine is only a child', declared the first of the Mapoon missionaries. Another declared, 'Satan has them in his power. They are the children of the Father of lies. For this reason their whole existence must also be a lie.' [23]

To discipline such children 'some harshness would no doubt be necessary' [24] but as Aborigines 'have a much less highly developed nervous system . . . they feel pain to a much less extent than we do.' [25]

The missionary on the next reserve at Weipa stated:

'In our dealing with the blacks we are always aware of our great duty—the lifting up of the black race to a higher standard of life; I may say, from the animal life to the human life.' [26]

But not to lift them up to the level of the whites!

The government inspector, a renowned humanitarian, noted with satisfaction after talking with a missionary in 1903:

'He is in agreement with me that no practically useful results can possibly occur from teaching our . . . blacks any subjects that will in any way enable them to come into competition with Europeans . . . A not unusual source of trouble, fortunately now, I believe, nipped in the bud, has been letter writing by more enlightened blacks to mission inmates, with ill-concealed attempts to make them dissatisfied with their lot, as compared to the apparent freedom of the outside world . . . Cricket matches–Rev. Scharz put down any attempt at competition with Europeans.' [27]

Similar attitudes were widespread among the missionaries at Jigalong in Western Australia sixty years later. The anthropologist, Professor Robert Tomkinson, reported in his book on Jigalong:

'They (the missionaries) view the Aborigines as the children of the devil, lost in the great darkness and steeped in sin. Aboriginal culture is thus the work of the devil and the antithesis of Christian virtues, principles and behaviours . . . the (Aboriginal) law must be destroyed and replaced with the Christian way of life. Because justice does not have to be ministered to the devil's people, acts such as the degrading and painful punishment of Aboriginal offenders, mainly children, are not considered cruel or unchristian, but rather are regarded as merciful acts performed for the recipient's ultimate good . . . In addition the missionaries hold steadfastly to the belief that the local Aborigines are low in intelligence . . . and this helps them to rationalise their lack of success at Jigalong . . . the Aborigines are like children and should be treated as such.

'The missionaries in fact regard the adults as largely beyond redemption. They concentrate

their greatest efforts on the more malleable school children . . . by partially segregating the children in dormitories.' [28]

Attitudes at the Catholic Kalumburu Mission were less extremely expressed but similar in the late 1970s. The mission diary recorded:

'Arrogant members of the native community say cattle belong to them–they forget . . . both cattle and Aborigines belong to the mission.' [29]

'It must not be overlooked that the remnants of the Kimberley society were dying . . . In the process of moral and social revolution, they had proved themselves the most cunning and daring . . . the Aborigines perpetuate their unhealthy attitude towards laziness, rivalries and personal reprisals.' [30]

'Selfish as always', according to the missionaries, the Aborigines 'absconded for days' rather than help re-open Kalumburu by moving the supplies back in after it had been evacuated because of a 1944 Japanese bombing attack. [31]

'These people are very sentimental, yielding easily to their emotions. They have little or no will power except for revenge.' [32]

Direct attempts were made to destroy the most sacred of Aboriginal ritual objects from the beginning. Thus Rev. Hagenaur of the Victorian Remahyuch Mission burnt Aboriginal ceremonial objects, banned corroborees and promoted marriages against Aboriginal law. [33]

And this still happened in 1947 at the Catholic Kalumburu Mission. When, in July 1947 Aboriginal Elders brought in the most sacred ceremonial boards there was much excitement and dancing. The missionaries reported:

'They went completely wild. It was disgraceful to discover that the instigators of the unhealthy unrest, the guardians of the boards–which are not emblems of native culture, but symbols of a most degrading practice–were Christians

Catechism class at Pago, Kalumburu Mission, (Kalumburu Mission).

Footnotes

1. Letter to Secretary of New Zealand Mission, 24 February 1819.
2. Letter to Rev. R. Watson.
3. R.M. Berndt, *Aboriginal Man in Australia*, 1965.
4. La Trobe to Colonial Secretary, 18 November 1848.
5. N.S.W. Select Committee on Aborigines, 1849.
6. Keith Willey, *When the Sky Fell Down* (Collins 1979), p. 217, and elsewhere.
7. Fr Perez, *Kalumburu*, 1977, p. 111.
8. R. Tonkinson, *The Jigalong Mob: Aboriginal Victors of a Desert Crusade*, 1974.
9. Perez, p. 91.
10. Report of Dr Penny to Home Secretary, 2 February 1901.
11. Meston to Under Home Secretary, 27 August 1901.
12. Jan Roberts, *Mapoon Book Two* (International Development Action, 1975), p. 20.
13. Perez, p. 13.
14. Perez, *Kalumburu Mission Diary*, 15 March 1915.
15. Evans, Saunders and Cronin, *Exclusion, Exploitation and Extermination* (ANZ 1975), p. 381, quoting McNabb's letter of 28 October 1879.
16. Christie, *Colonization of Aboriginal Victoria* (1980).
17. *ibid.*
18. Jan Roberts, *Mapoon Book Two*, pp. 24-26.
19. *ibid*, p. 52.
20. Messenger, 1 June 1912.
21. Perez, p. 90.
22. Roberts, Book 2, pp. 24-26.
23. *ibid.*
24. Evans, pp. 115-116.
25. Evans, pp. 114-116.
26. Roberts, *Mapoon Book Two*, pp. 24-6, 52.
27. *ibid.*
28. Robert Tonkinson *The Jigalong Mob*, 1974, pp. 121-2. He is describing the situation in the 1960s.
29. Perez, p. 122.
30. Perez, p. 116.
31. Perez, p. 115.
32. Perez, p. 92.
33. *The Christian Times*, 18 August 1860.
34. Perez, pp. 122-23.
35. Perez, p. 123.

from the mission. *The 'boards' in their possession were destroyed before their eyes.*

'The missionaries could not take lightly this misbehaviour of their Aborigines and announced in good time that there would be no sports and no distribution of gifts of clothing in the forthcoming Christmas of 1947...' [34]

In 1950 the Kalumburu diary records:

'The few Kularis here ... are making new arrangements for their Krang-anda amusements ... They already have the boards prepared. That such boards have semi-religious significance is open to question, what cannot be denied is the degrading influence which this practice has on our Christians, and on the work of the mission. It cannot be denied either that such practices have contributed to the destruction of their race.' [35]

Thus for over one hundred years missions in Australia attempted the destruction of Aboriginal culture while they deplored and tried to stop the physical destruction of the race.

There were a few individuals who fought for land rights and justice for Aboriginal people, but they were in the minority. The missions were operating in the context of the invasion of Aboriginal lands, and they often took a leading part in this themselves, carving out fiefdoms where 'their' Aborigines could be both 'protected' from the influence of others and gradually 'civilised'.

The role of missions in the 1960s and 1970s and the change of attitude on some missions is further described in Chapter 10 below.

8 ATOMIC BOMBS AND GARRISONS

One of the first threats to the larger Aboriginal reserves came from the cold-war military demands of Britain. An area of 'worthless' land was being sought for testing atomic bombs and firing intercontinental missiles. What could be more useless than the lands of the desert Aborigines!

Two sites were chosen on Aboriginal lands for nuclear explosions—Emu Junction and Maralinga. The precautions taken were pitiful. For example, a sole government officer was given the responsibility for warning Aborigines off a vast area of tribal land needed for the nuclear explosions at Emu Junction. He obviously could not do this task. All that he did in fact was warn those at the various mission stations and settlements. This officer had as his patrol thousands of square miles in three States.[1] The actual boundaries of the test-zone were patrolled by 20–30 men. One of them, Patrick Connolly, since has said: 'It was ridiculous to expect 20 or 30 of us to patrol an area that size. It was just a token attempt. It was just a question of whistling at a guy two miles away.[2]

Many Aborigines listened, but still had to go out into their lands. Some of the Aborigines were still living in trackless parts of their lands out of contact with whites. The government made public assurances that the area was clear, and Britain exploded approximately eight bombs over a period of time. A terrible fear was sent out into the desert.

The full consequences for the Aborigines living nearby is still unknown—but some accounts have surfaced recently.

Jim Lester, the blind Director of the Institute of Aboriginal Development in Alice Springs, was a young Yankunyatjara boy living at Wallatinna west of Coober Pedy when Britain let off two atomic blasts at Emu Field 170 km south of the station. He remembers,

'I looked up and saw this black smoke rolling through the mulga. It just came at us through the trees like a big black mist. The old people started shouting, "Oh, it's a mamu, a mamu" (a devil-spirit)... After that, maybe a day or two, everyone was vomiting and had diarrhoea... Next day people had very sore eyes, red with tears and I could not open my eyes. Some were partly blind and I lost the sight in my right eye and could only see a bit with my left eye... Five days after the black cloud came, the old people started dying.'[3]

The wife of the station owner at Welbourne Hills reported that the cloud reached them five hours after it covered Wallatinna. She later lost her husband and two Aboriginal employees from cancer. The trees around the station were covered by the cloud with a sticky dust and died.[4]

Darwin anti-war demonstration (N.T. News).

An army engineer, Mr Kevin Woodland, who served at Maralinga in 1957 recalled that he and three others were out in asbestos suits working in a highly radioactive area when an Aboriginal family walked up:

'We were wearing asbestos-lined protective clothing. The Aboriginal woman was wearing a sack-dress, the man a loin-cloth and the children were naked . . . We ran a geiger counter over them. The readings were pretty frightening.[5]

Patrick Connolly, who served in the RAF at Maralinga between 1959 and 1962, stated:

During the two and a half years I was there I would have seen 400 to 500 Aborigines in contaminated areas. Occasionally, we would bring them in for decontamination. Other times we just shooed them off like rabbits.[6]

Both Kevin Woodland and Patrick Connolly have received warnings from Government security agents telling them to remain silent about Maralinga's effect on Aborigines.

Dr Hedley Marston, late Director of CSIRO's Division of Biochemistry, researched the fallout pattern. He concluded: 'extensive areas of Australia have been contaminated . . . Some of the most heavily contaminated were 1500 to 3000 miles away on the north-eastern seaboard'. Rockhampton's radioactivity level increased 3000 times. Drums containing radioactive waste were also dropped from the air into waters off the Great Barrier Reef near Rockhampton. Some burst on impact.[7]

In 1956—several years after the bomb testing started, the authorities decided to evict 62 Aborigines from Forrest Lakes area. The Government Security Ranger at Woomera moved them to Loogara on the East to West Trans Australia railway line. Then, as they bothered the passengers on the trains by their presence, they were moved to the mission at Cundeelee where they still are, with no water supply apart from a dam. This dries up in every one of the many droughts so that water has to be brought in by tanker.

Plutonium dust was left unprotected on the ground until four years after the tests, being blown across the land. Then, in 1963, the surface of the ground was lightly ploughed and the fences and warning signs removed.

After ploughing, in one area of fifty acres there was in the top 1.5cm of soil an average of 15 micrograms of plutonium for every kilogram of soil. (This dust is capable of causing a cancer for every 1.4 micrograms breathed in.)

Five large drums were buried more deeply. They contained concentrated waste. One of the drums contained a half-kilogram lump of plutonium! After the presence of these drums became public knowledge, the British came and, in March 1979, took the five drums back to England. However they left behind a legacy of plutonium dust, other radioactive wastes and cancers.

The Aboriginal people who continued to walk the plutonium dust-blown plains must be suffering from cancers. Some were given salvage rights to the Maralinga base. They too may be affected. According to Phillip Toyne, lawyer for the Pitjantjatjara Land Council, it is hard to discover the full consequences as medical records are not available since they have been placed under the Official Secrets Act. An urgent Royal Commission, or other public enquiry, into the health consequences is clearly called for. Proper compensation should be given.

It is by no means just Aborigines who could benefit from such an inquiry. Many cases have been reported of Commonwealth Police who guarded the bombs, and of military and other testing staff, falling ill with cancer and dying. The survivors have been claiming compensation. But, although the South Australian government decided to have a low-key inquiry, the Federal Government, on 15th May 1980 decided that a Federal Inquiry was not desirable.

The Woomera rocket range was set up to fire missiles out over one thousand miles of land unused by anyone—but the Aborigines. The southern part of the great Central Australian Aboriginal Reserve was 'officially' evacuated and the missions shifted. Some missionaries even seemed pleased by this.

The 1957 Queensland Presbyterian Assembly report stated:

'Scientific research on guided missiles for defensive and offensive global warfare at the Woomera rocket range is projecting civilisation [sic] into the dead heart of Australia where hitherto nomadic Aborigines roamed at will.'

They went on to say that the eviction of 'our mission folk' from their tribal land into exile has made them 'leap forward a generation or two in their progress towards assimilation.'

Many Aborigines were also affected by the garrisoning of the north during the Second World War. About 100,000 troops were moved into the Northern Territory alone, into areas where the pre-war white population was a fraction of this, perhaps 2,000. Many of the pre-war white inhabitants were evacuated to the south but not the Aborigines. After 1942 over 700 Aborigines were employed by the Army for civilian support work. The Army established Aboriginal camps near its own and supported up to two dependents per worker. The Aborigines acquired a reputation for hard work, and on the whole the army treated them far better than the cattle station bosses. However army attitudes were confused.

For example, Australian Military Regulation No 177 forbad the acceptance into the forces of people who were not 'substantially of European origin or descent'—and thus forbad the recruitment into Army ranks of Aborigines. On 6th May 1940 a Military Board Memo reiterated this.

However wartime needs made some commanders ignore this to recruit a few Aborigines. But many who tried to enlist were rejected. Once in the Army, they were however treated more equally than was normal in Australian society. A few were promoted—Reg Saunders rose to the rank of lieutenant during the course of the war because of his exceptional bravery. He eventually reached the rank of captain, but he was very much an exception to the norm.

This equality was not accorded to Aborigines recruited into specifically Aboriginal and Islander units. The members of the Torres Strait Defence Force mutinied in January 1944 because they received half the pay given to the newest white private. (In the Torres Strait Defence Force a corporal only received four pounds fifteen shillings a month—while minimum pay for a white private was eight pounds a month).

The enquiry that followed this mutiny calculated that the Aborigines and Islanders had been underpaid by a total of thirty million pounds—but decided not to restore this to those to whom it was due by military regulation because it would not be good for them! A pay rise was given, but not up to equal standards.

The reconnaissance and guerrilla force recruited in Arnhemland received even less pay. They received just three sticks of tobacco a week! They were fifty renowned warriors from different bands who were fighting until the 1930s to protect their tribal lands. Some had served prison sentences for this. If the Japanese were to land they were to recruit other members of their tribes into a guerrilla force to attack the Japanese. However the Army refused to issue them with guns—they were only to use spears and other traditional weapons! Perhaps there was some fear as to who would be shot at! Similarly, an Aboriginal unit trained by the Army in the Kimberleys was refused guns.

Many in the Army and among the civilians saw Aborigines as a security threat, perhaps out of guilt feelings over the treatment of Aborigines. Also the Japanese in S.E. Asia were attempting to undermine the prestige of the white colonial powers and to assert the interests of indigenous populations.

This particularly affected Army policy in Western Australia where they moved to treat Aborigines almost as enemy aliens. In 1942 Army Orders restricted Aboriginal movements throughout Western Australia, forcefully confining them to reserves or into the 'care' of cattle station owners. [8]

Generally speaking, Major Hall argues, the most repressive Army policies orginated in the southern cities—the decision to underpay

'Let's advance Australia and give it all we've got? I thought we did that 200 years ago!'

the Torres Strait Defence Force was made in the Melbourne Headquarters. The least racist policies were originated on the spot in the north where civilian influence was least. The army had for a few years disrupted Aboriginal society by removing coastal communities, by building large camps on Aboriginal lands, by bringing so many white 'aliens' onto Aboriginal lands and by its suspicions. But it was to move the bulk of its troops out after 1946 to leave Aboriginal lands for the cattle station owners and missionaries—until it wanted vast areas of tribal lands for testing the new and frightful weapons of the atomic bomb age.

Footnotes

1. Phyl and Noel Wallace, *Killing Me Softly* (Nelson, 1977), pp. 29-30.
2. Adrian Tame, 'Maralinga: Britain's Atomic Legacy', *Penthouse,* November 1980.
3. *The Adelaide Advertiser*, 3 May 1980.
4. *ibid.*
5. Tame, p. 38; also *Perth Daily News*, 27 December 1976.
6. Tame, p. 41.
7. Tame, p. 36.
8; Major R.A. Hall, 'Aborigines and the Army' in *Defence Force Journal* Sept/Oct 1980. This is the source for information used in the rest of this chapter.

9 LIFE ON QUEENSLAND RESERVES

We will first of all consider what life is like for Aborigines on Queensland Reserves because:
1. This state has the largest Aboriginal population.
2. Unlike other states it has refused to relinquish control over Aboriginal Affairs to the Federal Authorities.
3. It currently embodies its oppression of Aborigines in an Act of Parliament solely concerned with Aborigines.

As this book goes to press, Bjelke-Petersen, the State Premier, has moved to abolish this act and, along with it, Aboriginal reserves. This chapter also examines the implications of this change.

The structures of oppression

The Aborigines Act of 1971 is administered by a Director of Aboriginal Advancement [sic] responsible only to the Minister. The law makes the Director a virtually omnipotent figure to blacks. He appoints the managers to reserves, or else permits a church to appoint the manager. All managers are whites.

Each reserve *may* have an Aboriginal council of five; two of these are appointed by the Director, the other three are elected. But he may appoint all five if he deems those elected to be unsuitable. He can veto all election candidates.

No residence rights

No Aborigine has a legal right to live on an Aboriginal reserve—even if it is on his own traditional tribal territory. He or she can be expelled at any time by the white manager who governs every reserve in the name of the Director of Aboriginal Advancement.

Control of movement

The Director, or the reserve manager, can forbid anyone to visit a reserve, notwithstanding the Aboriginal Council's permission, even to visit a relative. This power is widely used to ban blacks from visiting one or more reserves, even their homes, if they have oranised protests against these laws.

Blacks on reserves need permission to have any visitors—and there is no appeal against the manager's veto.

Control of communications

It is common for telegrams to be only sent after vetting by the manager. Lawyers representing Aborigines have found telegrams to be delayed for up to five days.

Mineral exploration authorities and mining leases

These may be issued by the Director as 'trustee' without consultation with Aborigines.[1]

Low wages and forced labour

Law Professor Nettheim of the University of New South Wales stated that:

'The Queensland Government has simply chosen to ignore overriding Commonwealth law. The law says that Aborigines employed on reserves should get full award wages, those employed by the department do not.'[2]

In 1980, people on Yarrabah Reserve, with the support of the North Queensland Land Council, fought and won a legal battle to get the same wages as whites. But the Queensland Government has so far not implemented this (as of January 1981). Aborigines now get the official minimum wage of around $90 a week but not award rates. This leaves them on rates one third or more less than whites.

When, in June 1980, the Federal Government raised this issue in a Brisbane meeting with the State Government, the Director said if there were equal pay for Aborigines the State would raise Aboriginal rents 500% and sack at least half the reserve workers. Killoran dismissed a letter from the Deputy Prime Minister, Doug Anthony, offering to help fund equal pay, as a 'write-off'.

Other regulations

The manager appoints, and sacks, Aborigines to serve as police in the reserve. The Director, or anyone acting on his behalf, may enter any home on the reserve. Dogs can be shot, no matter if they are Aboriginal owned and loved, on the manager's authorisation, and often in front of children.

Examples of common regulations:

'A person swimming and bathing shall be dressed in a manner approved by the manager'.[3]
'A person shall not use any electrical goods, other than a hot water jug, electric radio, iron or razor, unless permission is first obtained from an authorised officer.[4]
'A person shall not, without permission of the manager exhibit advertisements or distribute handbills . . . anywhere in the community/ reserve area.'[5]
'A person shall not, without permission of the manager, engage in any trade or business . . . anywhere in the community/reserve area.'
'Parents shall bring up their children with love and care and shall teach them good behaviour and conduct and shall ensure their conformity with these by-laws'.[6]

The manager can make or suspend any by-law, and can detain anyone without formal charge.

These laws were to be 'revised' in 1977 but in 1978 they were given extended life (May 1978). In fact, many of their discriminative clauses are now illegal under Federal law, but the Federal authorities are not attempting to enforce these Federal laws.

The by-laws quoted above are from the 1977 report of the Australian Commissioner for Community Relations. He concluded:

'many provisions in the by-laws, if not the whole of the by-laws, restrict and deny Aborigines basic human rights and fundamental freedoms.'

However, it seems that the Commissioner is powerless to do much about this.

Despite the illegality of the Queensland Act under Federal law, the Federal Government has not (as of July 1981) moved to end the racist Queensland legislation.

This is despite a major clash in the first half of 1978 between the Federal and Queensland Governments over developments at two Queensland mission reserves—Aurukun and Mornington Island. These events are described in the following chapter and in the chapter on Aurukun (Chapter 20).

In response to this, the Federal Government passed its 'Queensland Aborigines and Torres Strait Islanders (Self-Management) Act 1978'. This was based on the Queensland Act and gave Aborigines little more than the possible option of having their lives managed by the Federal Government rather than the Queensland Government.

The Queensland Government showed its hand by abolishing the Aurukun and Mornington Island Aboriginal Reserves before the Federal Act formally became law. (Mick

Mornington Island dancers at World Environment Week, Cairns 1980 (Jan Roberts).

Miller, Chairman of the North Queensland Land Council, had publically warned the Federal Government of Bjelke-Petersen's plan—but to no avail.) The Federal Act was thus rendered totally ineffective insofar as these former reserves were concerned.

Since then, despite fears that the Queensland Government would repeat this manoeuvre, several reserves have applied to be removed from Queensland control. But the Federal Government has ignored their application.

The new Queensland legislation for Aurukun and Mornington Island, the 'Local Government (Aboriginal Lands) Bill 1978' makes them into a unique form of Aboriginal 'local shire'. It includes these provisions:

1. *All the former Aboriginal reserve is being leased to the communities for fifty years.*
2. *Only Aborigines with a residency permit valid on 5th April 1978, plus their children and marriage partners, have any right to reside in the shire.*
3. *Nobody in the community has any title to land or dwelling. About 40% of the houses were built by, or bought from, the mission by the Aboriginal occupants—but the council has now been granted the right to* lease *these houses to their occupants.*
4. *Mining company staff are granted right of residence. The Aborigines have no power over mining facilities, over access to the mining area or over any mining authorised by the Government.*
5. *The Aboriginal shires have the power to control entry—excepting government officials and parliamentarians.*
6. *Aborigines resident in the shire have no right to invite any guests to enter the shire without council permission excepting missionaries 'doing spiritual work', suppliers of goods, medical staff, government officials and parliamentarians.*
7. *The Director of Aboriginal Affairs, Killoran, no longer has the power to exclude people from Aurukun.*
8. *The Shire Clerk is employed by the council and can be sacked by them. However they cannot appoint someone who is not approved*

by the Minister for Local Government. He also has considerable authority as the interpreter of law for the council. The Government can also veto any by-law.
9. *A 'Co-ordinating and Advisory' Committee is appointed—of three members (all non-Aborigines), two appointed by the Queensland Government and one by the Commonwealth Government. This is present at and takes part in every council meeting. It constitutes a 'shadow government' with its power to 'assist the shire in its financial affairs' and 'assist' the Queensland Government in 'the controlling and management' of the shire.*[7]

In August 1978, Bjelke-Petersen, the Premier of Queensland, sacked the Aurukun Aboriginal Council under this legislation. Instead, he moved in the police and appointed his own administrator. He did this because the Aborigines refused to accept his expulsion of the missionaries and insisted on demanding a freehold title to their tribal lands.

The Aborigines under this new Act were at first refused the right to stop alcohol entering their lands. The Government minister declared that everyone has the right to drink—and that the people would have to allow a 'wet canteen' or 'hotel' to open. However, after much protest from those of the community who knew the social devastation this 'whiteman's poison' can bring, an agreement was formally made that no one, neither white nor black, can bring in more than one carton of beer a week and that wines and other alcoholic drinks remained banned.

No 'wet canteen' has been opened. The two white police now moved into Aurukun inspect all incoming beer to ensure this agreement is kept.

When, in February 1979, Aboriginal representatives from communities all over N.E. Australia gathered at Aurukun for a 'Unity Conference', the following resolution was passed:

'... *Recommend to the Federal Government that* FREEHOLD *land titles to Aboriginal reserves in North Queensland and the local shires of Aurukun and Mornington Island be granted.*

'We recommend that full mining rights be given to the respective Aboriginal communities in North Queensland and the local shires of Aurukun and Mornington Island.

'We recommend that full fishing rights be given to the respective Aboriginal communities in Northern Queensland including the right to set their own limits . . . We want assurance from the Federal Government that the Department of Fisheries do their job and stop illegal fishing in Aboriginal reserves and the local government shires of Aurukun and Mornington Island.

Note: Illegal fishing includes:

1. *The illegal netting in rivers on reserves.*
2. *The use of vehicles by fishermen to get to sacred lagoons, clearing out of the lagoons in half a day leaving nothing alive until the next wet season.*

'We demand the right for each Aboriginal reserve in North Queensland and the local government shires of Aurukun and Mornington Island to be able to fully govern themselves in their own way and make the major decisions concerning day to day living.

'We demand just and fair compensation for land already taken away from the Aboriginal people in Northern Queensland.

'We demand that Aboriginal culture be taught in all schools both black and white in the whole of Australia.'

This was signed by forty-eight community representatives including two representatives of the North Queensland Land Council.

Although we have considered the laws affecting Aboriginal people in just one of the Australian States (that of Queensland in which live more of the Aborigines than in any other State) the practice in other States is often appalling. All the reserves are run under white supervision; in all reserves the lives of the Aboriginal people are regulated and institutionalised. In the Northern Territory some 60% of the Aborigines live in such institutions, in Western Australia some 12%, and in Queensland some 25%. In Western Australia, until

quite recently, it was illegal fo. any 'half-caste' child to remain with its mother and not be sent to a mission.

The situation in the other States will be examined in the chapter on 'State Governments and Aboriginal Land Rights.' For more on the Aurukun people and their struggle to protect their land from a massive mining project, see Chapter 20.

POST-SCRIPT: Although Bjelke-Petersen announced in 1980 that he will be doing away with the Aborigines Act, some Aboriginal communities in Queensland have said that they do not want the act repealed by Bjelke-Petersen until they have been guaranteed their reserve lands. They see this as a trick by the State Premier to rob them of the last of their lands under the pretext of ending discrimination. He has now stated that he will indeed be abolishing all Aboriginal reserves and instead giving 50 year leases as at Aurukun. He has refused to allow freehold rights over these areas to Aborigines.

Footnotes

1. *Aborigines Act*, Clause 29.
2. *Age*, 26 September 1977.
3. By-law 10/1.
4. By-law 13/2.
5. By-law 17/2.
6. By-law 24/3.
7. This does not include the 1,200 sq. miles taken from the Reserve for future bauxite strip mining, for the Aborigines have been granted no powers to control mining, no rights over minerals, which they would have under Aboriginal Law. Before this new Act, Aborigines had indefinite use of their tribal lands. But still they are not given any legal recognition of their right to *own* traditional land.

10 CO-OPERATION AND CONFLICT BETWEEN CHURCH AND STATE

The churches in Australia have mostly reformed their policies in recent years—but there is still much to be changed before Aboriginal people see Christians as genuinely respecting in practice their culture and their rights.

There are some occasions when the church authorities have come out strongly. One such was in January 1977 when the Queensland State authorities, cancelling their usual grant to the annual Catholic Aboriginal and Islanders Conference, said:

'We have grave doubts about the role of the council . . . we believe, some of the ideologies they are preaching are not helping the advancement of the Aborigines.'[1]

They particularly objected to the advocating of land rights.

In reply, the Catholic Bishop of Townsville stated:

'Land rights are tied up with religion—and one of the aims of the Conference is to make Aboriginal people feel more confident in their religion. Aboriginal people still derive inspiration from their land, and a meaning for their existence from it.'

The 1978 Catholic Social Justice Statement said:

'In Australia the church must stand with the Aboriginal people, and insist that mere financial considerations cannot take precedence over the rights of a people to protect their society and all that is sacred to them from destruction.'

In February 1980 the Adelaide Catholic Diocesan Pastoral Council strongly supported the recognition of the land rights of the Pitjantjatjara people.

'The whole community must respect the spirituality of the Aborigines. We must support in every way we can the Aborigines' right to seek their own betterment, to conserve their language, culture, ancestral customs and way of life.'

The Anglican Archbishop in Perth in 1977 was fined in court for allowing homeless Aborigines to camp in church grounds. He denounced Australia for its racism at the court hearing. The Uniting Church too has come out with strong official policies on the recognition of Aboriginal land rights and for Aboriginal control over their reserves and has implemented these policies as far as they feel able. Today its missions have the reputation of being some of the most enlightened, if not the most enlightened, in Australia.

The Catholic Bishops in their September 1980 Pastoral Letter stated:

'The Aboriginal can make a unique contribution to our world. To allow him to do so, we will need to be more intent on listening than on talking, more concerned with respect than criticism, more willing to learn than to teach.'

They also spoke of the intrusion of the major mining companies onto Aboriginal lands, 'It is this thrust that could crush Aboriginal peoples.'

But this pastoral letter could be criticised on three points.

Firstly: the bishops seemed to show an inadequate knowledge of the pastoral industry when they distinguished it from the mining industry as somehow more justified. They distinguished 'the pastoral thrust which was primarily an expansion of settlement' from the mining thrust which 'is purely an exploitative development which does not necessarily include permanent settlements'. Why it is morally better to settle on stolen land permanently rather than temporarily is not explained. Many massacres were caused through the

'The Sisters', near Stawell, Victoria — an Aboriginal sacred site.

pastoral industry's 'thrust' into Aboriginal lands. (See Chapter 4)

Secondly: the Catholic authorities still unfortunately feel a need to use euphemisms. In this pastoral letter they spoke of how 'settlement was commenced'. Others might call it 'invasion'. The massacres that followed were called 'the trauma of contact'. The fighting and killing were never mentioned. However the bishops are far from alone in choosing to use such terms. Most academics, anthropologists and historians in Australia use similar euphemisms—most Aborigines do not.

Thirdly: they did not look critically at the role played by the various Catholic missions but had only praise for them.

Bishop Jobst in Broome, Catholic bishop for the Kimberleys, was not so clear in his support. In an article in *The Record*, September 4–10, 1980, which he said reflected 'the general thinking of the staff and several Aboriginal people in our care', he questioned the giving of freehold rights to Aborigines as possibly not beneficial to Aborigines because the land could be sold. (He did not also question freehold title for non-Aborigines on the same grounds.) He stated that he was against the

giving of 'sovereignty' over land to Aborigines but did not say why. He was also obviously worried about the 'genuineness' of Aboriginal claims that Aboriginal sites are sacred.

The Kimberley Catholic Missions have come in for criticism. In 1976, documents tabled in the Federal Senate on Beagle Bay Mission stated that Beagle Bay had to repay the government a considerable sum of money and that the mission was run financially for the benefit of the mission order.[2]

More recently a member of the administration of Balgo Mission was convicted for wrongful use of funds. Kalumburu Mission has been attacked too for its paternalistic policies. (See below)

It should not be surprising that church actions do not always match up to their words—especially at the local level of mission administration. Many of the people whose actions and attitudes in the 1960s were described in the earlier chapter on 'The Mission Reserves', still retain positions of influence. Sometimes their views have not changed very much.

As a recent example of this, when Father Seraphim Sanz of the Roman Catholic Benedictine mission at Kalumburu released a book on his mission in 1977, he was reported as saying that the white man was pushing the Aborigines beyond their ability and capacity to cope with the 'civilised world'. The Western Australian deputy premier at the book launching said that the book explained some of the problems associated with civilising the Aborigines.[3] Obviously the mission and government still believe the Aborigines are like savage children—in need of protection and gradual 'civilising'.

The conclusion of the mission book stated:

'It would be naive and over-optimistic to expect the Australian Aborigines to reach within one or two generations the level of civilisation which has taken thinking man centuries to achieve.'[4]

Apparently Aborigines are not part of 'thinking man'.

He went on to say,

'Young men have practised various trades . . . but they are careless and unreliable when left to themselves . . . Young women . . . seldom use their abilities on their own initiative. Aborigines are slow to appreciate the need to exercise their skills and energy to improve themselves individually, let alone collectively as an Aboriginal minority.'[5]

Sir Charles Court, West Australian State Premier, introduced the book:

'The mission represents the most sustained attempt by Western Australians to incorporate Aboriginal people into the community at large. This record spans the years in which, with great compassion, patience and understanding, the Kalumburu Aborigines have been gradually introduced to the rewards and the responsibilities of the civilised Christian way of living.'[6]

So much for the co-operation between mission and state in the Kimberleys.

One of the Kalumburu Aborigines graphically described conditions at the mission in June 1981. He stated that Fr Sanz, the Administrator, treated Aborigines like children, refusing them any role in the running of the mission. He said that those who complained

were fined one month's social security payments and allowed no petrol. If they left the mission to complain to the outside world they were not allowed back. At meal times, people had to line up with billies or plastic buckets while a sister ladled 'slop' through a hole in the kitchen wall.

There are nine girls locked in the dormitory each night, a padlock on the door, and a nun sleeps inside with them. Two girls were taken away from their mother because she is living in sin with a man not her husband . . . Fr Sanz wants us to be dumb all our lives. The children who go to school in Broome are not encouraged to use their skills to take control of the office or money . . . He makes them do the worse jobs like pulling up weeds, so they forget what they learn in school. We want to be allowed to train as mechanics, bookkeepers and pilots, but he says we are not capable. Here at Oombulgurri, it was once a church mission and now control is being handed over to the Aborigines and they run it well. Aborigines are not stupid; we can run our own lives.[7]

In Queensland the Lutherans have co-operated at Hopevale and at another mission because, according to the North Queensland Land Council, 'the Lutheran Church does what Bjelke-Petersen, the State Premier wants' (the Premier is a Lutheran).

The Hopevale Mission in North Queensland has a major beach sands mining operation on the Aboriginal reserve conducted by Mitsubishi. This mine is the most cloaked in secrecy in all Australia. It is not listed in most mining reference books. The Hopevale Aborigines never consented to it, get no royalties and have no access to the mining area. These missionaries are still government officials responsible for enforcing the racist Aboriginal Act and by-laws.

The Uniting Church once had the missions of Mapoon, Weipa, Aurukun and Mornington Island. They gave up the first two voluntarily. (The 1963 story of how they forced out the Mapoon Aborigines is in Chapter 7.) But, in recent years they had difficulty in co-operating with the State Government. An incident illustrating this occurred in 1975.

Two Aboriginal women of high standing in the Mapoon community came down in 1975 to advise on incidents documented among mission records. On their return to the Weipa Reserve they were interrogated for over two hours by the Director of Aboriginal Advancement, Mr Killoran. Their legal adviser, an Aboriginal field worker with the Cairns Legal Aid Office, was refused admittance. He was allegedly told by the manager that Killoran has a policy of not seeing more than two Aborigines at once as he's found that if more than two saw him together, they got hysterical!

During the course of this interrogation Mr Killoran was told that they knew the truth because they had his official report on Mapoon (as they had). Killoran hit the roof. He immediately contacted the Presbyterian mission authorities and threatened them with the loss of their missions, if they allowed Aborigines access to mission records.

It is threats like these that kept the mission authorities from outrightly challenging the legislation and regulations concerning Aborigines in Queensland. The churches felt that it was better for the Aborigines that they control the missions than that the missions fall back under government control.

Eventually the growing split between church and state could not be papered over and concealed. The last straw seemed to have been church support to Aborigines going back to live on their tribal lands on out-stations on various parts of the reserve. This was contrary to State assimilation policies. It also could hinder planned mines.

So, in 1978, the State Government took from the Uniting Church its two Queensland missions, Aurukun and Mornington Island. The Uniting Church and most of the other churches however still retain today the shares they have in mining companies dispossessing Aborigines. In 1976 one of these shareholders, the Jesuits, challenged Comalco with exploiting Aborigines. The Jesuits concerned could get no other church shareholders to join in their action, nor to return the shares they hold in mines on Aboriginal tribal lands to the real owners, the Aborigines. A Jesuit delegation of three went to the Comalco mine site and produced a report critical of Comalco from two of their members, and another report from the other member which was circulated both by Comalco and by the Australian Mining Industry Council, with *no* reference to it being a minority report opposed by two of the three Jesuits.

Similarly, the Australian Mining Industry Council is circulating today a critique of the Aboriginal Land Rights Bill by one of the Lutheran Missionaries at Hermansberg in Central Australia, Rev Paul Albrecht. In it he calls the Land Rights Bill, based on the Woodward recommendations,

'*both socially destructive and politically damaging . . . divisive and lead(ing) to long term social problems resulting from the antipathy which such action would engender among whites.*'

He recommended granting legal title to traditional owners through the Northern Territory Government's land office:

'*Disband the Aboriginal Land Councils as they are completely irrelevant in Aboriginal terms. Remove [Land Councils] which could be and would be politicised without benefit to the Aboriginal people. [Instead create] a secretariat within the Lands Department to service group leaders.*[8]

These recommendations would have kept Aborigines further from being able to control

their own lives and dependent on the Northern
Territory Government for any recognition of
their rights.

In defence of their culture, Aborigines are
walking off the missions all over Australia,
and setting up out-stations back on their
tribal lands.

The book, *The Jigalong Mob: Aboriginal
Victors of the Desert Crusade*,[9] recorded how
Aborigines protected their culture despite all
that one group of Protestant fundamentalist
missionaries, the Apostolic Church of Australia, could do. The Aborigines were aided in
this by the missionaries' avoidance of the
Aboriginal living area as 'a place of vice, sin and
filth',[10] to quote the Superintendent. At times
the missionaries did visit the Aboriginal camp
—but they came en masse to conduct brief
prayer meetings virtually ignored by the Aborigines. The missionaries believed the Aborigines were 'the children of Satan lost in
darkness.'[11]

Another recently produced book *Aborigines
and Christians* by Fr. Howe, attacked the failure
of the churches. He stated:

*'There would be some justification in a claim
that the position of the church in 1977 is
little, if any, distance ahead of its position in
1869'.*[12]

He likened the present attitude of church
authorities to the way in which the churches
were once 'deeply involved in the reinforcement
and perpetualising of the slave trade.'

However, the production of books such as
this, and the Catholic-Australian Council of
Churches jointly-sponsored book *Land Rights:
a Christian Perspective* (D. Carne, 1980), are
in themselves a sign of positive change and
open debate within the churches.

Internationally, people are increasingly
aware of how Aborigines are treated in Australia. However this was not reflected in the
organisation of the first international conference organised in Australia by the World
Council of Churches Department of Mission
and Evangelism in 1980. Despite the topic of
'Missions' and despite the issue being raised

Kimberley Land Council News

with the Council many months before, representatives of Aborigines were not invited
from the missions nor from the land councils
representing these missions. (These land councils have been partly funded by the Program
to Combat Racism of the World Council of
Churches.

One Aborigine was included, after some
discussion, in the Australian Council of
Churches delegation, and other Aborigines
went under their own initiative to try to
raise support. Because of this a strong motion
was passed supporting Aboriginal rights.

*'The Aboriginal Australians have brought to
our attention the way in which the Aboriginal
people have been robbed of their own land and
spiritual heritage and have experienced racial
and spiritual genocide, and then been denied
any fair share in the fruits of the society
constructed with their resources.*

*'We are concerned about the continual
oppression and suffering of the Aboriginal
people and the blatent racism in Australia
which is a denial of the Kingdom of God.*

*'Whilst we recognise the attempts made by
some sectors of the Australian churches to
support Aboriginal Australians in their struggles,
we are particularly concerned by reports of
church co-operation in maintaining and condoning racist and oppressive policies of governments in Australia, failure to support action
against second-class citizenship for Aboriginal
Australians and reluctance to give adequate*

OF COURSE YOU REALISE THAT — IF THE CHEQUES WENT DIRECTLY TO THE ABORIGINIES — IT WOULD CHANGE THE FINANCIAL POSITION OF THE MISSION . . . .

Kimberley Land Council News

financial assistance to communities, organisations and projects controlled by the Aboriginal people.'

Several recommendations from an Australian Council of Churches' Conference on Racism (19th May 1980) were endorsed. These included:

'that the churches return some of their land and property to Aborigines', and that *'the churches refuse to participate in the bicentennial of European settlement in 1988 unless adequate land rights legislation is adopted in every State prior to that date.'*

In June 1981, the World Council of Churches Program to Combat Racism sent a team to investigate the situation of Aborigines in Australia. This attracted widespread press coverage — and many attacks. The Premiers of Western Australia and Queensland, and the Northern Territory Administration, refused to meet with them. But they received much Aboriginal support.

In the Kimberleys, the Catholic Bishop, Jobst, refused permission for the delegation to visit Kalumburu Mission saying that the Aborigines did not want them to come. Bishop Jobst is reported to have told the Aborigines that the WCC team had themselves decided not to have come so as not to aggravate the situation. This angered the delegation. Father Sanz, to make sure they would not come, threatened to barricade the airstrip with tractors and 44-gallon drums and to fine them

$2,000. However one reporter did pilot his own plane in and learnt that the Aborigines were sorry not to meet up with the delegation.

One week before the delegation was due to arrive, Father Sanz told a rebellious Aboriginal group who had walked off the mission that he would let them purchase from the mission the Carson River Station. This was their first chance to regain control over any of their tribal lands. The community was scared that if the WCC team came, Father Sanz would withdraw his offer.

The continuation of the conflict between church authorities and Aboriginal religion and culture was brought into the open with the treatment received by the only Roman Catholic Aboriginal priest, Father Pat Dodson, in June 1981.

He had been put in charge of the Waderr Aboriginal Mission in the Northern Territory. He found the Aborigines there had been forbidden to practise their traditional religion and told to forget their sacred grounds. He said:

People had been told to burn their sacred objects, the elders had been pushed into the background. I let them bring back the traditions and their self-esteem. This was followed by a move to take boys out of the Catholic school for periods, to be taught the traditional Aboriginal values of manhood . . . I put self-determination into practice. I let the thousand people on Waderr take back control of their own country, and gave them power to hire and sack staff . . . It led to enormous conflicts. The education authorities claimed that I was putting the children in jeopardy: the church claimed it was causing irreconcilable ideological problems . . . they said I was taking them back into the pagan era. There isn't much sympathy for the way I think in the Catholic Church.[13]

The Most Reverend John O'Loughlin, Bishop of Darwin said in reply:

Support for the revival of old Aboriginal customs has come from certain artistic people who see some value in it because they can get some

nice films of corroborees. There is also a group of old black people who are anxious not to lose their authority. They are brought hundreds of miles to initiate the young men into their wicked ways.[14]

He accused Father Dodson of encouraging these initiations.

Father Dodson told what happened to him:

Six weeks ago I was transferred to Alice Springs and told not to get involved in politics. Waderr has been put back to what it was before I arrived.

He believes despite all this that there are real Christian values and beliefs that can be combined with traditional Aboriginal values and beliefs to the enrichment of both.

My grandfather was kicked off the Catholic mission for keeping up Aboriginal ceremonies. He could combine both Christianity and traditional religion in his own spiritual life with no hassles.

The Bishops of Brazil have called on their country to learn from the Indians for they present alternative values, more human values, than those of capitalism.

Likewise in Australia, these conflicts cannot end until justice is restored and the churchmen and women sit down with the Aborigines as equals to share with one another what each holds most sacred—ready to give up the trappings of affluence and power and live in equal poverty and communal sharing and to fight for justice.

But what hope is there of such a solution, embodying perhaps the best of Christian traditions? Such values are not obvious even in the relations between clergy and the non-Aboriginal lay-members of the churches!

Footnotes

1. *Courier Mail*, 7 January 1977 and 11 January 1977.
2. *Nation Review*, 16 December 1976.
3. *West Australian*, 9 September 1977.
4. Fr Perez, *Kalumburu*, Kalumburu Mission 1977, p. 149.
5. Perez, pp. 149-150.
6. Perez, Preface.
7. *Age*, June 1981. The speaker is living at Oombulgurri but comes originally from Kalumburu.
8. Document dated 10 February 1976.
9. Robert Tonkinson (Cummings, USA, 1974).
10. Tonkinson, p. 124.
11. Tonkinson, p. 89.
12. Fr Morgan Howe, *Aborigines and Christians; an introduction to some of the issues* (Foundation of Aboriginal and Islander Research Action, Queensland, 1977).
13. *Age*, June 1981.
14 *Age*, June 1981.

"BUT REVEREND, the meek shall inherit the earth — after we've extracted the bauxite!"

11 LIFE ON THE CATTLE STATION

The dispossession of the southern Aborigines by the squatters was spurred on by the fortune to be made from wool. Most of the squatters did not try to use Aboriginal labour for they had a free supply of convicts.

In the north, this was not the case. Even today, the vast cattle stations depend largely on the labour of the people they have supplanted. The bloodshed that surrounded the carving out of these stations from Aboriginal lands has been described in the earlier chapter on 'The Resistance and the Massacres'. The Aborigines were usually allowed to stay on the station for the sake of the cheap labour they provided. On these cattle stations, it was nothing better than slavery for the Aboriginal people. They often were paid nothing and were not allowed to leave.

Mr R G Kimber said at the Warlpiri Land Claim hearing,

My understanding is that if any Aboriginal left a cattle station he could expect to be either flogged or shot and that policy would have been carried out until at least the Coniston massacre. From discussions with Aboriginals and with other slightly more disinterested white people, I would say that that policy continued into the 1940s without a doubt, with the very careful hiding of any evidence of that.[1]

The pastoralists in 1965 argued against equal pay for Aborigines saying

Because of their state of cultural assimilation, communities on the cattle stations were not equal to free competition on the labour market.[2]

The Aboriginals knew, however, that it was on their backs that the stations were built. They provided the skilled stockmen, tended the animals, tracked and mustered them. The author has heard this expressed forcefully by Aborigines throughout Northern Australia.

It has been recognised in Government reports that Aborigines were 'the backbone of the grazing industry in the Kimberleys and Territory.'[3]

Up until 1968, Aboriginal stockmen were fortunate if they received over eight pounds a week. A 1965–8 survey of thirty stations, selected as representative with the help of the Northern Territory Cattle Producers Council and located in every part of the Territory, gave the following details of weekly wages:[4]

Aboriginal:	
Stockman	3–8 pounds
Head Stockman	3–12 pounds
Boundary Rider	3–4 pounds
Domestic (women)	1–4 pounds
Part Aboriginal:	
Stockman	6–12 pounds
Head Stockman	5–18 pounds
Boundary Rider	none
Domestic (women)	2–5 pounds
White:	
Stockman	17–23 pounds
Head Stockman	20–30 pounds
Boundary Rider	18–20 pounds
Domestic (women)	8–12 pounds

Part Aborigines were preferred to Aborigines. Out of the 446 Aboriginal male employees surveyed, 289 were stockmen and only two head stockmen; out of the 36 part-Aboriginal males surveyed, 23 were stockmen and 9 head stockmen. The thirty stations employed 202 Aboriginal women as domestics, but only three part-Aborigines and 35 whites were so employed. The stockmen received about two pounds worth of food and supplies a week. They received in cash usually only about one pound a week–the rest went into the 'store account'.

When the equal wages case came up in 1965, the pastoralists said that they had not paid real wages, but mostly just cheap rations of

Aboriginal stockmen demand equal pay in 1960s.

food and tobacco. This was admitted by the spokesman of the Cattle Producers' Council in 1965. He went on to say that if the government ordered equal pay for Aborigines 'the pastoralists would move away from Aboriginal labour to white labour.' He said that one-fifth of the Aborigines could be registered as slow workers —and thus entitled to only a small allowance.[5]

In 1965, the government arbitration court ordered equal pay for Aborigines (but *excluded* women and 'slow workers') with the result that, undefended by any union, thousands of Aborigines were sacked and evicted from their tribal lands. These people are now living in the refugee camps surrounding Darwin and Alice Springs.

The major American cattle company, King Ranch, stated that on their 4,730 square mile Brunette Downs cattle station on the Barkly Tableland, they would 'retain about one-third of the Aborigines.' They had one hundred Aborigines in the labour camp on their station three-quarters of a mile from the whites' homestead.[6]

Even after equal pay was introduced, the official minimum pay only rose to $82 a week— less $17 for 'keep'. In 1979, Christmas Creek Station in the Kimberleys paid stockmen $80 a week.[7]

However, many stations paid Aborigines far less. If the Aborigines were too insistent on correct pay and conditions, they would be thrown off the station. Aborigines reported that in 1976 they earned just $45 and rations for four months work on Kurundi Station near Tennant Creek. After this, they walked off the station and set up their own camp on some vacant crown land, vowing never to go back to work for the station.[8] This walk-off was caused not only by the bad working conditions but also by the wish of the people to live independently on their own land.

More and more, the cattle station owners carried out the threats made at the equal wage hearing to evict the Aborigines.

The King Ranch Company at Nash River has tried again and again to evict the Aborigines from the tribal land the station has taken. The most recent effort was in 1979. This was stopped by the Aborigines with a Supreme Court injunction. Some of the Aborigines had worked for the station for over forty years— and many of these years for no pay. In 1948, they went on strike for a wage—and won ninety-two cents a week!

At Vestey's Gordon Downs Station, only six Aborigines were permanently employed in 1980 as against 42 in 1967. Vestey's also refused to allow anyone but the thirty Aborigines they defined as dependants of those they employed to shop at the station store. The other thirty to forty Aborigines in the community were obliged to drive over 200 kilometres to the next store even to cash their welfare cheques.

This Vestey's Station covers over one million acres. It was rented to them by the Government for $18 a week. (Not per acre, not per square mile—but $18 for the whole station!) In all, British-owned Vesteys had over 20,000 square miles of Australia in 1979. In 1980 Vesteys sold Gordon Downs, their other

Western Australian properties and several of their Northern Territory stations. But they retain Wave Hill (16,000 square km), Helen Springs (5,000 square km) and their Queensland properties. They still run about 200,000 cattle, 65,000 of these in the Northern Territory.

The new owners of Gordon Downs evicted the Aboriginal community on 2 January 1981. They killed all the Aborigines' dogs. Many of those evicted had lived all their lives on the station.

The Aborigines are now trying to rebuild their settlement at Ringers Soak, four kilometres from the station homestead. They are endeavouring to secure a legal right to this part of the station so they can live independently away from white control.

What is life like today for Aborigines on the cattle stations? The dispossessed Aborigines often still provide a vital pool of casual labour that can be laid off at no cost in the wet season. In return for this, the station boss permits them to remain on a small patch of their land near, but not too near, the homestead.

The land allotted to them usually amounts to no more than a squalid camp-site with scarcely any facilities. Perhaps they may have a tap for water supplies and a little shelter.

In the Northern Territory, the homestead is often built on a small hill. The white employees all live clustered around the homestead in a fenced or walled compound. Within this, there is a carefully maintained garden and perhaps a tennis court and barbecue area; this area is solely for white use and barred to the blacks unless they are servants.

Immediately outside this area would be the garages and tool-sheds. Then may come the house allotted to a probably half-caste head stockman. The Aboriginal camp would be still further away at the foot of the hill.[9]

In 1979, the London *Observer* reported conditions on the Vestey Gordon Downs Station:

The station provided nine 20 by 12 foot one-room tin huts for the Aborigines. There was no piped water. The one pump was broken and water had to be carried from over 200 yards away. But the lawn sprinklers were working at the homestead! Professor Hollows, the eye specialist, commented that when he visited the station in 1977 he had asked the manager's wife why the Aborigines had no taps. She replied, 'We can't give them taps. They leave them on.'[10]

Aboriginal people remember well the earlier massacres:

Aborigines can drive you around and point out the people responsible for the shooting.

This 1976 report was from Geoff Eames, a lawyer with the Central Australian Aboriginal Land Council. He went on to say that the attitudes of the pastoralists vary from

the paternal who talk about 'my Aborigines', to a group of stations north-west of Alice Springs which have banded together for 'self-protection'. On one of these stations an Aborigine was shot in the back and crippled. You have to understand that these people are armed to the teeth, and it's not just pastoralists.

I recall one policeman ... had a gun in every room in his house because he believed that savages were about to come and 'get him'. This is quite typical. Our Aboriginal field worker recently broke his collar bone ... He spent the night without blankets lying in the scrub near the Aboriginal camp ... [because] the station owner's wife refused to have an Aborigine in the house.[11]

There have been many Aboriginal strikes and walk-offs. One of the earliest of which there are good records was that of the Pilbara Aborigines which started in 1946. It was led by Aboriginal men such as Dooley and Clancy, with the assistance of a non-Aborigine, Don McLeod, who threw in his lot with the Aborigines. This strike hit at many stations and was co-ordinated right across the Pilbara. It lasted three years and when it ended about 600 of the Aborigines decided to stay clear of white-controlled cattle stations in future. Instead, calling themselves the 'Nomads', they supported themselves by such activities as small scale mining. Indeed, up until 1960, they were a major prospecting force in the Pilbara. At the same time, they preserved and strengthened their culture.

Today, some of them live on their own cattle station at Strelley where they have organised what is probably one of the best bi-cultural Aboriginal schools in Australia.

Aboriginal strikes and walk-outs rarely get reported in the newspapers. An exception to this was a strike on a Vesteys cattle station.

In 1966 almost all of the 170 Aborigines on the Vestey 6,000 square mile Wave Hill Station walked off in protest against the appalling working conditions and exploitation. They were people of the Gurindji tribe and their name became famous as forerunners of the modern Aboriginal struggle for land.

They were eventually to obtain from the Whitlam government 1,000 square miles of their country back but only as a leasehold. They were probably the only Aboriginal group to obtain even a lease over their land before the Whitlam government fell. Vesteys were paid for the 'sacrifice' of this land.

A folk song tells the story of the Gurindji struggle:

Poor Bugger me
Gurindji
Me bin sit down this country
Long time before Lord Vestey
All about land belongin' me
Long time work no wages we
Work for good Lord Vestey
Little bit flour, sugar and tea
for the Gurindji
From Lord Vestey
Oh Poor Bugger me . . .
Spose we buying back country
What you reckin proper fee
Might be flour, sugar and tea
From the Gurindji
to Lord Vestey
Oh Poor Bugger me.

The Yungngora Community at Noonkanbah also went on strike for three years in the early 1970s before they obtained control over the station through new policies initiated by the Whitlam Labor government. This government set up an Aboriginal Land Fund to purchase stations from willing sellers so that large Aboriginal communities could once more exercise greater control over their lives and future. Stations were purchased in many parts of Australia and handed over to Aboriginal ownership.

Another strike was at Christmas Creek Station in mid 1979. This is near Fitzroy Crossing in the Kimberleys. It was 'allegedly' occasioned by an assault by the manager and head-stockman on some Aborigines. When the Aborigines brought them to court, the magistrate dismissed the charges on 'insufficient evidence' . . . perhaps because all six witnesses for the prosecution were Aboriginal!

Inspector Styants of Broom dismissed the strike as a 'walkabout'. (The way many Aboriginal strikes have been dismissed.) The strikers were supplied with fresh meat by Noonkanbah— and when the Christmas Creek management offered jobs to unemployed Aborigines at Fitzroy Crossing, they refused to work for them.

The Christmas Creek Aborigines have now picked themselves a site for their own settlement nearby at Pinnacles—but the Minister for Housing was reported as saying that if they did not go back to work and to live nearer the station, they would not get the promised new houses.

At Christmas Creek Station there is now only seasonal employment for ten Aboriginal men and five women—out of an Aboriginal population of 200.

However, the Aborigines went ahead, building up their settlement at Pinnacles and calling it *Kroonull*. The Commissioner for Community Relations called Kroonull 'one of the biggest success stories of the region.'

The Aboriginal Land Fund Commission tried to buy Laurel Downs for the Junjuwah community at Fitzroy Crossing, but they were knocked back by the State even though theirs was the biggest bid. Instead it went to a neighbouring American-owned station.

Malan Station, at Lake Gregory on the

Aborigines are the backbone of the cattle industry.

by a new Australian owner and they were forced like refugees from their own land into Halls Creek. Their dogs were shot or poisoned. Later, the people moved camp to land they claimed some four kilometres from the homestead, planning to build their own community, like the people of Noonkanbah.[12]

Since 1977, not one pastoral lease has been obtained for Aborigines in Western Australia. Charles Court threatened Noonkanbah:

If this attitude persists, then it would mean that no government in its right mind or in the public interest could ever give a pastoral lease in the name of Aborigines again . . . nor could it give Aboriginal reserves.[13]

In Queensland, the State Government vetoed the purchase of pastoral properties for Aborigines in line with a Cabinet decision of September 1972:

The Queensland Government does not view favourably proposals to acquire large areas of additional freehold or leasehold land for development by Aborigines or Aboriginal groups in isolation.[14]

Such a purchase would be seen as hindering 'assimilation'.

Action was taken by the Commissioner for Community Relations, Mr Grassby, who considered this illegal under the *Racial Discrimination Act*, 1975. But a compulsory conference convened by the Commissioner under this Act was illegally ignored by the Queensland Government. Further action was prevented by Federal Government intervention. Queensland showed that it could ignore Federal laws on Aboriginal matters with impunity.

Only one Queensland pastoral property, Murray Upper, has been bought for Aborigines by the Aboriginal Lands Fund Commission; this is now occupied by over 100 Aborigines. In this case, the purchase was mostly of freehold property and difficult for the State Government to block.

Mining companies have also acted to hinder the work of the Aboriginal Land Fund Commission. Mount Isa Mines (MIM) purchased

edge of the desert, was one of the last obtained by Aborigines in 1977. It is flourishing.

The Djaru people of Gordon Downs requested some land of their own in 1975 but they still have none. They asked for one small poor part of the station, some crown land nearby and a part of a neighbouring unused station lease. The West Australian government said the crown land was being sold to Gordon Downs and the unused station would not be viable in the future if divided. Gordon Downs Station then was sold by Vestey. In January 1981, all the Aborigines were evicted from Gordon Downs Station three cattle stations near Borroloola to stop Aborigines regaining the land. MIM thus secured land around a proposed mine. Mount Newman Mines likewise outbid Aborigines for Ethel Creek Station, depriving Jigalong Aborigines of part of their traditional lands.

The position of the pastoralists in the Northern Territory is secure—guaranteed under the terms of the 1976 Aboriginal Land Rights (NT) Act! None of their pastoral land is to be returned without the pastoralists' consent.

In 1979, the Northern Territory Government wrote to all the Aboriginal-controlled stations and gave them twenty-eight days notice of forfeiture of lease for poor 'cattle-management'. However, the Aborigines organised a public outcry that forced the government to back down.

Today, Middle Eastern, American, British and Asian interests control vast cattle empires throughout the north of Australia. But some have gone back into Australian hands—to the Aborigines who have now gained about eleven stations in Western Australia and about seven in the Northern Territory. These support large Aboriginal populations and are centres for the revival of Aboriginal culture. They are also economically successful despite much government harrassment.

This is exactly what I've done for you in the past. I've built you up to what you are today in

the cattle empires in the bloody North. Criticise me not for standing up for what I, as a black full-blood Aboriginal of the North, believe what I am doing now is my own freedom of wants, my own freedom of choice, and that is asking you, the white man, as a well-educated gift-of-the-gab man, leave me alone and help me in my wants, and you and I can make it together, you in your white surroundings and we, as the full-blood Aboriginal people, in our own surroundings.

You've taught us nothing by coming up on to the face of our continent, but we, the full-blood Aboriginal people of the North, have helped you, the white man, in more ways than one to get what you wanted. You've given us nothing in return, not even understanding or co-operation, give us land rights so we can put into effect what's being done on Noonkanbah now and other stations in the North, if not in the continent. You've failed miserably to recognise us as human beings. You've failed miserably with your white ideas of the past right up to the critical present moment. [15]

Footnotes

1. Walpiri *transcript*, p. 2037, quoted in C.L.C. *Land Rights News*, June 1978.
2. *Conciliation and Arbitration Act*, application by North Australian Workers Union, p. 62 (Case 830 of 1965).
3. *West Australian*, 25 June 1959.
4. Frank Stevens, *Aborigines in the Northern Territory Cattle Industry* (1974).
5. *West Australian* 25 June 1959.
6. *ibid*.
7. From wage statement in author's possession.
8. Diane Bell, *For our families: the Kurundi walk-off and the Ngurrantiji venture*, Aboriginal History, Vol. 2 (1978).
9. See Stevens, p.
10. For further information on the conditions in these camps, see chapter 13.
11. Geoff Eames, 'Aborigines and the Law, in Legal Service Bulletin (Melbourne), December 1976.
12. *Age*, 15 January 1981.
13. Michael Doyle of the *'Age'* quoted in *KLC Newsletter* (April 1980).
14. See below, chapter 27.
15. Robert Bropho, *Fringedwellers* (1981), p. 15.

Kimberley Land Council News

12 RACISM AND DISCRIMINATION

Many of the racist excuses used today to justify the continued dispossession and exploitation of Aboriginal people have been in use since the start of colonisation.

A 1977 report on Western and South Australia, by the Federal Community Relations Commission, stated that blatantly racist talk about the Aborigines is considered normal. One view repeatedly expressed was that the most practical solution was to 'put them all on an island and bomb them.'[1]

In both States, the report said, racial discrimination affected nearly every aspect of Aboriginal life. Another report by the same Commission stated:

Aborigines remain the worst discriminated against group in the Australian community . . . Most Australians have never met an Aborigine . . . there is, however, an easy assumption by the non-Aborigine Australian that he knows all about them. The dominant part of this so-called knowledge is contempt.[2]

It goes on to quote studies made of Australian school textbooks. For example, *The World and Its People*, a recent series of geography readers published by Nelson, in which these passages occur: 'The blackfellows form one of the lowest races of mankind in existence . . . They are fast disappearing, before the onward march of the white man.'

A Hunt and Marshall textbook widely used in New South Wales says of the Aborigines, 'They were lazy individuals, apparently devoid of morals, and always prepared to lie, cheat and steal.'

Most of the history and social studies school textbooks currently used in Australia give a totally derogatory picture of Aborigines, and completely white-wash the history of European settlement.[3] They turn invaders into heroic explorers and governors of prison camps into devoted missionaries.

This general despising of the Aborigines is often reflected in the press where Aborigines are sometimes depicted as lazy drunkards living off the social services. Even the more enlightened newspapers such as the Melbourne *Age* sometimes forget the existence of Aborigines. On 2 February 1981 it reported the renaming of the Johnston Street Bridge in honour of Charles Grimes, 'the man who discovered the Yarra River.' A few days earlier it reported the 'discovery' that Aborigines near Portland lived in stone houses before whites came. The *Age* did not interview the nearby Aboriginal community which could have told them at any time about these houses. Instead a white archaeologist was given all the attention for his 'discovery'.

Racism and Evolution

But more basically, whites commonly justify their treatment of Aborigines by saying that they are only just one little step up the evolutionary ladder from animals, and far inferior to whites.

Thus, a 1977 report that some Aborigines would be given $5,000 a year each for the uranium mining on their land, was banner-headlined 'Stone-Age Millionaires'. The inference was that this was a great blessing for so primitive a people.[4]

Another example of the continued use of Darwinian theory against Aborigines is this letter in the *West Australian*, 10th September 1977:

May I bring to the attention of the Minister of Aboriginal Affairs, one very definite way of life was decreed by Mother Nature: the strong will always dominate, thus ensuring a strong and virile environment . . . At no time does she tolerate a species or form of life that has to rely on the good graces of a powerful friend without some form of payment to its protector.'

Aboriginal culture is despised, misunderstood,

reviled and rejected by many whites who regard themselves as having an 'advanced' civilisation. Thus, an article in the *National Times* of 6th June 1977, stated:

There is no room in a civilised country like Australia for the standards of that (Aboriginal) tradition, they just do not conform to the basic human rights of society . . . what may have, perforce, been acceptable to a mob of half-starved vagrant hunters cannot be permitted when it (Aboriginal land) is provided at enormous expense by the taxpayer.

A letter supporting this said that to allow the Aborigines to go back on to their tribal land would be to facilitate

the increasingly rapid descent of our native people into a state of savagery, squalor, sickness and sloth. [5]

A 1970 reprint of the 1964 edition of *The Squatting Age* by Professor Stephen Roberts, stated:

It was quite useless to treat them (the Aborigines) fairly, since they were completely amoral and usually incapable of sincere and prolonged gratitude. [6]

Even those who think of Aborigines more positively, often presume that Aborigines will 'progress' towards a European way of doing things by their own choice.

In the more remote northern towns where Aborigines still constitute a high proportion of the population, attitudes have not changed much since the days, easily remembered by many Aborigines, of the outright genocidal massacres.

One statement, quoted by a Melbourne paper as typical, was: 'If the government declared an open season on the coons tomorrow I would be the first in line for my hunter's licence.' Other whites present 'gave every sign of approval.' Aborigines are also called 'niggers' and 'mongrels'. 'Total hate is the order of the day.' [7]

Another comment from another part of Australia was that Aborigines could be put under 'the Blackfeller's act for 100 miles from Adelaide, or box them up and send them over to the CSIRO (Commonwealth laboratories) for use in experiments instead of rats.' This was reported to have been said by a Port Adelaide town councillor in September 1977. [8]

Aboriginal voting rights

But the prejudices against mixing with Aborigines is shared at the highest level of government responsibility. For example, the West Australian Minister for Aboriginal Affairs, Mr Ridge, had his own election to Parliament declared invalid in 1977 because Aborigines had been deliberately prevented from voting by his campaign workers. Ridge wrote that

It was a degrading experience to have to campaign amongst the Aborigines to the extent

that I did. It offended me to know that whilst I was concentrating on these simple people over the last couple of weeks, I was neglecting a more informed and intelligent section of the community.[9]

After the elections he wrote as follows:

'I believe that we now have enough evidence to try and convince people of the necessity for amending the Electoral Act in relation to illiterate voters. If this is not done I would anticipate that by the next election there could be 3000 to 4000 Aborigines on the roll and under such circumstances the Liberal party would be doomed to failure.

He was eventually defeated by an Aborigine, Ernie Bridge, in a campaign which had the State Government changing electoral practices to make things harder for Aborigines. The police unsuccessfully charged those whites who worked with the Aborigines with 'electoral violations'.

Two whites in the Kimberleys on election day in 1980 drove with a drum of wine to the local Aboriginal community and left it in the entrance. One of them was reported as saying: 'I wanted to get them drunk because they are the most illiterate race in the world. They don't have the brains to vote . . . I tried to stop them voting in the best way I could.'

In the Northern Territory there have been other abuses of the electoral process. A letter from a member of the governing Liberal-Country Party alliance, Mr MacFarlane, to the Aboriginal community of Hodgson Downs, about 180 km south-east of Katherine, said: that as all voters on Hodgson Downs had not voted for him, he had 'cancelled all the things I promised such as electricity, airstrip, bores, etc. He knew how they had voted, because the Aborigines 'hung their heads and looked guilty'.

Mr Les Stoneham, executive officer of the Yulngu Association, stated that the people were shocked. 'As people still new to, and still struggling to understand, the basic concepts of European democracy, the community is now totally confused.'[10]

Police violence

Degradation and discrimination based on white prejudices are a simple fact of life for all Aborigines in Australia. A policeman stated that Aborigines are frequently beaten up in the Northern Territory:

One policeman fancies himself with the baton and uses that on the Aborigines with great effect. Another practises his karate. They don't care about hurting them. They just regard them as rock-apes.[11] Another expression used by police for Aborigines is 'protected animals'.[12]

The Aboriginal Legal Service estimates that about 90% of all arrests in the Northern Territory are of Aborigines—although they are but 30% of the population.[13]

In Western Australia, Aborigines make up 2% of the total population, in South Australia only 1% and in Victoria even less. In these three states 64% of all the women prisoners are Aborigines and 33% Aborginal men.[14] In Western Australia, 70% of the children in State institutions are Aborigines.[15] The New South Wales Bureau of Crime statistics stated that unrepresented Aborigines on drunkenness charges are 34 times more likely to receive penalties of imprisonment than are whites on the same charge.

Phil Slade of the Victoria Aboriginal Legal Service reported that a Victorian Aborigine had 45 times more chance of going to gaol than whites. Another report stated that an Aboriginal child in Victoria was 26 times more likely to be put into care.[16]

The evidence that the Aboriginal Legal Service gathered of police shootings, brutality, cell beatings and false arrests convinced the Whitlam Government that a Royal Commission should be called to investigate the Alice Springs police force. However, before this could be constituted, Whitlam was sacked by the Governor-General. The Fraser Government has publicly cancelled this Commission.

Another Royal Commission was set up earlier on the treatment of Aborigines by police at Laverton, in central Western Australia. This reported in mid-1976 that the police had beaten up Aborigines going to sacred ceremonies and fabricated evidence against the Aborigines. The state government refused to accept the Royal Commission and no further action was taken against the police.

In Brisbane, many Aborigines are scared to leave their homes. They are scared of the police who, it has been reported, have thrown elderly Aborigines in the river, attacked Aboriginal hostels, and beaten up black prisoners.[17]

The Federal Member of Parliament for Brisbane (Mr Peter Johnson) reacted to complaints about this police brutality by saying the Aborigines were an 'overfed, overprotected minority.' He added—'Queensland is not a racist state and never will be.'[18]

Magistrate Kenneth Quinn of Wilcannia, New South Wales, said in court, 'Your race ... must be the most interfering race of people ... you are becoming a pest race in Wilcannia ... There is only one end for pests.'[19]

General discrimination

Racist attitudes affect not only the treatment the Aborigines get from the police but also from medical staff.

Professor Hollows, conducting an anti-trachoma programme in 1977 in Central Australia, was reported by a nursing sister with him as saying 'If the Northern Territory Medical Service treated animals the way they treat the blacks, the RSPCA would be on to them.'[20] He reported that many of the white health workers, 'hate blacks'.[21]

These attitudes make white people avoid Aborigines. In most northern pubs the Aborigines are not welcome in the main bar. Instead they are sent to a small side window, or 'dog window' as it is known, or to a dingy minor bar. In the 330 miles between Alice Springs and Tennant Creek all but one of the pubs has a 'dog window'. (However dogs, unlike Aborigines, are let into the main bar.)

Some outback hotels serve Aborigines with glasses with a black spot painted on so that white lips face no risk of contamination.[22]

Others will serve Aborigines from a swill pot in to which the dregs of everyone's drinks are thrown. (However, pubs in southern cities are not nearly so blatantly racist.)

Aborigines, too, are not often wanted as neighbours by white people. For example, in 1977, a meeting of over 200 whites forced the cancellation of plans to house a few black families in Brunswick Junction in Western Australia.[23] An old Aboriginal woman was forced from her home in Morwell, Victoria, because she put up itinerant Aboriginal friends.[24]

Such attitudes among the whites actually stop the government's assimilation policies. Another example, in 1977, was the reaction of the town council when the Anglican Church in Guildford, Western Australia, allowed homeless Aborigines to pitch tents on church land in the city. The tents were slashed by vandals, and the city council ordered the tents' removal, prosecuting the church for allowing their land to be thus used. Yet every year up until then, Aborigines had slept under bridges in the city during the winter.

The Anglican Archbishop, fined in court for allowing the tents, said, 'We'll break the law again if needs be. Australia is a racist country. We must fight racism wherever it appears.'[25]

In the *West Australian*, 29 March 1980, a letter said: 'I had plenty of opportunity to observe and study ... the Aboriginal. My impression was that he had little to recommend him, and that impression has not altered. I am not a racist but I do claim to be a realist. Can anyone imagine what this beautiful city of Perth and its environment would be like if the white man had never come here?' Letters in a similar vein are frequently published in this paper. This letter concluded: 'You hear only what the white man has done to the Aborigines but not a word about what they have done on many occasions to the white man.'

Many whites resented the recognition of Aboriginal rights in the Northern Territory Land Rights Bill. The *Central Australian Advocate* said that this law had saddled them with a liability which many see as the most divisive and politically destructive law ever made (29 June 1978). The *Age* reported that a typical remark was: 'Before long there'll be a pandanus (palm) curtain dividing whites and blacks and we won't be able to use half of our own bloody country' (10 August 1979). (The *Age* also noted that the person saying this had been in the Northern Territory less than two years and was not born in Australia.)

White backlash

Any attempt to treat Aborigines as people with equal rights and needs is met with an instant outcry, typified by a Queensland MP saying, 'No white man in Australia is advantaged as much as the Aborigines'.

Other examples of this white backlash can easily be given. The former leader of the Northern Territory Assembly, Dr Letts, threatened violence from whites if Aborigines were allowed to control some of their tribal lands. He said this would give them an unfair advantage since whites had to purchase any land they wanted. The Queensland Government vetoed the return of land unused by whites to Aboriginal traditional owners, using exactly the same reason. A uranium company, Queensland Mines, objected to a freeze on developing a deposit while traditional Aboriginal claims were considered. It placed advertisements declaring boldly '50,000 Australian shareholders claim equality with Aborigines.'[26]

1. London *Evening Standard*, 4 January 1977.
2. Commissioner for Human Relations, *Reports*, 1976, 1977.
3. Fr Morgan Howe, *Aborigines and Christians: an introduction to some of the issues* (Foundation of Aboriginal and Islander Research Action, Queensland 1977), pp. 13-14.
4. Sydney *Telegraph*, 26 August 1977.
5. *National Times*, June 1977.
*6. Professor Stephen Roberts, *The Squatting Age*, 1964 (1970 edition).
*7. *Herald*.
*8. *News*, 28 September 1977.
9. *National Times*, 21 November 1977.
10. The *Age*, 2 February 1981.
11. Justin Maloney, *Resumé of Aboriginal Position in the Northern Territory*, 1976, p. 23 (Unpublished manuscript).
12. Maloney p. 23.
*13. Geoff Eames; Central Land Council.
14. The *Age*, 16 September 1976, quoting Senator Bonner.
*15. Peter Tobin, 'A Meeting of Nations: Aborigines and the Law' in *Legal Service Bulletin*, Melbourne, December 1976.
16. Nunawading *Gazette*, 26 October 1977.
17. *Nation Review*, 18 August 1977.
18. *Courier Mail*, 15 August 1977 and *Age*, 16 August 1977.
19. *Australian*, 7 August 1980.
20. *Morning Herald* 3 August 1977.
21. *Age*, 2 July 1977.
22. Melbourne *Herald*, 5 September 1977 and Sydney *Sun*, 8 September 1977.
23. *Western Australian*, 30 June 1977.
24. *Australian Report*, CIMRA No. 1, p. 6, and the *Age*, 29 January 1977.
25. *Australian Report*, CIMRA No. 1, p. 7, and the *Australian*, 19 August 1977.
*26. Queensland Mines.

13 THE ILLS OF COLONISATION – POVERTY AND DISEASE

Poverty

The full hypocrisy of the demand by whites for equality with Aborigines can only be realised if one is aware of just how desperate Aboriginal living conditions are today.

The Aborigines, forced off their lands, discriminated against, and persecuted, have been driven from a self-sufficient rich way of life into becoming malnourished supplicants, dwelling alongside an affluent, wasteful, white community.

Their economy is wrecked, the heart of their culture torn away, by their expulsion from their land. Their only hope of survival is to work for the people who have stolen their land. To do such work they are expected to adopt a completely alien culture and to be obedient to the invader.

But the whites do not want to employ Aborigines except at extremely low wages. Few jobs, usually only the lowest, are offered to them.

Government estimates in 1976 showed a national Aboriginal unemployment rate of 57% and a rural Aboriginal unemployment rate of over 80%. These figures had not improved by 1980. Indeed between 1978–9 Aboriginal unemployment rose by 12%!

Aboriginal people who follow their traditional culture may well find it difficult and unpleasant to adopt the European life-style necessary in the eyes of many employers. Aboriginal culture demands that a considerable amount of time is given to religious work and often companies (such as Comalco, owned by Rio Tinto Zinc and Kaiser) refuse to give time off for important communal religious ceremonies. The companies only allow time off for Christian festivals such as Easter.[1]

When they do find work, it is often only for minimal pay. Despite the equal pay award for the cattle industry, many Aborigines only get around $80 a week on the stations. In Queensland, despite legal battles, Aborigines are still paid the minimum pay rates in government funded jobs on the reserves ... $60 to $80 a week.

One of the most widespread myths among white people about blacks is that they are commonly 'bludgers' living off social security payments, living off the white tax payers. In fact fewer blacks take social security than whites, despite ten times as much unemployment among blacks as among whites! This myth is just another example of the way whites tend to denigrate the Aborigines.

Thus at Yuendemu, a large settlement 300 km north-east of Alice Springs, with an Aboriginal population of about 1,000 and an adult male population of 300, over 150 of the males of working age were unemployed in 1976. Of these, only seven were receiving the dole. *Per capita* income at Yuendemu came to less than $12. At Borroloola, another Aboriginal settlement of some 400 mostly unemployed inhabitants, only twelve received unemployment benefit. The Northern Territory Aboriginal *per capita* income was about $780 a year in 1976.

In 1978, a Government inquiry into 'The Economic Development of Aboriginal Communities in the Northern Territory' listed the social welfare payments received per person in Aboriginal communities. Three typical examples would be: Oenpelli–$1.22 per person; Yirrkala–$1.19 per person; Bamyili (population 600)–just 64 cents each.

Extra benefits Aboriginal people have access to–ones not available to whites–are allowances for secondary education, and less than 1% of Aborigines receive this benefit.

Birth control is being encouraged among Aborigines, because whites fear the increasing Aboriginal population. Nobel Prize winner, McFarlane Burnett, said, 'Aborigines must limit the size of their families if Australia is to avoid racial problems like those in the USA.[2]

Another myth is about free government housing on settlements. This is much more true of the whites than the Aborigines. Thus at Papunya in 1975–77, twenty-eight houses were built for white staff and seven for Aborigines. At Yuendemu, of the 45 completed houses, 34 were occupied by whites. The vast majority of Aborigines live in humpies that make the shanties of Soweto look luxurious. They are without water or electricity, with bare earthen floors and walls made of rubbish from the tip.

If conditions are so bad, why do people stay in the settlements? Originally, many did try to leave. People had been trucked into the settlements by police. They escaped and were brought back again time after time, walking 200 or more miles to escape and return to their lands. But their lands were by now in the hands of whites.

Today Aborigines are no longer forced to remain in these settlements. Many are leaving to live in their own 'outstations' back on their tribal lands. Thus, at Hermannsburg Mission 77% of the Aborigines have left and at War-burton at least 55%. Health on these outstations is reported to be vastly better than in the main settlements. Yet it has been estimated that the government only spends in services to the outstations about 2% of what it spends in the main settlements.

Aboriginal housing

Housing has been officially seen from the start of colonial settlement as a means by which tribes could be 'settled' and thus brought under closer control. Housing policies have consistently been used as a tool for the destruction of Aboriginal culture and the assimilation of Aboriginal people.

'Raising living standards' usually meant (and still means) requiring Aborigines to behave and live like Europeans. For example, the Queensland Native Affairs Annual Report of 1957 stated:

Housing has always held a very strong priority in State Government policy aimed at the ultimate assimilation of the Aboriginal people into the white community.'[3]

Such a policy is ultimately based on the notion that Aboriginal society is inferior, and to 'progress' Aborigines must abandon their culture and enter the mainstream of Australian life.

It is usually completely forgotten that Aborigines have an extremely long tradition of housing themselves. (The wide range of different traditional housing types has been indicated.) It is also assumed that Aborigines today are incapable of developing their own forms of housing, even when they have their land returned.

Housing in Towns

In towns the assimilation policy works through the imposition of rules that do not suit the Aboriginal way of life and conflict with Aboriginal culture. For example, two common rules are that no visitors may stay overnight and that no one may keep a dog.

The houses offered to Aborigines were often carefully selected so as not to be too close together. The West Australian Housing Commission, had a policy of dispersing houses 'ideally in any one street, say two Aboriginal houses situated at diagonal ends.'[4]

In 1979, when Aborigines looked like, for the first time, obtaining adequate housing in Alice Springs, a number of alarmed townspeople formed themselves into 'Citizens for Civilised Living'. (Now known as 'The Alice Springs Citizens Association'.) They petitioned against the location of Aboriginal homes near to their own homes. They had the support of over one thousand Alice Springs whites.

They argued that the Aborigines were, 'Tenants of substandard nature . . . unacquainted with the work ethic . . . incapable of simple household duties.' They said having Aborigines living near them would cause them 'financial loss' by devaluing their homes.

The Northern Territory authorities agreed

to their petition. It announced a policy of not siting any house for an Aborigine next to a private white residence. It also cut the number of houses to be built for Aborigines from 20 to 14.[5]

Who are the officially homeless?

The Department of Aboriginal Affairs sent out a survey form around 1977 to determine just how many Aborigines were homeless. But the instructions that went with it stated, 'Do not include people living in improvised dwellings'. Improvised dwellings were defined elsewhere in the form to include 'wiltja, lean-to, shed, shanty, car body'.

Presumably, the Government believed that only Aborigines living under bridges or the night sky are the genuinely homeless.

Aboriginal housing in outback Australia and on reserves

In order to gradually 'assimilate' Aborigines, a system of 'transitional housing' was developed.

In the 'first stage', Aborigines were allotted a simple metal roofed and walled hut. The 'second stage' housing was also made out of galvanised iron—but had water and electricity. The 'third stage' was similar to a housing commission house—as given to non-Aborigines.

However funds were always so sparingly provided, that most Aborigines never had the opportunity to sample more than 'stage one' housing. Often these houses were and are abandoned in desert regions because they become like ovens. Experiments have shown that at night they can be ten degrees centigrade hotter inside than outside, thirteen degrees hotter than in a spinifex humpy.[6]

They also could not be adapted to the normal traditional way of living. Usually a family built a house that could be moved within the camp as relationships changed or people moved. The strain caused by the im-mobility of this housing was and is a major reason why these houses are often abandoned. They are a particularly inconvenient and

House and dog kennel at Jigalong 1979. The dome marks the failure of one housing 'expert's' idea. The canvas cover proved too expensive to replace. (Jan Roberts).

uncomfortable form of housing for traditional Aborigines.

Under the Whitlam government there was a sharp rise in the funds given for housing Aborigines, but not enough even to keep up with the rising birth-rate. Despite a self-determination policy, whites remained firmly in control of Aboriginal housing and there was little actual study of what Aborigines wanted.

Aborigines, in fact, increasingly left the settlements where houses were being slowly provided to go back to their traditional lands.

Much of the money provided went to white professional advisors. For example, between 1972 and 1975 at Oenpelli, $21,000 was spent in fees to architects, $401,000 went as a housing grant, and no houses were built. In all 76 houses were built for Aborigines in the Northern Territory from 1972—75 for about $210,000 each.[7]

Sometimes houses were built for the white staff and not for the Aborigines. For example, the Pitjantjatjara people at Pipalyatjara Out-station told the Department of Aboriginal Affairs that housing aid was not a high priority. They didn't want their white adviser to have a permanent house as they did not want to have a permanent white advisor. But in 1978—79, the aid they received from the DAA had to be mostly spent on building a conventional home for this adviser.[8]

With the Fraser Government, self-manage-ment became a catch-cry, but, the Government added, only if Aborigines maintain proper cost controls and observe set standards! Aborigines are not permitted 'self-management' as they have practised it for thousands of years.

At places like Tennant Creek Mulga Reserve unlined two room iron huts are still being built for Aborigines with Commonwealth funds. Money is not provided for anything better.

Malnutrition and disease

Poverty can lead to the most chronic malnourishment. A 1977 survey in Sydney found that currently: 25% of Aboriginal children are suffering from serious malnutrition; 80% of the 1,500 malnourished children were under three years old and therefore likely to be brain-damaged. Of these 64% were anaemic, 60% had a parasitic bowel infection and 32% had at least one perforated ear-drum.

The report noted that all this was in an area with the 'highest density of health care facilities in the State'. (The report was put out by the Sydney Aborigine Medical Service—an organisation founded by Aborigines.)

In Sydney there are some 20,000 Aborigines living in slum conditions. Thirty per cent are diabetic, as against two per cent of whites. The average life span is twenty years less than for whites. The national figure is fifty years for Aborigines, as against a general national average of 69.3 for men and 76.3 for women.

The Australian Freedom from Hunger Campaign announced that it would give a small grant to help feed the Sydney Aboriginal children. The Alice Springs whites immediately stopped giving their support to the campaign, saying they did not want their money to be poured away.

Similar conditions occur in other Australian cities. Thus Melbourne Aborigines only live to an average of 49 for men and 51 for women, and malnutrition is rife. Over half of the 8,000 Aborigines in Melbourne are unemployed. [9]

A 1977 Victorian survey by Dr Mal Dobbin determined that 22% of Aboriginal children in Melbourne and 56% of the Aboriginal children in East Gippsland were undernourished by United Nations standards.

A survey of Aboriginal children admitted to a Perth hospital showed that over 50% were malnourished. This was the main reason for ill health. All but one were under 15 months old. [10]

Health conditions in the outback are still worse than in the cities. Many of the dispossessed refugee Aboriginal communities live on the cheapest and worst of white man's food—on white sugar, white bread and flour, tea and canned soft drinks.

A medical officer with the Sydney Aboriginal Medical Centre recently warned: 'Don't immunise black children.' Malnutrition means that they don't have enough resistance to take even the tiny amounts injected and thus are dying. [11]

Inoculation campaigns in central Australia in the early 1970s, coupled with cut-backs in government funding of Aboriginal welfare programmes, led to a leap in the infant mortality rate to 296 per thousand. In one three-month period, over half of the Aboriginal babies died. [12]

The official statistics for the Northern Territory show that from 1965 to 1975 infant mortality rates among Aborigines dropped from 143 per thousand to 50 per thousand, but by 1977 it was up to 75 per thousand. Queensland had a rate of 54 per thousand in 1977. The general Australian average is 13.8 per thousand (1976).

Such horrifying statistics are not unique to the North. A 1980 report on the Shepparton-Mooroopna area of Victoria found that stillbirths were 42 per thousand among Aborigines, as against a Victorian average of 9.6 per thousand. [13]

An Aboriginal baby is thus four to five times more likely to die as an infant than the child of a white Australian.

A major reason for these appalling figures has been the failure to provide an adequate water supply for outback Aboriginal communities. At Jigalong, in 1979, most of the community had to walk 100 yards to the nearest tap—and this tap only had water in the evenings! This did not affect the white staff whose houses had tanks that refilled in the evenings. At Umbalkumba, Northern Territory, 325 people share seven communal taps. The Department of Aboriginal Affairs reported that in 1975, 15% of Aboriginal communities had no water supply.[14]

These are communities that would not be gathered into these reserve and mission settlements if it were not for Government policy. For millenia Aborigines managed their own water supply by living in groups where there was water naturally sufficient to support them.

These settlements also bring sewerage problems. Sixty-three percent in the Northern Territory have no access to a functioning toilet near their home.[15]

Diabetes

The above inquiry quoted a South Australian survey between 1969 and 1974. Diabetes was found to be twenty times more prevalent among the Aboriginal population 20–39 years old, and ten times among those 40–59 years old, than among whites.

Leprosy

Leprosy is still virulent in Northern Australia. In 1977 the Northern Territory had 740 lepers of which all but thirty were Aborigines. That year there were fourteen new cases among Aborigines in the Northern Territory and four among whites. In the Kimberleys and Pilbara there were sixteen more cases. The West Australian rates are twice as bad as in the poorest of Third World nations.

In 1981 between 1500 and 2000 people had leprosy in Australia—nearly all Aborigines. This estimate was given by a world authority on leprosy, Dr Charles Shepard. He said that the number of new patients in the Northern Territory had only fallen by twenty per cent in fifteen years, as against an eighty per cent drop in China and Upper Volta. One in twenty eight of Northern Territory Aborigines has or has had leprosy.

Tuberculosis

West Australian Aborigines were three times more likely than non-Aborigines to catch TB in 1976—but this is half what it was in 1971.

Syphilis

There is a growing epidemic of this disease. One Kimberley community was 38% infected. In the Northern Territory in 1971 there were two Aboriginal cases notified and eighteen non-Aboriginal. But in 1977 there were 703 Aboriginal cases and 164 non-Aboriginal.

In 1981 Professor Hollows, a leading expert on Aboriginal Health, estimated that thirty per cent of Aborigines between fifteen and 49 years old had syphilis. [16]

Trachoma

Trachoma was eliminated among Australian whites some 30 years ago. But in a survey of Aborigines living in the southern part of Western Australia in 1977 it was found that between 50% and 83% of the children under 11 had this disease.[17]

Trachoma is a very severe form of conjunctivitis, causing scarring on the eyes and eyelids. It causes pain in bright light and eventual blindness. Only in the last two years has any national publicity been given to this disease. Its prevalence is indicative of the acute impoverishment of the Aborigines, and the prevalence among them of other diseases typical of the poor of Third World countries.

A national survey of eye-disease among Aborigines organised in 1977–78 by Professor Hollows, Australia's leading eye-specialist, has provided for the first time a broad survey of health conditions on outback Aboriginal settlements. He says: 'It is clear that Aborigines have the worst ethnic blindness rate in the world.'[18] His team found that one in every four Aborigines over 60 is blind and another has poor vision. One in every five blacks needs an eye operation. There is twenty times as much chance for an Aborigine to go blind as there is for a white.

These are general statistics. Some outback Aboriginal settlements are far worse—in some most of the old people are blind.[19]

One report in a respected newspaper describing the Balgo Roman Catholic Pallotine Order mission station visted by the team stated:

The Mission lies in one of the most isolated and arid parts of the Tanami Desert in the north of West Australia. A handsome stone church dominates the central area which boasts a sports ground, basketball courts, an outdoor theatre and two impressive community health buildings which house a small hospital. Housing for white mission staff—there are about thirty—ranges from attractive stone units and pre-fabricated houses to caravans . . . The black camp, 200 yards from the hospital, is a sprawling mass of tin huts, ramshackle shelters erected out of old sheets of corrugated iron and petrol drums and a few flimsy canvas shelters strung over insecure frames . . . When the national trachoma and eye health team arrived . . . there were 353 blacks camped in the tin huts and shacks.

Twenty-two of the 353 blacks were blind, 41 had 'poor vision', 103 had well developed trachoma follicles and 78 had badly infected ears. Seventeen required eye surgery . . . none of the 24 white people on the mission tested had any eye problem Nursing sisters employed on the mission by the government were unaware that 12% of the adult Aboriginal population were blind and that 51% of the black children had trachoma follicles, which if left untreated would eventually cause blindness.[20]

But this mission is one of the *better* places for the Aborigines to live. The situation in the black camps at the cattle stations, where the Aboriginal stockmen live with their families, is far worse.

One cattle station—Gordon Downs, owned by the giant British company Vesteys—was described in a newspaper report thus:

One hundred yards from the homestead—a beautiful green oasis . . . —fifty blacks are camped in an ugly dustbowl. The housing includes rusty car bodies. The nearest water is 300 yards away at a communal ablution block . . . The trachoma team was told it was hopeless putting in plumbing in black camps because blacks waste water . . . At nearby Sturt Creek, another Vestey property, the situation was similar.[21]

There has been some recent improvement in death rates—but this was due to the institution of an air ambulance system for serious cases rather than from an improvement in health. Still the Northern Territory death rate is over three times the national average at 50 per thousand. In Western Australia the Aboriginal Medical Service Director stated that the infant mortality rate among blacks in West Australia is now six times that among whites—and yet, incredibly, the Aboriginal Affairs department returned $16.6 million in unspent money to the Treasury in 1977.[22]

There are no Aboriginal, university qualified, doctors in the whole of Australia. There are only a few Aboriginal graduates to date and most of these have general arts degrees. Only 2% of the Aborigines were educated beyond third form secondary school in 1977.[23]

Professor Hollows blames the terrible health not just on the pauperisation of the Aborigines and the wrecking of their economy, but also strongly on the racism of the whites. He said that it would be better if some of the

white health workers just got up and left. Most are doing virtually nothing for black health and some are actually setting back any chances of improvement. Some of the whites delivering health care to Aborigines actually hate blacks, which is like an architect sabotaging his own design or a reporter trying to get the facts wrong.[24]

On 18th August 1978, the UK *Australasian Express* reported that the Australian Broadcasting Commission had been asked by the Federal Director-General of Health to cancel a film on Aboriginal blindness in the Northern Territory ... because it might damage the Territory's tourist trade!

This film reported the work of Professor Hollows. In it, he said that one in thirty Northern Territory Aborigines had leprosy, and one in twenty had VD. He stated, too, that some Aboriginal health workers were treated as nothing more than 'glorified cleaning ladies'. The Director-General claimed the film exaggerated the ill-health of the Aborigines and the attitudes of the white health workers.

It is particularly worrying that similar attitudes seem to extend to governmental level. Professor Hollows had a dramatic example of this when the Queensland Premier, Bjelke-Petersen, got the Federal Government to stop the anti-trachoma programme in Queensland because two of the Aboriginal field-workers with the team were 'enrolling Aborigines to vote'. Professor Hollows was stunned. He said, 'They are the best two field workers we have ever had. The eye health problems of Aborigines here are so horrific.[25]

The anti-trachoma team decided that they would move temporarily into New South Wales until after the elections and then return to Queensland. However, the Federal Minister for Health, Mr Hunt, is reported to have tried to ban them in New South Wales too, until after the elections. It seemed that one of the first areas the team intended to visit was Mr Hunt's own electorate where there are several thousand Aborigines. He did not want any embarrassing publicity on Aboriginal health in his electorate. A leaked report said that the Government was prepared to move against Professor Hollows himself if he did not accept this.

The Queensland Government was reported as insisting that the programme would not be allowed to restart in that State until Aboriginal members of the team were sacked and replaced with others selected by that government.[26] However, the existing workers had the confidence of tribal blacks. An official committee recently recognised that such confidence was essential if any health programme among Aborigines was to have hope of success.

The violent cutbacks in Federal funding of Aboriginal health programmes since Fraser took office shows the lack of concern the Fraser Government has for Aborigines. The proportion of the national budget spent on Aboriginal Affairs has dropped by a third from that appropriated by the Whitlam Labor Government to the level of the pre-Whitlam Liberal Government, back to about 0.65% of the national budget. In 1976-77 they *underspent* the total appropriation for Aboriginal Affairs by ten per cent, returning $16 million to consolidated revenue. In 1975–76 they underspent by $32 million.

It should also be noted that State Governments also frequently return to the Treasury large sums of money originally provided for Aboriginal Affairs.

It is not that the Aboriginal communities are not providing for their own health care. It has been amply demonstrated by the Aboriginal Health and Legal Services, established in recent years in many parts of Australia at Aboriginal initiative, that Aboriginal people can bring good health to their own people far more effectively than non-Aboriginal services. These have carved for themselves a claim for official funding–and are funded. But these funds are grudgingly and sparingly given. Far more goes to much less effective agencies that are not Aboriginal controlled.

As an example of this, the Victorian Aboriginal Dental Service received $140,000 to treat 6,500 cases in 1979. But the Department of Aboriginal Affairs also gave the Victorian Health Commission $70,000–for the treatment of only 512 cases. Another example is the refusal of promised funds by Senator Chaney in December 1980 to the Victorian Aboriginal Child Care Agency for a carefully planned and much needed hostel in Brunswick on the grounds that it was 'expanding faster than its ability to manage'.

In 1980, the Fraser Government was still

spending less than had been allotted to the Department of Aboriginal Affairs in 1975, even before accounting for inflation. After accounting for inflation, the Government had cut funds spent by 30.7% overall. They had cut Aboriginal health by 15%, Aboriginal housing by 24%, Aboriginal education by 25%.

Fraser had explicitly promised Aboriginal communities (by telegram before he was first elected) that there would be no cuts. Once elected, he cynically broke his promise and slashed the overall Aboriginal Affairs spending by about a third in real terms.

Many Aboriginal communities have found themselves totally unemployed with the closure of the housing co-operatives they were establishing with Federal support . . . not only unemployed but with far less possibilities of social security support. Unemployment pay is very often not paid if the Aborigines refuse to leave their tribal lands to look for work.

The violent cut-back in aid has devastated the work of the Aboriginal Health and Legal Aid organisations. For example, the staff of the Victorian Legal Aid office has been halved (as of 24th June 1977).[27]

Mick Dodson, Victoria's first Aboriginal law graduate, stated: 'Expectations have been killed, there's total frustration and Aborigines are losing sight of any future for themselves'. A barrister who had worked with the Service stated:

'Aborigines are totally and utterly deprived from the beginning of their lives and while the

law can never solve Aboriginal problems it can keep social oppression at bay . . .

Australian whites are sophisticated racists— there's no overt opposition. They just pat you on the back and cut off the money . . . the white people have been practising genocide in this country for 200 years. What does one legal service matter? Who'd care?[28]

Footnotes

1. Discussion between J. Tonkin (Comalco) and Church officials, 14 June 1963.
2. Fr Morgan Howe, *Aborigines and Christians: an introduction to some of the issues*, Foundation of Aboriginal and Islander Research Action, Queensland, 1977, p. 15.
*3. M. Heppell (ed.), *A Black Reality: Aboriginal Camps and Housing* (AIAS, 1979). I am largely indebted to this excellent book for the information on housing in this section.
4. Royal Commission into Aboriginal Affairs, *Report*, 1974, p. 223.
5. *Nation Review*, 26 July 1979.
6. C. Tatz, *Aboriginal Administration in the N.T.* Unpublished Ph.D. thesis, A.N.U., 1965.
7. N.T. Dept. of Aboriginal Affairs paper, January 1976.
8. Heppell, p. 23.
9. *Australian Report*, CIMRA, No. 1, p. 14, and the *Age*, 30 August 1976.
10. Aboriginal and Islander Forum, July 1977, p. 6.
11. *Australian Report*, CIMRA, No. 1, p. 5, and the Brisbane *Courier Mail*, 14 June 1977.
*12. Dr A. Kalokeimos, *Australia's Expendable Babies*, 1972.
13. *Age*, 30 March 1979.
14. D.A.A. Statistical Bulletin 1979.
15. House of Representatives Standing Committee, 1979 Inquiry.
16. *Age*, 14 May 1981 and 23 May 1981.
17. House of Representatives Inquiry.
18. *Aboriginal and Islander Forum*, Perth, November 1977, p. 10.
19. *Age*, 2 July 1977.
20. *Age*, 2 July 1977.
21. *Age*, 2 July 1977.
22. *Age*, 2 July 1977.
23. *Aboriginal and Islander Forum*, Perth, November 1977.
24. *Age*, 2 July 1977.
25. *Age*, 8 November 1977.
26. Brisbane *Courier Mail*, 9 November 1977.
27. *Age*, 24 June 1977.
28. *Age*, 24 June 1977.

14 THE DEVELOPMENT OF THE ASSIMILATION POLICY

It was not until after the Second World War that the whites of Australia realised that they were going to have to live with Aborigines. It was not until then that it became clear that the Aborigines were not going to die out. The goal of a racially homogeneous Australia, a white Australia, began to look harder to achieve.

More particularly, it was discovered that the reserves set up on what was thought to be worthless land, in fact contained valuable minerals. It was thought inadvisable to leave these resources unused in Aboriginal hands. It would also be 'wasteful' to leave the Aborigines in such isolated places when they could be a useful part of the working force.

A new strategy had to be devised to dispossess the Aborigines and to move them to the cities and townships. A policy of 'assimilation' was adopted. This, like all previous policies, would have the effect of placing further Aboriginal lands in white hands. It was a nominal rather than a real change.

It was defined to Parliament in September 1951 by Paul Hasluck, Minister for Northern Development and a future Governor-General:

The recent Native Welfare Conference agreed that assimilation is the objective of native welfare measures. Assimilation means, in practical terms that, in the course of time, it is expected that all persons of Aboriginal birth or mixed blood in Australia will live like white Australians do. We recognise now that the noble savage can benefit from measures taken to lead him in civilised ways of life.

Prior to this new policy,

there was considerable neglect of the Aborigine, due largely to the acceptance of the idea that his inevitable end was to lead a low and primitive life until his race died out.

The assimilation policy was totally opposed to the recognition of Aboriginal land rights from its very conception. Hasluck stated that the alternative policy of leaving them alone on their reserve lands would:

create a series of minority groups living on little bits of territory on their own . . . it would result in the very situation in Australia that we have always sought to avoid, namely the existence of a separate minority group living on its own.[1]

These same assimilation policies were to be used to justify the destruction of the remaining Aboriginal reserves for mining.

This policy was still in force at Federal level in 1972 when the Minister for Aboriginal Affairs, reacting to the establishment of an Aboriginal tent embassy outside Parliament House, stated to Parliament:

The government is not prepared to see a separate race within a race developed in Australia, with an embassy for the Aborigines as though they were a foreign power . . . We have a long way to go to help these ancient people into the 21st century.[2]

The South Australian Government initially adopted the same policy, with legislation in 1962 giving superintendents of reserves powers to search homes, fix wages, order people into training schemes—all to forcibly assimilate them.

But they were the first to abandon this policy. In 1971 their Minister for Aboriginal Affairs rejected the assimilation policy because it viewed Aborigines 'as a primitive and backward people . . . who must be taught the white man's ways and be made into an indistinguishable part of the white community'. He stated 'the principle objective should be the integration of the Aboriginal people into the community upon the basis of respect for their culture and their right to live in their own ways.'[3]

Although the Federal Government has since made similar statements, in practice efforts are still being made to destroy the separate cultural identity of the Aborigines. They have officially espoused 'integration', allowing Aborigines to choose to live in accordance with their culture in communities of their own. But in practice the eviction from land continues, assimilation continues.

Since Whitlam, the Federal Government has been sharing the administration of Aboriginal Affairs with the States (except Queensland). Both the Whitlam and the Fraser Governments strongly resisted pressure to give the nationally elected Aboriginal Congress, or Consultative Committee, set up by the Whitlam Government, any real power to administer their own people's affairs.

Whites still take a dominating role in all Departments of Aboriginal Affairs, whites manage all reserves. The Federal Government is

An unidentified Ngarrindji woman and children, c. 1910. Their land is by the mouth of the Murray River.

currently setting up an Aboriginal Development Commission with senior Aboriginal staff but this is still subservient to the Government.

Land has only been returned to Aboriginal community ownership, to any significant extent, in the Northern Territory under Labor Government-initiated legislation, and in South Australia, again under legislation initiated by a Labor Government.

The principal policy still seems to be to take the remaining land in Aboriginal use away from the Aborigines, to close the reserves, to disperse the Aboriginal population, and to hope that they will thus lose all sense of being Aboriginal; that is, to assimilate them out of existence as a people. When Aborigines are rehoused from the reserves into white townships, they are scattered around so that they may assimilate better. They are usually rented houses by State housing authorities with rules that completely violate Aboriginal culture: such as forbidding putting up travelling relatives, and the keeping of dogs.

A report in the leading Melbourne evening paper, the *Herald*, 12th November 1977:

Aboriginal leaders are not optimistic. Genocide, more politely called assimilation, was government policy for so long that it is difficult for any Aboriginal to regard a white man's promise as worth more than a tinker's cuss . . . assimilation—'breeding out', . . . the problem would simply find its own genetic solution . . . It didn't work. [4]

Also, by orders of the Federal Government, the Aboriginal Lands Council for Victoria was abolished at the end of 1977. It was obviously thought that the 7,000 Aborigines in Victoria, many living in desperate fringe camps, had no need to have any land returned. They are just to be assimilated. However this Council was in the first place appointed by the Government and not elected.

In a similar manner, the Aborigines of Tasmania are refused anything but assimilation by policy of the Government. Scarcely any land is being returned to them, they receive little recognition as Aborigines.

Also, on 21st October 1977, the *Daily News* reported:

The Federal Government is moving to close down all town-fringe Aboriginal reserves in Western Australia . . . Mr Viner (the Minister for Aboriginal Affairs) hopes to extend the programme to other states, particularly New South Wales . . . He said he had decided that one of his major tasks is the elimination of these reserves which are a major source of infection and disease . . . [5]

In Perth, Aboriginal Land rights campaigner, Mr Robert Bropho, bitterly opposed the abolition of reserves:

The reserves represent security to the Aboriginal people. They are being thrown off their own land into places where they'll get kicked out if a white neighbour complains. [6]

He went on to say that the Aborigines were opposed to the move but were being forced to go into the white townships.

Robert Bropho, a spokesman for the fringe dwellers of Western Australia.

To help in 'assimilation', the Federal Government decided 'to make Aboriginal shanty dwellers in the Northern Territory pay rates on their tin huts'.[7] The government cannot so easily close these settlements under the new Northern Territory Land Rights Act, but in every way they are now making life difficult for the people on them by slashing financial help, and by taking money from them. The danger now is that the Aborigines could be starved on their new-won land, which, after all, is only the land that the whites had not previously taken and, therefore, the poorest.

Despite the terrible conditions that Aborigines are forced to live in on the settlements and camps of the north, despite the Federal Government cutting by over 50% in real terms the re-housing programme from 1975–77, the government deemed it necessary in 1977 to start charging Aborigines rates for garbage collection and 'parks and gardens'. For anyone who knows their living conditions, this is unreal. The people often don't have a piped water supply let alone parks and gardens. Rates were payable for 'dwellings of one room with four or fewer walls'!

For people whose average weekly income is about $20–$30, with malnourished children, these extra charges were severe. Many of their houses were made just of old kerosene tins and strips of corrugated iron. They were going to be charged for electricity too if they were lucky enough to have it—$1 a week for each power point!

Aboriginal officials in Alice Springs claimed that the Federal Government would take from the desperately poor some $600,000 a year this way. The price for meals for the unemployed was to go up by 300%. Aboriginal community leaders sent a protest telegram to the government, which read in part:

Aboriginal people are being robbed. We have got nothing and you are taking it away from us. We are waiting for deadness. That's all. Mr Viner it is a terrible thing you say. We are still waiting under trees and bits of tin. Many people do not have enough money for food. We are trying hard for employment but

Women and children at Noonkanbah, Kimberleys (Jan Roberts, 1979).

many people do not have jobs . . . we are still waiting for the money you promised. You are not troubled for Aboriginal people. White people dump rubbish near our camps. Nobody takes it away. What services do we get? When it rains we get wet and sick. Some children die and old people die, our humpies [shacks] *can't keep water out.* [8]

Leaked Cabinet documents have since shown that the Federal Government decided that the annual cost of 'services' to Aboriginal communities in the Northern Territory will in future be recovered from Aborigines, the poorest sector of the Australian population. It was also revealed that this was to be the basis for future policy towards all Aborigines in Australia.

The Minister for Aboriginal Affairs, Mr Viner, said in his submission to Cabinet:

At present, some $350,000 p.a. is being collected in the Northern Territory. It is estimated that an additional $600,000 p.a. will accrue from the present proposal. Figures for the States will not be available until the scheme has been running for a while in the Northern Territory.

As well as providing an opportunity for Aboriginals to move towards self-sufficiency, *the introduction of economic rentals and service charges should be favourably received by the Australian community* [i.e. whites]. *The rents and charges proposed in this submission approach those applicable to the Australian community as a whole . . .*

It is proposed to offset against future grants to communities, organisations, etc . . . the revenue they should collect under this scheme so as to encourage efficient collection . . . a family head living in a traditional humpy will pay $2 a week.

The Federal Government has shown a marked reluctance to return Aboriginal land, despite the land rights legislation for the Northern Territory. By the beginning of 1978 no land had, in fact, been returned to Aboriginal ownership. And, despite the fact that this land is supposed to be the freehold possession of Aboriginal communities, the Northern Territory legislature has insisted on supplementary legislation to control what the Aborigines can do on their land.

The Federal Government is also refusing to return land required by Aboriginal communities on the basis of need rather than traditional claim. Many communities are in exile from their land because their land is held by whites. Many have left their land because of their desperate need for food and medicine. They are now living in camps around the townships. They, too, need land and their right to this was recognised by the Woodward Commission into Aboriginal land claims. But the Government is refusing to follow its recommendations on this except in a nominal way. The land rights legislation does not return land now in white hands, only 'unallotted' Crown land. Again, land for these communities would be hindering 'assimilation', but, paying rates as white people do, helps 'assimilation'.

The Federal Government in 1980-1 is cutting in half the funds previously allocated to help Aboriginal communities re-establish themselves on tribal land. The Federal Government has continued some previously introduced schemes for funding the purchase of land for Aboriginal communities when they have a traditional claim on this land and the owners are willing to sell. However, even this scheme has been strenuously opposed by Bjelke-Petersen, the Premier of Queensland. He has stated that his government's policy was 'the eventual elimination of Aborignal and Islander reserves.'[9] He has vetoed the purchase of cattle stations for return to the Aboriginal tribal owners.

The Queensland Minister for Aboriginal Affairs was reported as 'disturbed' because Aborigines are returning from the cities to their reserves. He said 'reserves were meant to prepare Aborigines to go out into the world, not the reverse.'[10]

The Queensland Premier accused Fraser, the Federal Prime Minister, of instituting apartheid by returning to some Northern Territory Aborigines their tribal lands and forsaking assimilation.

The assimilation policy is diametrically opposed to the Aboriginal demand for land on which they can preserve their culture. As will be seen later, the mining companies, especially Rio Tinto Zinc's companies, heavily relied on the 'assimilation' argument to justify their taking of Aboriginal lands. (See Chapter 17.)

Footnotes

1. Sharman Stone, *Aborigines in White Australia: documentary history* (Heineman Educational), 1974, p. 193.
2. Stone, p. 236.
3. Stone, p. 231-2.
4. *Herald*, 12 November 1977.
5. Perth *Daily News*, 21 October 1977.
6. *ibid*.
7. *Age*, 24 November 1977.
8. Central Land Council.
9. Cairns *Post*, 2 August 1976.
10. *Courier Mail*, 4 August 1977.

15 THE PEOPLE OF THE LAND – LAND RIGHTS AND APARTHEID

There have been comparisons made between the apartheid system in South Africa, and the oppression of blacks in Australia. There are obvious similarities; the privileged position of the white settlers, the dispossession of the people of their land.

However the more apt comparison is with the North American Indians, the Bushmen of South Africa, the Amazon Indians and the other aboriginal people who have lost most of their lands to colonists. These are people who have been the victims of similar genocidal assaults. They groan under the same assimilationist attacks on their culture and, above all, share in the same vital basic attachment to their land.

American Indian leaders have spoken about their land in words that could equally have been spoken by Australian Aborigines. Cecilo Blacktooth explains why her people refused to leave (c. 1900):

When God made those mountains he gave us this place. We have always been here. We do not care for any other place . . . If we cannot live here then we want to go into the mountains and die.[1]

A Northern Blackfoot chief, when asked for his land, said:

Our land is more valuable than your money. It will last forever. It will not perish by the flames of fire. As long as the sun shines and the waters flow, this land will be here to give life to men and animals; therefore we cannot sell this land. It was put here for us by the Great Spirit, and we cannot sell it because it does not belong to us . . . As a present to you, we will give you anything we have that you can take with you; but the land never.[2]

American Indians sometimes call themselves the 'natural people' because they see themselves as part of nature, one with nature, living in harmony with nature. Perhaps this is a better descriptive title for these people than the imposed anthropological term 'Aborigine' or the misnomer 'Indian'–a name born of Columbus' geographical error.

Many of the first colonists to come to Australia also referred to the resident Australians as 'Indians'. But in Australia the inhabitants soon became known either as 'Blacks' or as 'Aborigines'.

They themselves had their own name for their own people. In Queensland today Aboriginal people commonly use the name 'Murri', in the South-east–'Korrie' and in West Australia and South Australia–'Noongar'.

These people are generally despised by the much more recently arrived inhabitants of their lands, treated as 'savages' to be shot, kept in reserves as if in zoos, or exiled from their land to be 'assimilated'.

Only to the white man was nature a 'wilderness' and only to him was the land 'infested' with 'wild' animals and 'savage' people. To us it was tame. Earth was bountiful and we were surrounded with the blessings of the Great Mystery. Not until the hairy man from the east came and with brutal frenzy heaped injustices upon us and the families we love, was it 'wild' for us. When the very animals of the forest began fleeing from his approach, then it was that for us the 'Wild West' began. Chief Luther Standing Bear of the Ogala band of Sioux.[3]

Although now outnumbered by white immigrants, these 'natural people' are all desperately holding on to whatever lands they have left and seeking to regain lost land. Such is the meaning of their land to them that without it their culture and spirit would be killed. They are thus fighting for racial survival.

Since people in the West generally know far more about South Africa than Australia, they naturally ask if the recognition of Aboriginal land rights in some parts of Australia would mean in fact the creation of Bantustans.

The South African Government has continually tried to justify its policy of only allowing blacks political rights in set-aside regions called 'Bantustans'. It states its policy of 'separate development' allows both whites and blacks to keep their cultural heritage.

However, on analysis, apartheid is akin, not to the Aboriginal land rights movement, but to the Australian assimilation policy.

In South Africa, the Bantustan system gives the four million whites 87% of the land, leaving the fifteen million blacks with the remaining 13% in the form of fragmented 'home-lands' or 'Bantustans'. The blacks are wanted in the white areas, but only as migrant labour with no political rights. The blacks are not to marry whites or otherwise 'integrate'.

Vorster explained why this system was set up:

In the light of pressure being exerted on South Africa, the government would create Bantustans, a form of fragmentation we would not have liked if we were able to avoid it, thereby buying the white man his freedom and the right to retain domination.[4]

Botha, Minister of Bantu Administration, added,

As far as I am concerned, the ideal condition would be if we could succeed in due course in having all Bantu present in the white areas on a basis of migratory labour only.[5]

The South African Commission responsible for the details of the Bantustan policy reported:

The choice is clear. Either the challenge must be accepted, or the inevitable consequences of the integration of the Bantu and European population groups into a common society must be endured.[6]

Thus the Bantustan system of apartheid was set up to:
1. Guarantee the white minority most of the land.

2. Provide cheap labour for whites—while giving only migrant workers' rights to black employees.
3. Keep the white people and their lands white—preventing 'assimilation'.

Since 'assimilation' tends to subsume the minority into the majority, such a policy would be utterly distasteful to South African whites who, through it, would lose their identity. The Bantustan policy allows them to keep their racial identity as 'pure' as they desire, while allowing them to keep nearly all the resources of the country so they can maintain their obscenely high standard of living.

Australia is the other side of the coin. Just as 'assimilation' is denounced by the white South African Government, so nowadays apartheid is denounced by the white Australian Government.

The Prime Minister, Mr Fraser said in London on 9th June 1977: 'Racial policies and minority rule in Southern Africa were an offence to human decency and a scourge to the dignity of man.'[7]

In Australia this statement was attacked as hypocritical by Aborigines. The leader of the Aborigines on whose land Fraser's vast and rich grazing property is situated said:

Many of my people are below the poverty line. In Mr Fraser's electorate, Aboriginal people are dying by the time they are 35. [We have] just 600 acres to replace the thousands of square miles now owned by Australia's richest graziers.[8]

They are living in what one reporter described as 'a scene of squalor and despair similar to thousands I have witnessed in 17 years of reporting in Africa.'

With the development of the land rights movement, 'separate development' or 'apartheid' became abhorrent to the Premier of Queensland, a man notorious for his racist policies. He vetoed the return of tribal lands to Aboriginal groups. He said this

would create a 'Black State' across the whole of northern Australia, surely apartheid in the extreme and an introduction of the South

African Bantustan policy to Australia, a situation the Queensland Government would not tolerate. [9]

The former leader of the Northern Territory Assembly has echoed his words. [10]

Thus, the Australian authorities now reject apartheid, after using it in the early reserve system, as it would allow Aborigines to keep some land from the whites and maintain a separate identity.

In Australia, the high standard of living of the whites has always been based on the expropriation of Aboriginal land. All the policies evolved to 'deal with' Aborigines have had this as a major element—from 'elimination' to 'protection' to 'assimilation' and 'integration'.

Unlike the blacks of South Africa, Australian Aborigines are usually not particularly wanted by whites as a cheap labour force. First, because there are many more white workers than black. Secondly, and more importantly, because

Aboriginal housing in north-west Australia (Jan Roberts, 1979).

Aboriginal values conflict sharply with the Protestant work ethic.

Individual private property is not a basic social value in Aboriginal society. The Aborigines traditionally live a far more communal style of life, sharing the proceeds of their work with their kith and kin, and with others. They distribute goods according to need rather than rank.

They don't have a hierarchical system as does industry, nor do they like working under such a system. They give more importance to cultural and religious pursuits than to daily work.

Such attitudes and beliefs can be deeply disturbing or threatening to people imbued with the values of individualism, private property and hard work. The industrialist can find white workers to be money-motivated company-centred automatons, but he cannot easily find Aboriginal workers with similar motivations.

A major mining company (Comalco), seeking lower pay for Aborigines, stated: 'At this stage of their development, they are unintegrated to the industrial demands of our society.' [11] In the late nineteenth century, white Australians found it necessary to import South Sea islanders as slaves to work the sugar plantations because Aborigines were 'unsuitable'. In South Africa the parallel is with the Bushmen who cannot be used by the whites, as can the blacks.

The way Aborigines respect and use their land is very foreign to the capitalist. He sees it as just 'wasteful'. Aborigines who refuse to exploit their land are wasting resources needed to maintain his Western, high-consumption ways of living, and, in his eyes, people who waste things have no right to them. In 1977, when Bjelke-Petersen, the Queensland Premier, vetoed the acquisition by an Aboriginal community of a cattle station located on their tribal land, he gave as the major reason that they would not 'run it on profitable lines'— i.e. they would 'waste' it. [12]

The Australian assimilation policy was therefore evolved:

1. To secure all of Australian lands and minerals in white hands.

2. To make Aborigines live as whites, and thus possibly make them into workers.
3. To eventually remove all signs of a distinctive Aboriginal race and leave Australia white.

Like apartheid, it is aimed at maximising the white standard of living, at maximising the profits to be made from blacks and their land.

However, Aborigines do not want to keep their land in order to turn it into a black reflection of European society, with blacks seeing other people and every tree and rock in terms of maximum possible profits. Rather, they want their lands to be communally owned protected by Elders, a place where they can live as they want to live.

It seems that decisions have been made in many countries to destroy these peoples at least as land-holding races. This is a natural outcome of seeing these people as racially inferior, as useless and unprofitable, and as a hindrance to the maintenance of a high standard of life for the dominant race.

The Brazilian Catholic Bishops in 1973 spoke out in defence of all the Natural Peoples when they said of the Amazonian Indian:

What would Brazil be if it truly relied upon the Indians, rather than attempting to annihilate them as at present?

It is quite possible that many capitalist and imperialist minded Brazilians and authorities fear this question . . .

. . . they support the extinction of these people who, by virtue of their positive values, constitute a living denial of the capitalist system as well as of the 'values' of a so-called 'Christian civilisation'.

Without assuming the idyllic vision of a Rousseau, we feel it urgently necessary to recognise and make public certain values which are more human . . . than our 'civilised' values and which constitute a true alternative for our society:

1. The native peoples in general have a system of using the land for the community and not for the individual . . .

2. The economy is based on needs of the people, not on profit.

3. The only purpose of the social organisation is to guarantee survival and the rights of all, not just of the privileged few.

4. The educational process is characterised by the exercise of freedom.

5. The organisation of power is not despotic but shared.

6. They live in harmony with nature.

The time has come to announce, in hope, that he who would have to die is the one who must live.

The values of the Brazilian Indians are those, too, of the Australian Aborigine. White Australians can only gain by the survival of Aboriginal Australians and their culture. But for this to happen, land must be returned and Aborigines listened to with respect. This is as yet very far from happening.

For Aborigines, the idea of selling land is far more strange and unthinkable than selling air would be for Europeans.

Footnotes

1. T.C. McLuhan (ed.), *Touch the Earth* (Sphere, London, 1972).
2. McLuhan.
3. McLuhan.
4. Barbara Rogers, *Divide and Rule* (IDAF, 1976), pp. 8-11.
5. *ibid.*
6. *ibid.*
7. *Age*, 10 June 1977.
8. *Australian*, 15 June 1977.
9. *Sunday Mail*, 6 March 1977.
10. *Northern Territory News*, 7 March 1977.
11. Jan Roberts, *The Mapoon Books* (International Development Action, 1975), Comalco Arbitration Submission, 26 June 1963.
12. *Age*, 26 January 1977.

16 THE MINERS COME

We have seen how the Aboriginal struggle to retain their land led eventually, after over 100 years of massacres, to the white authorities conceding that a few large temporary reserves should be set up for Aborigines in north and central Australia. We now come to the dispossession of the Aborigines of these and other remaining lands.

By the early 1950s the centre and north of Australia had been brought firmly under the control of the cattle stations, missions, police and government administrators, or so they wished to think. In fact, because few whites lived outside a few small townships, the majority of the population was still strongly Aboriginal, and these people still retained much of their own law and culture and lived on their ancestral lands. There were indeed some few tribes who still lived independently of the white settlements such as the people south of Cape Keer-Weer on Aurukun Aboriginal Reserve.

The Aboriginal people in these regions were still recovering from the murderous epidemics of influenza, tuberculosis and other diseases. The frontier wars had taken their dreadful toll too and had not been long over for some of the tribes. At Kulumburu in the northern Kimberleys the last reported massacre was about 1944 when Aborigines reported twenty killed by the police. At about the same time at Kalumburu missionaries reported that the Aborigines would shortly die out since epidemics were so shattering the tribes. Not until 1974 did births equal deaths at this Catholic mission.

Miners had previously entered the North, notably in the Palmer gold rush in the late 1880s which had required large bodies of armed men to protect the miners from the people whose land they were invading. But in 1950 there was little sign of the rush that would soon be underway, master-minded by transnational corporations based in distant lands with the assistance of Australian investors and State and Federal Governments.

A world-wide rush

In the 1950s came a rapid expansion of Western and Japanese industry, fuelling and supporting the beginning of the consumer boom in the West, boosted by the Cold War, the Korean and Vietnamese wars. This boosted Western and Japanese consumption of minerals well beyond the capacity of domestic and existing colonial mines. Mining companies went out on a world-wide hunt for cheap, easily available mineral deposits.

Many of these companies were controlled by Anglo-Saxons, and so it was natural that they should first look to the countries controlled by their colonialists—to Australia, Canada and South Africa as well as unexploited parts of the United States. The United States also looked to the former European colonies of South America over which it had taken hegemony and Europe looked to Africa. But the dominant search was in the Anglo-Saxon settled colonies.

All these countries had in common the conquest of the previous inhabitants, the forcing of them off their most valuable lands and the leaving to them of the most barren regions as 'reserves'. These were the Dene, Inuit (Eskimo), Mohawks, Sioux and other nations of the North American continent, the Bushmen, Zulu and other nations of southern Africa, and the Kalkadoons, the Gunditj-Mara, the Pitjantjatjara and other nations of Australia. To these people were left only the most barren regions with the climates found most inhospitable by the white grazier or farmer . . . if they were left any lands at all.

The mining companies in their search noticed these lands. They were cheap, free of alternative profitable uses, unsettled by Europeans—and were available from white governments eager to encourage 'development'—that is, the extraction of resources and the making of taxable profits.

Nearly all the existing inhabitants of these lands had in common a self-sufficient, non-

The Gunditjmara people on part of their traditional land wanted for an Alcoa smelter, Portland, Victoria, 1980.

---

mechanical, non-materialistic way of life. Their lives and cultures were adapted to living from their own lands, and naturally, they had not destroyed these lands for the sake of international profit. To corporate and colonial eyes, this was waste.

Most importantly, all these people had no 'legal' way of protecting their lands since political power had been taken from them by the conquering settlers.

So, in the USA the coal and uranium companies moved onto ancestral lands and reservations belonging to the Indian tribes of the mid-West—opening vast coal strip mines and uranium mines in which many Indian miners were to die of radiation-induced cancers.

In Canada, uranium companies moved into Dene country, and hydro-electric engineers into Indian lands in the Rockies and Inuit land in the north.

In Australia the destruction of the northern reserves commenced with the awarding to Comalco of a vast 2,700 square mile mining lease over the largest Aboriginal reserve in eastern Australia in 1957.

The companies responsible

In all these moves, and in other recent moves onto the lands of kindred tribal peoples in the Amazon and Panama and elsewhere, the same corporate names come up again and again. For wealth is being increasingly concentrated in fewer and fewer hands.

Alcan has both started a bauxite mine on Indian land in the Amazon and taken 536 square miles of Mapoon Aboriginal Reserve. Amax is strip-mining Indian lands in the USA and planning oil wells on Noonkanbah and bauxite mines in the north Kimberleys.

One of the companies which has particularly taken tribal lands is Rio Tinto Zinc. This company, headquartered in London, is currently taking control over a copper mining venture that will displace thousands of Panamanian Indians; it planned a uranium mine in Labrador, Canada, despite strenuous objections from the nearby Inuit community; a bauxite mine for Amazonian Indian land; a uranium mine for occupied Namibia against United Nations sanctions; and in Australia it controls 61% of CRA, which is the leading company in the current invasion of Aboriginal lands in the Kimberleys.

In later chapters we will be particularly examining the role played by this company in Australia.

How large scale mines affect Aborigines

First let it be said that Aboriginal people are not necessarily opposed to all mining. They have worked mines themselves in a small way. Stone axes with particularly fine qualities were made from stone quarried near Melbourne's international airport. These axes were traded across Australia right up to the Kimberleys. Painting clays were also excavated forming large pits in some places. A few gold implements have been located in Western Victoria.

When Pilbara Aborigines walked off the cattle stations in the 1940s many of them joined together to organise small scale mining enterprises. Up until about 1960 the 'Nomads', as they called themselves, were the largest prospecting force in the Pilbara.

This mining was carried out in ways that respected Aboriginal concern for their land and all sacred places. It did not entail large-scale destruction.

What is now particularly threatening is the giant scale of the proposed developments in the North, the bringing of many whites onto

Aboriginal lands, and the insensitivity and lack of respect displayed by most miners towards Aboriginal culture and Aboriginal laws concerning ancestral lands.

It is these factors that have induced Aboriginal people to try every way they can to keep the mining companies off their lands. This to them could well be the final invasion. On the result of this struggle depends the survival of much of Aboriginal culture.

The next chapters will detail the impact of the mining and describe what Aboriginal people are doing to lessen this impact.

Sacred sites, land rights and mining rights

First it should be said that the right to protect sacred sites cannot be separated from land rights. Today many companies are prepared to protect Aboriginal sacred sites by putting a fence around them unless the sacred site is on top of a diamond pipe as it is at Argyle, CRA's major diamond prospect.

But these sacred places, centres of Aboriginal religion and spiritual beliefs, are desecrated and wrecked if they are separated from the land around them of which they are an intrinsic part. Indeed for Aborigines all their land is spiritually important.

It seems that Federal Government policy is today aimed at limiting Aboriginal land rights to 'sacred site rights' outside of the Northern Territory. By concentrating on these sites, government and companies alike hope to distract attention from the basic issue of justice—recognition of the land as rightfully Aboriginal.

Another fiction that is being spread around is that mineral rights always belong to the community through the state and that therefore Aboriginal land rights must exclude mineral rights.

Thus we have CRA stating in a 1980 leaflet on Aboriginal land rights:

Minerals in Australia are owned by the 'Crown', that is by the whole Australian people through their respective state governments . . . Giving mineral rights, in effect, to Aboriginals and not to other landholders is divisive. CRA believes that Aboriginal title to land should be held on the same basis as that of any other Australian.

This is simply not true. Thousands of people privately own mineral rights particularly in New South Wales where over 40% (soon to be 60%) of the coal is mined from private mineral rights. These pay the owners over 80 cents a ton royalty. These are rights originally issued before 1850. In Victoria, leases on land first 'alienated'—given to private ownership—before 1892 include rights to all minerals except gold, silver, uranium and thorium. In addition, all landowners own the rights to any limestone, slate or other building materials on their property and these cannot be mined without their permission. Also, the land owner is entitled to 10% of all royalties extracted by the State for any mining on his land. The same is true in the USA and in many other countries. Australia is nearly unique in not generally allowing the original inhabitants any rights to the minerals, rights that were theirs before Captain Cook put up his flag. Aboriginal mineral rights however are not the private ownership rights of the profit-centred West. They are rights that belong to an Aboriginal community and that entail strict laws of social responsibility.

A summary of recent moves by mining companies on to Australian Aborigines' lands

1953
Rum Jungle uranium mine established south of Darwin.

1957
Consolidated Zinc (later to merge with another British company, Rio Tinto, to form Rio Tinto Zinc—RTZ) took mining rights for bauxite over 2,270 square miles at the heart of the largest continuous Aboriginal reserve lands in north-east Australia, on the reserves of Weipa, Mapoon and Aurukun.

The rights secured, Kaiser Aluminium of the USA joined forces with Consolidated Zinc to form Comalco to mine the world's largest known deposit of bauxite (aluminium) . . . over 3,000 million tons. Management responsibilities for the mine were later held by RTZ's Australian subsidiary—Conzinc Riotinto of Australia (CRA).

The companies adamantly refused to pay compensation or royalties to the Aborigines. They took all timber, cattle and water rights too.

1965

Alcan, of Canada and the USA, took out an adjacent bauxite lease over 536 square miles of the Mapoon Reserve. The Queensland Minister for Mines stated in 1957 that the Alcan lease had on it 'just as much bauxite as the Comalco lease', an 'enormous deposit'. Again the Aborigines were not consulted and no compensation went to them.

1965–75

The iron ore mines of the Pilbara, in the northwest of Australia, were opened. These mines make Australia the world's leading exporter of iron ore and currently account for about 90% of Australian production.

This region is a major centre of Aboriginal culture and of Aboriginal resistance, yet few areas were set aside as Aboriginal reserves.

The major producers are Hamersley Holdings, controlled by RTZ of London, Mt Newman Mining Co. (owned by Australian, American and Japanese interests—BHP, CSR, Amax and Mitsui); Goldsworthy (American and British—Cyprus Mines, Goldfields, Utah); Robe River (Australian and Japanese—Cliffs Western, Englehard, Burns Philip and Mitsui).

An anthropologist reported that Newman Mines initially employed a few Aborigines but 'by 1970 the mining company was making quiet efforts to get rid of both Aboriginal employees and the small group of local Aborig-

Mount Newman — mining a sacred hill.

ines who were living on the edge of the town. Local police were telling Aborigines that they were not welcome in Newman.'[1]

In 1979 a company official told the author that they had six or seven Aborigines working there, but none from the local community for 'they wouldn't last five minutes.' He said that they had 'no training programme for Aborigines, that would be racist.'

Newman holds 777 square miles on their mining lease of land belonging to Aborigines at Jigalong. Aboriginal Elders there told the author that Mount Newman itself, now being turned from a hill 270 metres high into a pit 300 metres deep, was a very important sacred site.

1966

Broken Hill Limited, the major Australian mining company, took a 100 year lease over part of the Groote Eylandt Reserve to mine the largest Australian manganese deposit (500 million tons). This is on a major Aboriginal island reserve in the Northern Territory. This deposit is big enough to supply the whole world's needs at current levels of consumption for twenty years. Outside of Russia, it is the world's third largest manganese mine.

On Groote Eylandt, missionaries managed to retain for the Aboriginal community legal rights to minerals by taking out in the name of the Aborigines an exploration licence. As a result of this, BHP agreed to pay the Aborigines a one and a quarter per cent royalty on top of two and a half per cent due by Federal legislation for the Northern Territory to the Aboriginal Benefits Trust Fund, one tenth of which comes back to the community. However, the Aboriginal community were not consulted about the mining of their land, nor about the settlement of yet more Europeans on their tribal land.

1967

The Cape Flattery silica sand mine was established. It is owned by Mitsubishi and is on the land of the Hopevale Aborigines in North Queensland. There is no consultation with Aboriginal people over the areas to be mined on the reserve and the Aborigines have no access to the mining areas.

In 1979, the declared quantity shipped of the 99.7% pure silica sand was 490,000 tonnes, worth at the company's estimate $8 a tonne—a total of about $4 million. A royalty rate is paid at 25 cents a tonne, and an undisclosed percentage of the profits goes to the Department of Aboriginal Advancement. (In 1973 out of sales of $1.2 million the Department received $4,110.)

No royalties come to the Hopevale Aborigines. (This low declared price could well be a case of 'transfer pricing'. This means that since it sells the ore to a company based abroad but owned by the same people as itself, it charges an artificially low price in order to minimise taxes payable in Australia.)

1968

Alusuisse of Switzerland obtained a bauxite mining lease over the eastern part of the major Arnhemland Reserve, the largest Aboriginal reserve in northern Australia. Again the Aborigines did not consent and were not consulted. Aborigines could not fish within 30 miles of the Alusuisse refinery because of the pollution. Alusuisse have at least 250 million tons of bauxite reserves on this lease.

The Yirrkala people failed in a major legal battle to stop this mine going ahead. (See page 164)

1975

Shell (through its wholly-owned subsidiary Billiton), working in association with Pechiney (PUK) of France and Tipperary of the USA, took a bauxite mining lease over 736 square miles of the Aurukun Reserve to the south of the Comalco lease, on which there were over 1,000 million tons of bauxite. This lease was secured despite strong opposition from the Aboriginal community. Again no compensation is to be paid to the community. (A payment will go to the Director of Aboriginal Advancement in Brisbane for government expenses.) In October 1977 the British Privy Council heard a case alleging that the government had violated its trusteeship in negotiating this lease. They ruled for the government against the Aborigines.[2]

1976

RTZ (CRA) secured diamond mining exploration rights over the largest Aboriginal reserve in Western Australia, at Forrest River, Again the Aborigines did not want their lands destroyed and were dismayed at the rush of mining companies to secure entry on to their lands. (This is now called Oombulgurri.)[3]

1977

Mount Isa Mines (49% owned by Asarco of the USA) prevented the return of ancestral land to local Aborigines at McArthur River in the Northern Territory, near the coastal Queensland border. Here MIM has claimed the largest (200 million tons) lead/zinc/silver deposit in the world. There is much Aboriginal opposition to mining, especially since it will entail re-routing a river with important sacred places along it.

1978

The Federal Australian Government gave the go-ahead for three planned uranium mines on Aboriginal land on the western side of Arnhemland Reserve despite strong Aboriginal protests against the destruction of their lands. Mr Mahon, a British Government Minister on a visit to Australia strongly criticised groups in Australia opposed to the mining of uranium, saying that the British working man needed the uranium.

1979

CRA discovered diamonds on a very sacred Aboriginal site near Lake Argyle in the Kimberleys. Strong Aboriginal protests.

1980

Oenpelli Aborigines were stopped by Federal intervention from taking legal action to close the road to the Nabarlek uranium mine. Alcoa bulldozed sacred Aboriginal sites at Portland, Victoria, and had the police arrest and remove the Aboriginal protesters.

A police convoy escorted a drilling rig over 2000 km to Noonkanbah to drill on an Aboriginal sacred area against the strongest Aboriginal protests, taken even to the United Nations in Geneva.

Less environmentally damaging operations for oil and gas were agreed to in Central Australia after lengthy negotiations.

1981

CRA took control over major bauxite deposits in the northern Kimberleys on the Mitchell Plateau. No agreement was made with the Aboriginal Elders responsible for this land. Alumax and Alcoa are minor partners in this venture. CRA also drilled on a major Aboriginal sacred site on Christmas Creek station in the Kimberleys.

Uranium companies began an intensive lobbying campaign for government permission to greatly extend their operations in Aboriginal Arnhemland. Legislation was passed altering the boundaries of Kalkadu National Park to facilitate mining at Dennison's Koongarra prospect, despite this being condemned on environmental grounds by the Fox Inquiry.

Oilmin, Transoil and Petromin, all companies associated with the Queensland Premier, Bjelke-Petersen, found uranium on Lockhard River Aboriginal Reserve on Cape York.

There are many other developments in central Australia. At Tennant Creek there is a flourishing coppermine. From 1975 there has been greatly increased prospective activity, with the main emphasis on uranium. British, American, French and Italian companies are among those most involved. Firms such as Le Nickel, AGIP Nucleare, Afmeco—all associated with the European nuclear programme— have taken out exploration leases south-east of Alice Springs. According to a September 1976 report, none of these companies had then consulted Aboriginal groups.[4]

AGIP is an affiliate of the Italian state-owned corporation ENI, Le Nickel is controlled by the French Rothschilds and Afmeco is associated with the French Atomic Energy Commission. Aboriginal counter-claims to the land wanted by AGIP have been lodged in Alice Springs courts.

Uranium deposits have also been taken by Oilmin and Transoil, in association with Western Mining, owned by Phelps Dodge Corporation, USA. These deposits are at Beverley and Mount Painter some 500 km north of Adelaide. Nearby there are at least eight other significant uranium deposits including Honeymoon and the giant Roxby Downs copper-uranium deposit. (The latter owned by Western Mining Corporation and BP.) These are all to the north of the Flinders Ranges.

In Western Australia, the large Yeelirrie uranium deposit is likely to be mined. Aboriginal Elders, objecting to the desecration of sacred sites, have been totally ignored. (See page 134)

In Victoria there is much Aboriginal concern about the Benambra copper, zinc and gold

deposit owned by Western Mining Corporation and BP.

Many of these mines and mining prospects are described in the following chapters, for they all deeply concern the Aboriginal people whose land is being exploited with scant respect for their rights.

Footnotes
1. Robert Tonkinson, *The Jigalong Mob; Aboriginal Victors of the Desert Crusade* (Cummings California, 1974) p. 150.
2. *Courier Mail*, 27 October 1977 and *Mining Journal*, January 1978.
3. *Australia Report*, (CIMRA, London 1977), No. 2, p. 13.
4. Justin Maloney, *Resumé of Aboriginal Position in the Northern Territory* (unpublished ms.), September 1976, p. 23.

17 THE WEIPA BAUXITE MINE. PART ONE: DISPOSSESSION

Aluminium is one of the most common minerals in the earth's crust—it is a basic constituent of most soils and clays. However, it occurs in its richest concentration of 35% to 60% purity in a reddish clay, bauxite, formed under tropical or Mediterranean conditions.

It is a misfortune of many Aboriginal communities living along the northern coast of Australia, who still use their tribal lands, that these lands are underlaid by rich bauxite clays.

The Aborigines were in no position to use or benefit from these deposits even if they had been so inclined. The reserves were only theirs on sufferance until white people wanted them, the ownership of the reserve was vested in the Crown, not in them.

Thus, when Consolidated Zinc 'discovered' in 1955 vast bauxite deposits underlying by far the largest area of continuous Aboriginal reserve land in north-east Australia, at Weipa, Mapoon and Aurukun, they were able to move rapidly to take possession of these lands with the Queensland State Government's blessing.[1]

The method of mining the bauxite is by stripping two feet of top soil, then ripping out the twenty or so feet of clay from the land over literally hundreds of square miles. It is extremely difficult to restore land so treated, and it is of course impossible for Aborigines to maintain their traditional livelihoods of hunting and gathering on such land. It is nearly impossible, in fact, for them to retain their culture. (Thus no Aboriginal community has so far consented to the strip-mining of their land.)

The company received the full co-operation of the missionaries, the only whites previously stationed on these reserves. The church authorities reported:

The co-operation and facilities of our Weipa Mission and staff accelerated the company's plans so quickly that all the information necessary for a decision regarding mining potential was collected and correlated by Christmas 1956. The parent company, convinced of bauxite deposits in quality and expanse greater than anything known among the Western nations, is seeking a mining tenure of 100 years for a large area of the Mapoon and Weipa Aboriginal Reserves . . . The rising flood of mining industry flowing through the Cape York Peninsula will flow into the billabong of all our Missions and convert it into a rich broad tributary of industrial Australia.[2]

The church over-optimistically asked the company for new houses for the three most affected Aboriginal communities, a Native Welfare Fund from the royalties, pastoral grazing rights for the missions and guarantees for existing Aboriginal rights. What they actually received is described in the next section.

In 1956 Comalco was formed by Consolidated Zinc (Conzinc) to manage the proposed mine. Then, in 1957, Comalco obtained from the Queensland Government its enormous mining lease of which 1,000 square miles were to be selected by 1977. This could be strip-

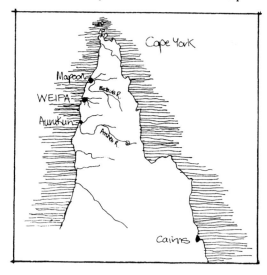

WEIPA: PART ONE 97

mined for bauxite, forming by far the largest bauxite mine in the world. The company found its one thousand square miles (2,590 square km) contained over 3,000 million tons of bauxite worth over $60 billion. (The 1979 world production of bauxite was only 74 million tons.)

In 1961 Comalco became a partnership between Conzinc and Kaiser of the USA. In 1962 Conzinc merged with Rio Tinto to form the English company Rio Tinto Zinc (RTZ), with its Australian subsidiary Conzinc Riotinto of Australia (CRA). This change brought no significant change to Comalco's management.

The attitude of the State Government towards Aborigines and their tribal lands was spelt out during the parliamentary debate on the *Comalco Bill* in 1957. The Minister for Aboriginal Affairs stated:

Sites for reserves were picked so that the development of known resources was not impeded. Since the Aborigines will be given jobs by the mining company, the amount of land available to them as the reserve [being loaned to them by the company out of its mining lease] *– 75 acres–is more than sufficient for their requirements. It could be argued that having suffered no loss there would be no claim for compensation.*[3]

The Minister for Mines said:

Does the Hon. Member not realise that many of these simple people have been living up there so long that they will be unemployable. Yet

---

The *Comalco Act 1957* gave the company:
— 2,270 square miles (5,780 square km) of Aboriginal reserve land on the west coast of Cape York and 1,982.5 square miles (5,135 square km) on the east coast, again land owned by Aborigines although not protected as a reserve.
—of the west coast lease, 1,000 square miles (2,590 square km) can be retained by the company for a minimum of 105 years; i.e. up to the year 2063. The other 1,270 square miles (3,190 square km) had to be relinquished by Comalco over a period of twenty years. The land the company keeps can be selected so that it contains up to two-thirds of the commercial grade bauxite found on the original holding.
—a royalty rate of 5 cents a ton, about the lowest rate in the world (Jamaica at that time had a royalty rate of 12 cents). This rate stood until 1965 when the rate on bauxite exported in the raw state was increased to 10 cents a ton.
—a rent of two pounds a square mile (2.5 square km) for the first six years, four pounds a square mile for the next ten years and fifteen pounds a year thereafter. This compares well with the normal mining rental at the time of three hun-

dred and twenty pounds per square mile.
—all cattle grazing, timber, water and farming rights over the mining lease with a right to perpetual leases over the areas used for the requirements of the mining town.
—government aid to cover the cost of building the harbour and some mining town facilities amounting to some 8.5 million pounds. (The company, in its turn, eventually gave one hundred and fifty thousand pounds for the rebuilding of the Aborigines' homes at Weipa which, the company stated, discharged in full the company's obligations toward the owners of the land.)
—exemption from the provisions of the Clean Water Act. Comalco pay for their 1,370 square mile cattle station under $5 a week ($250 p.a.) to the Queensland Government.

Comalco made a record $75 million after-tax profit in 1980. Financed by Weipa bauxite, the company has subsidiaries expanding into: New Zealand, Papua-Niugini, Hong Kong, Italy, United Kingdom, Luxemburg, Japan, and in the tax-haven West Indian island of Netherlands Antilles. It has partly owned associated companies also in the Philippines, Malaysia and Indonesia.

Australian bauxite mines

Name	Former Aboriginal Reserves & size of Mining Lease	Company	Production (million tonnes per year)	Reserves (million tonnes)
QUEENSLAND				
Weipa and Andoom Vrilya Point, Pera Head	2,590 sq.kms of Mapoon Weipa and Aurukun Reserves (1000 sq.miles)	Comalco Kaiser (USA) CRA (UK)	10 m.t. expanding to 14 m.t.	3205 m.t. + Aurukun unproven + Vrilya unpublished
Wenlock River	536 sq. miles of Mapoon Reserve	Alcan (Canadian)	not yet	unpublished
Aurukun	1,800 sq.kms of Aurukun Reserve plus 105 sq.kms adjacent	Billiton (Dutch) Pechinery (French)	1983 ?	1,016 m.t. est. (400 m.t. proved)
NORTHERN TERRITORY				
Gove Other claims on Arnhemland Reserve being made, esp. on Islands to N.E.	Arnhemland Reserve, —Yirrkala	Swiss Aluminium (Alusuisse) 70% Nabalco (30%) (= CSR 51.1% Peko Wallsend 12.64% AMP 12.1%)	2.2 m.t. increasing to 5 m.t.	221 m.t. proved
WESTERN AUSTRALIA **North**				
Mitchell Plateau	Aboriginal Reserve	CRA 52.5% Alcoa of Australia 17.5% Billiton 10% etc	1980s	235 m.t. proved
Cape Bougainville	Aboriginal Reserve	CRA 67.5% Alcoa of Australia 22.5% Billiton 10%	1980s	995 m.t.
Near Perth				
Chittering	Not Aboriginal Reserve	CRA	?	200 m.t.
Del Park and Huntley	12,627 sq.kms Not Aboriginal Reserve	Alcoa of Australia (= 51% Alcoa (USA) 33.1% WMC 12% Nth Broken Hill)	9 m.t.	500 m.t.
Wagerup	„ „ „	Alcoa of Aust (USA)	5 m.t.	750 m.t.
Jarrahdale	„ „ „	Alcoa of Aust (USA)	starting 1981 target 8 m.t.	2,200 m.t.
Worsley	„ „ „	Alwest = Reynolds (USA) 40% Billiton (Dutch) 30% BHP 20% Japanese 10%	starting 1981 target 6.4 m.t.	over 200 m.t. on just 2% of lease

One out of every eight tons of bauxite used by Western countries comes today from Weipa. Taken together, bauxite and alumina rank fourth among commodities in international trade, shipments totalling 32.5 million tonnes and 10 million tonnes respectively in 1974. Just over 50% of this is consumed in North America, about 30% in Europe and 15% in Japan ('Mining Journal', 16/4/76). In 1978 total Australian production was 27.6 m.t.

In practical terms bauxite is in unlimited amounts in Australia with the major deposits around Weipa and Aurukun alone being able to supply the entire world's current demands for over 50 years—or to be mined at present levels for over 400 years. There are also vast deposits in Latin America and Africa.

The total Australian reserves would therefore amount to at least 9,000 million tons. The above figures are taken from the Queensland Government Mining Journal of March 1974, and from the 'Register of Australian Mining', 1981.

This states that the Weipa, Mapoon and Aurukun reserve figures are for bauxite averaging 52% alumina content, and Gove deposit averages 50%, the North Kimberleys deposit has 235 m.t. on the Mitchell Plateau at 47% and 995 m.t. on Cape Bougainville at 36%, and the Darling Range deposits vary between 30-35% pure. The Weipa bauxite is mined up to 58% pure.

Comalco are going to build homes for them too. How fortunate they are! Is this not an opportunity for them to live as human beings should? He will be able to buy things . . . In time the unemployable will be employable.

He added that Australians would be getting *a solid town which would mean defence of the country in a place where it would be badly wanted. We are going to rehabilitate the aborigines.*[4]

On 5 September 1957, at a conference between Government and church officials the Director of Aboriginal Affairs, Dr Noble, advised:

The mining company was legally responsible only for compensation to the mission for the transference of the mission village and native huts from the present site to another site to be chosen.

The company was adamant that it could not under any circumstances confer with the Government and the mission on the compensation claimed as set out in the church's earlier submission.

The company was anxious that the mission should trust it to do the right thing over the years.

As the mining of bauxite did not allow for a great margin of profit, it was mainly agreed that the company might find it difficult to attract white labour to the Weipa development . . . therefore for economic and practical reasons alone the company would be happy to employ native labour.

There is going to be no chance of legislation granting royalties to Aborigines.

The Queensland Government was most anxious to encourage any company to develop the Far North . . . The best way to defend the North was by development and settling of as large a population of white people as possible.

The defence of the North from attack from the Far East was in the best interests of the Aborigines.

Sir Maurice Mawby, a director of Consolidated Zinc, wrote on 21 August 1957 to advise the church mission:

We do not consider that native protection and welfare can be properly cared for by a negotiated settlement of a 'claim for compensation' and accordingly our attendance at the proposed conference will not be for the purpose of entering upon such negotiations.

In this same letter he made it clear that Comalco and the State Government would be collaborating in assimilating the Aborigines. He wrote:

There is no conflict between our plans for large scale development of the area and the well-established objectives of policy on native affairs in Queensland. We aim to provide a gradual and satisfactory means of assimilating suitable natives.

In the name of the company he listed the support they were prepared to give. They were prepared to pay the eviction expenses of the Weipa Aborigines and the costs of rehousing them, to 'accelerate' native education, to give 'employment opportunities for selected natives' and provide accommodation for these in the mining town. As for the Mapoon Mission, the site of this mission was not immediately wanted. They would assist with the eventual removal of the Mapoon Aborigines and allow this mission, until the land is needed by the company, to continue grazing on parts of the mining lease.

The Queensland Government has assured Parliament in the debate over the Comalco Act, that the Aborigines would not need any compensation for the loss of their land since Comalco would be giving all of them jobs.

However, once Comalco has secured the Aboriginal reserve land in exchange for these pitifully small promises made to the church and Government authorities, they immediately began moves to have most of the Aboriginal community removed, offering only a few permanent work.

Rev Stuckey, the church General Secretary wrote concerning this to Mr Hibberd, the Comalco Managing Director:

In brief, what I have maintained is that the Queensland Parliament accepted and passed the Commonwealth Aluminium Corporation (Comalco) Bill in 1957 on the basis that there would be ample employment for the native peoples, and that they therefore stood to gain by the coming of Comalco to the area, to such a substantial extent that it did away with the need for compensation, for royalties or anything but the building of a village which would enable them to be housed in terms of some parity with the European population of the proposed Weipa township. In connection with this I would refer you to page 1,431 and following, of the parliamentary debates of the 35th Parliament, number 18, for the dates Thursday, 28th November and Friday, 29th November 1957.

The then Minister for Health and Home Affairs who was the Minister for Aboriginal Welfare at the time stated: 'In regard to the question of the alienation of almost the whole of the Weipa Mission Reserve, it follows then that the land required by them, is to all intents and purposes only the same amount as would be required by the same number of families in any suburb,'—thereby implying that all of them would be employed under Comalco or in the town, and therefore that no other means of livelihood would be necessary.

On page 1,432, in reply to a question from Mr O'Dare, 'Does the Agreement contain a provision that the natives will still be employed after it is signed? Could the company dump them after the signing of the agreement?'—Dr Noble replied: 'We have the assurance of the company that it will employ all the natives. . .'

I do not think it is possible to hide the conclusion that this was one of the factors that enabled, despite the protests of the mission and the church authorities, the Bill to be passed without any written-in provisions for the welfare of the people. I could quote you at length of the number of occasions when, in discussion with the Government at the time, the mission authorities were assured 'You can trust the company' . . . But it has become obvious that the employment potential is now reduced to the employment of a very few.[5]

In 1976 Comalco stated that they employed only 40 of the 650 Aborigines on Weipa Aboriginal Reserve, and about 40 from elsewhere, including some Torres Strait Islanders. Many of the Aborigines now living in Weipa Aboriginal Reserve are not from Weipa but recent arrivals, so they employ probably well under 40 of the original inhabitants. (In March 1978, a Weipa missionary reported that Comalco employed only eight Aborigines from the reserve.)

However, employment of all the Aborigines is not the answer. It would not remove the necessity to return stolen land and pay compensation for damage. Few Aborigines would want to be employed by a company that has taken their land and heritage from them.

Few want to be employed ripping up their sacred land. By taking the Aborigines' land, Comalco had destroyed any chance the people had of developing an alternative economical base more in keeping with their culture.

In 1964 the church mission authorities had decided to resurrect the issue of royalties to compensate the Aborigines since they were not getting jobs. So they sent a copy of the above-quoted letter of the 13th March to the Director of Aboriginal Affairs together with a letter saying they really intended to 'persist with this matter.'

The mission authorities were also annoyed because they had believed that Comalco had promised them one hundred and fifty thousand pounds to build new houses for the Aborigines. But the company had recently said that, since the Aborigines were not going to be moved from Weipa, the grant would now only be one hundred thousand pounds.

This later matter seemed to be more important in the eyes of the mission authority than the winning of any just royalties for the Aborigines. On the 23rd April 1964, the General Secretary of the Mission Board was invited to the company headquarters. What went on at this meeting is unknown. What is known is that immediately after this visit, the following letter was dictated over the telephone to the Mission Board by a high executive of Comalco, John Tonkin. (A man still responsible for

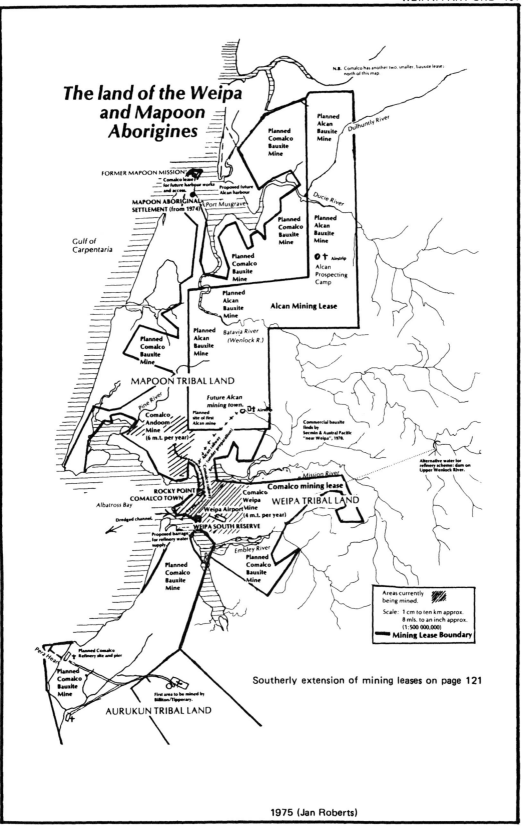

The land of the Weipa and Mapoon Aborigines

N.B. Comalco has another two, smaller, bauxite leases north of this map.

Planned Alcan Bauxite Mine

Dulhuntly River

Planned Comalco Bauxite Mine

FORMER MAPOON MISSION
Comalco lease for future harbour works and access.

Proposed future Alcan harbour

Ducie River

MAPOON ABORIGINAL SETTLEMENT (from 1974)

Port Musgrave

Planned Comalco Bauxite Mine

Planned Alcan Bauxite Mine

Gulf of Carpentaria

Planned Comalco Bauxite Mine

Airstrip
Alcan Prospecting Camp

Planned Alcan Bauxite Mine

Alcan Mining Lease

Planned Comalco Bauxite Mine

Planned Alcan Bauxite Mine

Batavia River (Wenlock R.)

MAPOON TRIBAL LAND

Pine River

Future Alcan mining town.

Planned site of first Alcan mine

Airstrip

Commercial bauxite finds by Secmin & Austral Pacific "near Weipa", 1970.

Comalco Andoom Mine (6 m.t. per year)

Alternative water for refinery scheme: dam on Upper Wenlock River.

Mission River

ROCKY POINT COMALCO TOWN

Comalco Weipa Mine (4 m.t. per year)

Comalco mining lease

WEIPA TRIBAL LAND

Albatross Bay

Dredged channel.

Weipa Airport

WEIPA SOUTH RESERVE

Proposed barrage for refinery water supply.

Embley River

Planned Comalco Bauxite Mine

Planned Comalco Bauxite Mine

Areas currently being mined.

Scale: 1 cm to ten km approx.
8 mls. to an inch approx.
(1:500 000,000)
Mining Lease Boundary

Planned Comalco Refinery site and pier

Pera Head

Planned Comalco Bauxite Mine

First area to be mined by Billiton/Tipperary.

AURUKUN TRIBAL LAND

Southerly extension of mining leases on page 121

1975 (Jan Roberts)

company/Aboriginal relations at Weipa in 1977.)

This letter was signed by Rev. Stuckey for the Mission Board and returned unchanged on 30th April 1964. They had their grant back—and royalties were forgotten. The church accepted that the housing grant was a full discharge of the company's obligation to the Weipa people.

Mr D. Hibberd,   30th April, 1964
Managing Director,
Comalco Industries,
95 Collins Street, Melbourne, Vic.

Dear Mr Hibberd,

I refer to my letter of 13th March. The Board of Missions has requested that your Company:

(a) make a cash grant of 150,000 pounds in three annual payments of 50,000 pounds starting this year, and

(b) express its intent to allow the Weipa Mission to use for grazing the areas of special bauxite mining leases as are not being used and which are agreed upon.

I now confirm that the Board of Missions regards such a contribution as a full discharge of the Company's obligation to the Weipa people.

I further confirm that:

(1) Our recent submissions to the Queensland Government on the payment by Mining Companies of bauxite royalties to Aborigines are not intended to be a reopening of the above negotiations.

(2) The Board of Missions or its contractors will undertake the work.

(3) The grant will be devoted to the benefit of the Weipa Aboriginals in respect to the creation of both accommodation and means of livelihood.

It is understood that the granting of our request to your Company must still be subject to the agreement of the Queensland Government.

Yours sincerely,
James M. Stuckey,
General Secretary

This letter was then submitted by CRA to its other partner in Comalco for approval, to Kaiser Aluminium of the USA. On 11th June 1964, Comalco replied to the Mission Board thus:

Commonwealth Aluminium Corporation Limited (incorporated in Queensland)
95 Collins St., Melbourne.

11th June 1964

The General Secretary,
The Australian Presbyterian Board of Missions,
GPO Box 100, Sydney, NSW

Dear Sir,

Weipa Mission

I am pleased to report that approval was given at a Board meeting on the 8th June to the granting of the request of the Board of Missions as set out in your letter of the 30th April, 1964.

We have today written to the Hon. J.C.A. Pizzey, Minister for Education, requesting the Government's sanction for our agreement with you, and we attach a copy of our letter.

Subject to Government approval we now formally confirm that this company, in consideration of your Board's firm intentions as set out in your letter—

(a) will make a cash grant to the Australian Presbyterian Board of Missions of one hundred and fifty thousand pounds payable in three annual instalments of fifty thousand pounds on each the first day of July 1964, 1965 and 1966, in full discharge of the company's obligation to the Weipa people; and

(b) expresses its intent to allow the Weipa Mission to use for grazing and/or associated purposes such areas of special bauxite mining leases as are not being used, and which are agreed upon.

Yours faithfully,
S. Christie,
Managing Director

Encl.

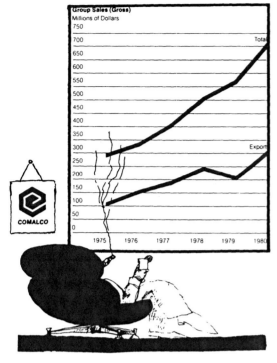

Thus the church board, acting in the name of the Aborigines without any proper authorisation from them, agreed that, in return for a grant to the mission for Aboriginal housing, Comalco had no other obligations towards the Aborigines. In fact this sum of money turned out to be quite insufficient for the most elementary housing (see 'What did the Weipa Aborigines get?' below). The housing in any case, at the insistence of the government, was rented to the Aborigines and not given, and the people's previous homes which they owned were bulldozed by the company as 'unsuitable'. So, in fact, the people were left poorer than before.

For this, Comalco received Aboriginal land containing some $60 billion worth of bauxite. By 1980 they had earned from this over A$340 million net profit (after tax) and built Weipa into the biggest bauxite exporting port in the world.

What happened to the Aborigines?

All the land granted by the Queensland Government to Comalco was the tribal ancestral land of a number of Aboriginal clans or tribes living in and around the Weipa, Aurukun and Mapoon Presbyterian Mission Stations which are situated 50 miles apart on the west coast of Cape York.

One Mapoon Aboriginal Elder, Mrs Rachel Peter, described what the land meant to her thus:

I was born here, my father was born here, my mother, my great grand-parents. This is our tribal land . . . I hope we will never leave this place. Here in our home, our Mapoon, there's plenty of everything for us to eat. Everything that you can think of: pigs, wallabies, kangaroo, oysters, and crabs, arrowroot, wild yams and much else that we were taught to eat by our grandparents and our fathers and mothers . . . In our home, in Mapoon, we just get these things freely. We don't have to buy them. Here we are free to go anywhere and everywhere we wish. There is no block to us around . . . Nobody is here to say: 'you can't go over there, that is not your place to go.' That's why I like to be at home here—because it's so free. We don't have to spend money on anything.[6]

The devastation caused by the Comalco mine and by Government and church policy can best be described if the Weipa and Mapoon Aboriginal communities are taken separately. The Aurukun Aborigines will be considered in Chapter 20.

What happened to the Weipa Aborigines?

Despite many efforts by Comalco and the church to persuade them to go, the Weipa Aborigines refused to leave their ancestral lands. Initially, in 1957, Comalco suggested that the Aborigines be moved away to protect them from the white workers they would be bringing in.

A document headed, 'Comalco Industries. Internal Memorandum' recorded a leading Comalco executive, John Tonkin, (still with the company in 1978) as repeating this on the 11th July 1962:

J.T. emphasised that the company had intended and would wish primarily to use its funds to place the Weipa people in a situation where the white workers could not corrupt them.

Comalco suggested that the people be exiled to the tribal area of the Aurukun people, to Aurukun Mission. This was opposed by both the Weipa and Aurukun Aborigines.

Comalco in 1960, on their own initiative, constructed a model of a settlement at Hey Point, on the other side of the mouth of the river from their proposed mining headquarters. The company tried to sell this proposal to the mission authorities. (At no time did they first approach the Aborigines.) The Aborigines refused again to leave their tribal land.

A letter from the Brisbane church mission authorities to the Weipa missionaries recorded this:

The latest information is that they have built a large scale model of the new village at Hey Point in the hope that they can sell this suggestion to the mission authorities and later to the native people. There is no doubt that it is time they commenced doing something to honour their promise [of housing for Aborigines][7](our emphasis)

Failing in this, the company suggested that Hey Point might be too close. A letter from Jim Winn, the Weipa missionary, to the Rev Stuckey, General Secretary of the Australian Board of Missions, 20th December 1961, stated that a senior member of the Comalco executive said, 'The quicker that we get rid of these coons from here the better it will be.' (It was later denied by the company that such a word as 'coon' would have been used.) He was also reported as saying the company will not fulfil its promise of giving work to the Aborigines. The church, too, then suggested a plan to remove the Aborigines.

However, the Aborigines adamantly refused to move. The Director of Aboriginal Affairs for the Queensland Government, Pat Killoran, decided to permit the Aborigines to remain since the close proximity of the blacks to the white workers would promote assimilation.

The church eventually decided against moving the Aborigines. It could not in any case persuade them to go and could not make them go without the support of the Queensland Government. Comalco, however, still tried to move the Aborigines, and blamed the opposition

of the Weipa Aborigines to any move on to the influence of the Weipa missionary. They had little idea of how Aborigines felt about their land.

A letter from the General Secretary of the Missions to Hibberd, Chairman of Comalco, on 14th February 1964, recorded,

Their [the Aborigines'] *reply was a flat refusal to even consider the amalgamation with Aurukun or . . . the move to Hey Point, and all negotiations since make it obvious that to seek to remove the Aborigines from Jessica Point* (Weipa) *would cause so much upset in the people's mind that I for one would not be willing to contemplate it.*

(The same churchman, a year earlier, had helped to forcibly evict the Mapoon Aborigines.)

What did the Weipa Aborigines get?

Today the Weipa Aborigines live in a tiny area set aside for them by Comalco some nine miles from the mining town. It is easy to see this area when flying into Weipa. It is a small green oasis by the Embley River, surrounded by vast red plains of exposed and barren bauxite, the pits of Comalco, pits that cover the reserve with a pall of dust in the dry season and isolate it with a sea of mud in the wet.

Their hunting lands are destroyed. The Aborigines remain as a pool of casual unskilled labour utilised by Comalco, or by the Queensland Government, on minimal wages. They live on just 308 acres surrounded by devastation,

Mrs Joyce Hall (left) and Mrs Jean Jimmy campaigning for their land, 1980 (Jan Roberts).

these people that own, in their law, hundreds of square kilometres.

Their traditional means of support has gone. They have to go considerable distances to find untouched bush. Even after they have passed the mined-out area, they have to go a long way through grid-roaded bush laid out for mining before they can hunt. Comalco has forbidden the use of guns, and dynamite used for prospecting has driven the animals away. Aboriginal mothers say they now fear to let their children go into the bush because of the dynamiting.

The devastation this means becomes plain if we think of the present ruin being extended by over 14 acres a week for over 100 years—if the last few years' mining levels remained steady at ten million tons a year. (They are currently being increased.) On Comalco's lease alone a minimum of 303 square miles of excellent grade bauxite exists. And adjacent to their 1,000 square mile lease there is a 536 square mile Alcan lease and an 832 square mile Shell lease. It is equivalent to excavating in England, an area from Dover through London to Bristol, and back via Southampton and Brighton.

The Comalco grant was totally inadequate to provide the Aborigines with the housing they were promised. Their old homes, which they owned, were bulldozed off the beach by the company as an eye-sore. Instead they were rented new houses built with the company grant. The missionaries wanted to give the houses to the people, arguing that they had been given to the people as compensation. The Director of Aboriginal Affairs, Killoran, refused to contemplate this.

He wrote:

Freehold title . . . would render null and void any rights of control by the Board of Missions or this Department . . . it is difficult to accept that these persons . . . should be given what is virtually a gift of several thousands of pounds which could be alienated at will. [8]

The Aborigines thus finished in a poorer and more vulnerable position than when they owned their own homes. When any member of the community travels south to protest at conditions at Weipa, they say they are often threatened by government officials with the loss of their homes and expulsion from their reserve and tribal lands.

The Comalco grant was only sufficient to provide them with shed-like homes without stoves, hand basins, sinks, plumbing or private toilets. Even so, the church authorities wrote, 2 March 1966,

Regarding stoves for pensioners: All pensioner amenities funds and child endowment funds have been used in the construction of the new village as the Comalco grant was inadequate.

Only in 1975, with the government paying half the cost, has sewerage been provided. Other better new houses have been totally government funded. Many Aborigines are still in the Comalco houses.

Comalco has been quoting Dr Coombes, as saying that the Weipa Aboriginal housing is the best he has seen. If so, this does not say much for Aboriginal housing elsewhere! They certainly do not compare with the vastly more expensive homes built by the company for white miners, that had, from the first, all facilities. Nor did they quote Dr Coombes' next remark—that still the Weipa people were amongst the saddest he has met.

Even if the company had built such homes for the Aborigines, this would still not amount to anything like just compensation for these impoverished people of Weipa.

Footnotes

1. J. Roberts (ed.), *The Mapoon Books*, Book Two pp. 54-5, Book Three, p. 6. These books are based on original documentation and are a basic source for this and the next two chapters.
2. Queensland Presbyterian Assembly Report, 1957.
3. Queensland *Hansard*, 1957 debate on Comalco Bill.
4. ibid, quoted in *Mapoon Book Two*, p. 65.
5. Letter dated 13 March 1964, quoted in *Mapoon Book Two*, p. 76.
6. *Mapoon Book One*, p. 23.
7. Mission authorities to Weipa Mission, 17 November 1960.
8. Killoran, Director Aboriginal Advancement Queensland, to Mission Board, 14 July 1965, quoted in *Mapoon Book Two*, p. 82.

18 THE WEIPA BAUXITE MINE.
PART TWO: LAND RIGHTS, APARTHEID
AND ASSIMILATION

RTZ and Kaiser share responsibility for what happened to these Aboriginal communities. Kaiser as the major profiteer, RTZ through CRA with nearly equal profits and managerial responsibility over their jointly owned mine-operating company at Weipa and Mapoon.

In the following section, extensive use will be made of Comalco's reply to the Mapoon Books. The Mapoon Books, published in June 1976, comprehensively documented company actions from internal company and mission memos, letters and minutes.[1] This was admitted by the company to be very damaging.[2] Comalco published in October of the same year a counter report entitled *Aborigines and Islanders at Weipa.* This they updated in 1978.

An uninhabited land?

As did Cook and the first colonists, the State Government and the company ignored the Aborigines and treated the land as an 'untamed wilderness' without inhabitants.

Thus the Queensland Government's Minister for Mines told the State Assembly: 'The area was desolate and without fences and the company will turn it into a township.'[3]

In 1975, Comalco's annual report described it as 'one of the most thinly inhabited parts of Australia, occupied only by a few large scattered cattle holdings.'

Comalco tried to shift the blame for any destruction of Aboriginal culture to the missionaries in their 1976 response:

Comalco's advent did not significantly change any traditional way of life among the Weipa Aboriginal people. They were already a missionised people.[4]

Yet it was not the church that took these people's land. It was Comalco. And the land

was not lying unused—a point which eventually, even Comalco had to admit.

In 1976 the company acknowledged that at the time of its arrival, the Weipa Aborigines

hunted and fished: they gathered yams, and the older ones kept alive traditional legends then as they do now ... within the mission environment they preserved family and clan relationships. These were and are identified with clan affinities for particular areas of land.[5]

Comalco's staff have documented the ... family structures and traditional land affinities.[6]

One wonders why Comalco have done this since they show no sign of recognising Aboriginal rights to the land they are mining. It could be, one supposes, for possible use if they are forced to acknowledge Aboriginal claims.

It would enable them to pinpoint the weakest link in the claims. They have distributed a monograph stating that, in such a situation, they should be fully compensated by the government for the loss of 'their' land.

A Jesuit who challenged the company at its Annual General Meeting in 1976, said after a meeting with leading Comalco executives: 'The company still basically refuses to acknowledge land rights, but this is essential to the identity of the people.'[7]

Comalco has always refused to use the word 'compensation' in its negotiations over Aboriginal claims or the claims made by missionaries on 'behalf' of the Aborigines. This is consistent with a belief that the Aborigines have no rights and, therefore, no compensation for loss of rights is payable. Instead they seek to show how good they are to Aborigines by detailing the 'gifts' they have made.

By the company's own calculations, by 1976 these gifts amounted to about $1 million.[8] To put this in perspective, the same report said they have spent a total of $130 million at Weipa on the mining town and mining facilities. Also the $1 million amounts to only $50,000 a year. This can be compared with the $10 million a year profits they are making from the Aborigines' land.

The 1976 statement by the company also tried to undermine any idea of paying the Aborigines more funds. It stated:

Critics of the company have never really out-lined what they thought it should be doing apart from paying more money to Aborigines themselves . . . [but] there is abundant evidence in recent years that cash alone has been socially destructive in many Aboriginal communities.

This is really extraordinary. They turn a completely deaf ear to the many calls to recognise the legitimate land rights of the Aborigines, but they can't pay any realistic compensation as money is harmful! Money indeed can corrupt—but the RTZ-Comalco directors obviously think themselves immune from infection! We are left to wonder just where they have found wealthy Aboriginal communities.

They obviously also make the presumption that Aborigines would not be able to spend the funds wisely. They do have yet another reason for not compensating the Aborigines. They say:

To make an exception for certain Aborigines who by chance live in proximity to a mining project is to create divisions within and between different Aboriginal communities and between society. Such divisions can only be to the detriment of Aborigines and their develop-ment. 9

Again the company in its solicitude for local Aborigines is ensuring that no divisions arise between them and other Aborigines, by ensuring that they all remain in poverty! It is also being careful that no divisions arise between the wealthy white community and the Aborig-ines through the Aborigines gaining wealth of their own!

The company is obviously on very weak ground indeed in its efforts to justify not returning any land or compensating the Aborig-ines whose land and livelihoods have been destroyed. It can only deal with land rights by totally turning a deaf ear to any mention of this subject.

Comalco and apartheid

Policies akin to apartheid showed themselves immediately Comalco began to develop the mine.

They first wanted to move the Aborigines' homes far from Weipa. They effectively kept out most of the Mapoon people. Weipa was to become practically an all-white area with some Aboriginal migrant workers in the mines. They used for this the pretext of 'protecting' the Aborigines. Similar reasons were used in the establishment of the South African Bantustans. Similar reasons were used in South Australia for the creation of reserves that were, according to Professor Rowley, prisons where the undesira-bles and unemployed could be kept out of sight and out of mind.

When they failed to evict the Aborigines and were faced with keeping their promise to give jobs, they developed Weipa along strong apart-heid-like lines.

Weipa now has the following features:

1. Separate white-black mining townships (except for nominal numbers of blacks in the white township).

"Australia's sons let us rejoice, for we are young and free
We've golden soil and wealth for toil, our home is girt by sea."

North Queensland Messagestick

2. Blacks used for lowest jobs and for a pool of casual labour.
3. Blacks treated as inferior.
4. Blacks under government laws to control movements to and from the reserves.
5. Comalco retains complete white control over black land and white townships.
6. Finally and most importantly—the ownership of most of the land is firmly in white hands.

The Aboriginal settlement was permitted to stay near the mining town at Weipa. Comalco developed the mining town as a nearly all white town with just a nominal number of selected Aborigines.

The policy for allowing a token Aboriginal presence was laid down at a church conference:

A carefully selected number of Weipa (Aboriginal) couples, perhaps three in number, should be given houses in the mining township. Both husband and wife must have qualities calculated to make their acceptance in a white community a guaranteed success.[10]

By 1975, there were just six Aboriginal families in a town of several thousand whites. In 1978 Comalco policy remained unchanged. They stated that Aborigines needed to be specially qualified before they would be allowed to live in the mining town.

They use the Weipa Aborigines as a pool of casual labour and for the lowest jobs. When in 1963 they tried to get half-pay for Aborigines they described the work thus:

The type of work involved has been varied in nature, unskilled in requirement and embraces such functions as sweeping, trench-digging, scrub clearing, wheel-barrow pushing, loading and unloading trucks etc. With the exception of three women and a few men doing specific jobs of limited occurrence, all these operations had to be performed under detailed and constant supervision.[11]

In 1978, company-provided figures suggest that nearly all the Aborigines employed from Weipa Reserve are on the company's lowest pay rates. The missionary there reported in March 1978 that Comalco employed thirty members of the community, but that only eight of these were Aborigines. The others were immigrant workers from the Torres Strait Islands.

At the 1980 Comalco Annual General Meeting, the Chairman, Sir Don Hibberd, said in a prepared statement:

We are employing as many as we possibly can fit into the workforce, having regard to the unhappy fact that, through no fault of their own, most of the openings are limited to unskilled or semi-skilled staff.

Comalco clearly see the Aborigines as culturally inferior and needing company help to 'advance' them. It states that it 'has for some years been pursuing a policy which has Aboriginal advancement as its central aim.'

The implicit racism of this becomes clear if we turn the situation on its head. Imagine the reactions of company executives if the Aborigines organised a reserve on which the executives were to be 'advanced' by Aboriginal-evolved programmes. The same argument of course applies to the title of Minister of Aboriginal Advancement in the Queensland Government.

Finally the company has secured the control of much of the Aborigines' land. Even their current small 300 acre reserve is on land loaned to them by the company. Thus whites secure blacks' lands here as in South Africa.

Church and state on the assimilation policy

The Government attacked the church mission authorities for supporting Comalco's efforts. They stated in Parliament:

Retaining Aboriginal able-bodied men on the mission 'to further their development and betterment'... could destroy the very thing that is the basis of the Aboriginal policy, that is, the assimilation of the Aboriginal into the community.[12]

At a meeting between church and Government authorities, the Government Director accused the churchmen of trying to 'keep the Aboriginal people protected and separate for ever', of trying 'to preclude people from assimilation with the white people at Weipa. The churchmen argued that 'the church does not envisage the Aboriginal people as needing protection for ever but some sections may be slow in developing, possibly up to several generations.'[13]

The churchmen added: 'There was a need to develop the whole community of Aboriginal people and assimilate them as a body into white ways.'

The church General Secretary further stressed:

the dangers inherent in always skimming off the cream of an Aboriginal community and moving them as family parties piecemeal into a white community [and] the need for Aborigines to be given the chance to develop their own land ... foreseeing the political dangers when Aboriginals and others learnt of how the Maoris and American Indians have been allowed to keep their land but the Aborigines have lost theirs.[14]

He said Aborigines would 'resist assimilation if it means the end of them as a distinct people.'

The churchmen saw the Aborigines as needing protection while they saw themselves providing this protection. But they also supported the Aboriginal people's right to survive as a distinct people, and it was here that their version of the assimilation policy parted company with the Government's.

The official Queensland Government assimilation policy is based on destroying the Aborigines as a race and on integrating the Aborigines into the white community strictly as individuals.

The Government wanted the Aborigines to remain at Weipa precisely because white workers were coming into reserve lands. In Government eyes this created an excellent opportunity to try and incorporate the blacks into the white work force.

It also profitably, for whites that is, divested the Aborigines of their land and thus removed from the Aborigines the economic resources needed for any community-based development. It was an ideal test of the assimilation policy. It was ideally calculated to break up Aboriginal culture.

Comalco and assimilation

It is indeed an apartheid policy modified for the worse by the insistence of the Queensland Government on the assimilation of the Aborigines. Comalco's original efforts to remove the Aborigines from their tribal land to distant reserves were frustrated not just by Aboriginal opposition, but by the Queensland Government.

Comalco promised to help with the Government's assimilation policy before it received the mining lease. Sir Maurice Mawby of Comalco said that their move on to these Aboriginal reserves

would prove to be the very opportunity that has for so long been necessary there to enable practical effect to be given to established policy on native affairs . . . there is no conflict between our plans . . . and the well established objective of policy on native affairs in Queensland. We aim to provide a gradual and satisfactory means of assimilating suitable natives.[15]

But once Comalco had secured the mining lease they attempted to limit strictly their assimilation efforts to a few Aborigines they judged 'suitable' and to remove the rest, but this was not permitted by the Government.

Comalco still could show no enthusiasm for employing the Aborigines. A trade school solemnly promised in 1957, had not materialised by 1980. Nor could the Aborigines find much enthusiasm for working for the company that had destroyed so much of their much loved and cared for land.

The minutes of company/church meetings recorded company complaints against Aborigines arguing their rights, calling the blacks 'bush-lawyers'. Not much love was lost on either side.

They found difficulties in incorporating the Aborigines as individuals given the Aboriginal communal culture. Comalco refused to allow Aborigines time off work for their vitally important religious celebrations and in 1976 they stated: 'Concepts such as regular attendance on the job and punctuality had largely to be learnt'.

They also said,

'The inducement to earn money and the ability to handle it were and continue to be problems. Earning just enough for immediate needs may well be an acceptable Aboriginal concept. The cultural background of the Aborigines has not prepared them to work for a living. The

immediate scope for employing Aborigines, even in unskilled jobs, was therefore severely limited.[16]

(Comalco ignored all their traditional occupations—hunting, gathering etc.)

They enquired of anthropologists visiting Weipa how they would recommend changing the Aboriginal culture so that the Aborigines would become more money and possession centred and thus more motivated to work for the company.

They tried to give the Aborigines a financial incentive to become good nine-to-five and overtime workers, by cutting the pay of those who did not attend regularly to far below that of white workers.

They applied to the Federal Government Arbitration Court for this system of incentives to be approved. In their submission they divided Aborigines into two types. These were 'integrated Aborigines' who were good workers, and 'non-integrated Aborigines'. They defined the latter as:

An indigenous Aboriginal inhabitant of Australia whose development from the primitive tribal life towards a Western type society has not progressed far enough for him to be able to comprehend and fulfil, among other things, the demands made of a worker by industry.[17]

They concluded:

At this stage of development the majority of Aborigines at Weipa are handicapped persons, being unintegrated to the industrial demands of our society.'

To them they would pay the legal minimum, about half of what they paid the whites.

Who would decide whether or not an Aborigine was 'integrated'? The company said this would be done 'by agreement between the employer and the protector of Aborigines [the government officer].'

John Tonkin of Comalco met with church mission officials to discuss this proposal, which the church also supported. He said that their criterion for 'integrated' would be 'a year's good attendance.' He did not mention that the company could not get some white workers to stay for more than three to four weeks! He stressed that the company could not allow the Aborigines to be absent for their corroborees, that is, for their major religious festivals.

However the company's efforts failed. First, they were embarrassed by the church suggestion of bringing two Aborigines down to the arbitration hearings. John Tonkin, Comalco's main negotiator on Aboriginal issues for the last fifteen years or more, was horrified at the idea:

One would first have to define whether the witnesses were 'integrated' or 'unintegrated' Aborigines. My mind boggles at the thought of having to do this in court.[18]

Secondly, they were opposed by unions concerned that their white workers might be undercut by cheap black labour. So Tonkin wrote back to Rev. Stuckey, the church General Secretary, saying:

Dear Jim, ... I consider it would be unwise for the company to run the risk of attracting a considerable degree of unfavourable publicity for something it could not hope to win. All we can do is to endeavour to get a reference to Section 48 included in the award and proceed from there as I discussed with you, Yours sincerely, John.[19]

So the company withdrew its submission. But, to this last letter, John Tonkin attached a copy of the 'Slow Worker's Permit' authorised under the Section 48 he had mentioned. This permit enables pay to an Aborigine to be cut on an individual case basis with the consent of the local State Aboriginal Department Office and the Aborigine—who might well know that only if he agreed would he get a job.

This company submission explained why the Aborigines were poor workers. It was because the Aborigines work communally, share their income and go back to their traditional occupations as soon as they have met their basic financial needs. It was this system, this communal culture, that the company was trying to break ... all in the name of 'assimilation'.

More recently they decided that if their assimilation policies were to be successful they would have to start with the children as did the early missionaries. They stated:

Particular attention clearly had to be given to children at pre-school age.[20]

They thus founded a pre-school for Aborigines at Weipa with the company retaining, according to a former teacher, considerable veto powers over the course content.

Comalco now declare that their formal policy on Aborigines is to teach them individualism, helping the Aborigines as 'independent individuals' to 'take their place in the Australian community on equal terms.'[21]

In this they see eye to eye with the Queensland Government.

However the Aborigines must start from the bottom, without their own land, without compensation. Comalco conclude that eventually the Aborigines will be qualified 'to choose the lifestyle they wish to adopt and the locality in which they wish to live'[22]—as long as they don't want to live on their own ancestral land, Comalco's mining lease! As long as the Aboriginal option to live their own lifestyle is effectively killed.

The actions of Comalco, under the managerial responsibility of Rio Tinto Zinc's Australian subsidiary, Conzinc Riotinto (CRA) and the 45% ownership of Kaiser Aluminium, amount to ethnocide.[23] They are deeply implicated, by their own admission, in enforcing the racist assimilation policies of the Queensland Government and of the Federal Government. There is no way that the responsible directors in England and America, can escape their responsibility by hiding behind immoral and unjust Australian legislation. They did just this in their 1976 statement on Weipa Aborigines when the Comalco Chairman concluded his introduction by saying,

It is important to remind ourselves, as we continue the task of implementing our policy towards Aborigines and Islanders at Weipa, that these aims were drawn up in close consul-

tation with the Commonwealth and Queensland Governments and continue to have their endorsements.

Yet, if tackled over their co-operation with the Queensland Government's racist policies, they will say, don't blame us, blame the Queensland Government.

But as Sir Maurice Mawby admitted back in 1957 at the start of this plunder of Aboriginal land, it is the company that enabled the assimilation policy to be applied to the Weipa Aborigines. It is also the company that took the Aboriginal lands.

The operations and employment policies of the company are in conflict with the way Aboriginal culture puts communal responsibility before private gain. It is the company that, by stopping the Aborigines using their land, destroys the foundation of their life, part of their very soul.

At the 1980 Comalco Annual General Meeting, the Chairman, Sir Don Hibberd, said they were suing the ABC for televising the film, *Strangers in their own land.* This film was made by Granada Television in the United Kingdom, and produced by Chris Curling, with the very active assistance of the North Queensland and Kimberley Land Councils and based on the manuscript of this book. It was shot on location in Weipa, in Noonkanbah and Oombulgurri. It has already been seen by many millions of people abroad.

When a company executive, Dean Bunney, was asked why they were taking action to prevent the circulation of this film, he said that it was because of statements made by Aborigines in the film on how Comalco had treated them – in particular, the remarks of Mrs Joyce Hall, a Weipa Aborigine and member of the North Queensland Land Council. This is expected to come to court in 1981. Obviously it is not a film that Comalco wants to be available in Australia.

Comalco may have learnt from the criticism of its Weipa operation. Its recent approach to the Pitjantjatjara Land Council showed much greater consideration of the Aborigines' rights

than they have shown at Weipa. But this is no doubt more because they legally have to secure Pitjantjatjara permission to mine their land. At Weipa, the Aborigines remain legally powerless over the land they own in their own law.

At the end of the film, *Strangers in their own land*, Joyce Hall of Weipa, said:

Why can't they give us back our land. If not, why can't they stop the mining or give compensation to the people so we could go back to our tribal lands. We can't ask them. I had a poor education and yet I know what is right and wrong. I don't think the white people know the Ten Commandments which they, the white people, have broken. 'Thou shalt not covet, thou shalt not steal'. (Recorded in 1979, televised 1980)

Senator Keefe, on 6 April 1978, stated in Canberra:

I shall read to the Senate a letter written by Joyce Hall, an active member of the North Queensland Land Council and an associate of a tribe which has been based in this area for generations: 'I am from Weipa and I feel that we

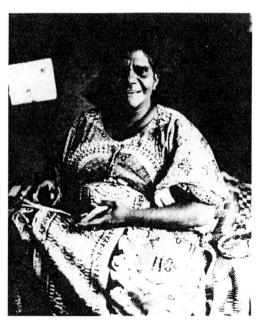

Joyce Hall on 1981 tour in London (Les Russell).

are too tired of the way the State Government has been treating us as babies or prisoners. The by-laws are not good, it's bad. No houses are built for the Aboriginals; more houses are built for the white people who are working in the mining area. Where is all the money the miners are making, taking minerals from our mother land which God has given us? We know that the Aboriginals were the first people who were in the North Gulf of Carpentaria. Since I was five or six years of age I did see our people get shot and whipped with stock whips. After, the bleeding wound was cured with coarse salt, chains round their legs and hands, they was led to the beach at Napranam (Jessica Point) on to the boat.

'This we feel should be changed, as it is still today our black police are doing to the prisoners in jail bash them up because they must take the orders from the State Government. The people of Weipa do not know how or why we are not getting a better deal. Comalco is not fair to the Aboriginals. I see the unfairness too. Still in them the greedy way of feeling they have and do not think of the people of the community. This is why the Aurukun people feel and has fears in them because they seen a lot of things happening to the people of Weipa. The drinking was brought by the white people and did make the people and children suffer by drunkenness and broken homes, deserted homes, mothers left with children and fathers left with children, children wandering away from the love of their father and mother which we know our homes before was the best Christian community. Now It's brought heartaches and pains, car accidents, fights and deaths.'

Footnotes

1. J. Roberts (ed.), *The Mapoon Books*. A basic reference for this chapter.
2. W. Smith, S.J., *Visit to a Bauxite Mine* (Comalco, 1975).
3. Queensland *Hansard*, debate on Comalco Bill 1957.
4. *Aborigines and Islanders at Weipa* (Comalco, October 1976), p. 6.
5. ibid, p. 7.
6. ibid, p. 12.
7. *Age*, 6 May 1976.
8. *Aborigines and Islanders at Weipa* (Comalco, 1976).
9. ibid.
10. *Queensland Presbyterian Church Assembly Report*, 1957, in *Mapoon Book Two*, p. 69.
11. *Comalco Arbitration Submission*, 26 June 1963.
12. Queensland *Hansard*, 4 December 1957, in *Mapoon Book Two*, p. 80.
13. Notes on a meeting of church and state officials in office of Director of Native Affairs, Brisbane, 30 June 1962, *Mapoon Book Two*, p. 80.
14. ibid, p. 80.
15. Maurice Mawby of Comalco, letter to Brisbane church authorities, in *Mapoon Book Two*, p. 66.
16. *Aborigines and Islanders at Weipa* (Comalco 1976).
17. *Comalco Arbitration Submission*, 26 June 1963.
18. John Tonkin of Comalco, letter to Rev. Jim Stuckey, General Secretary, Presbyterian Board of Missions, 9 September 1963. Quoted in full in *Mapoon Book Two*, p. 75.
19. John Tonkin to Rev. Stuckey, 30 September 1963.
20. *Aborigines and Islanders at Weipa* (Comalco 1976).
21. ibid.
22. ibid.
23. Genocide and ethnocide are very closely related concepts. Both mean the destruction of a race of people. However 'ethnocide' is applied more to one form of genocide – the destruction of a people by destroying the foundations of their lifestyle and culture without actually killing them.

19 ASSIMILATION AND THE BURNING OF MAPOON

At Mapoon Mission, 80 km north of Weipa, yet some 35 km within the northern boundary of the Comalco mining lease, the assimilationist aims of the Queensland Government and the purposes of the mining company coincided in supporting the eviction of the Aborigines.

The company said it would remove the Aborigines when the time came for the company to dig up the region around the mission. Once again the company refused to consider consulting or compensating the Aborigines. However they did say that, since they would take some years to extend their strip-mine to Mapoon, the Aborigines could stay until they arrived!

However they would make no objection if the Aborigines were conveniently evicted before the company wanted the mission site (which they had planned to turn into a port facility).

The church mission authorities had hoped that the company would pay some compensation to the Mapoon people for the loss of their lands, and that this would enable the church to reverse the earlier non-implemented decision they had made, on dubious economic grounds, to close the mission.

But the Government wanted the Mapoon Aborigines off their land so it could be profitably developed by the mining companies. The Government saw no reason to leave the Mapoon people on the land, for no white workers were coming to live there.

The mining company was going to house all its workers at Weipa. Therefore Mapoon was a bad place to leave Aborigines. There they would not assimilate and learn to live as whites. To leave them on their land would be to waste a possible financial asset to the European community of some more workers.

The Government certainly did not wish to grant more funds to Mapoon, for the development of an independent Aboriginal community was not considered desirable.

The church, too, did not care to retain its Mapoon mission. They provided for it in a miserly way according to two Government inspectors and a missionary. The attitudes of the missionaries then at Weipa are described towards the end of Chapter 7.[1]

The church authorities in a press statement issued in 1962, stated that the Government should not provide funds for Mapoon: 'It would not be in the future interests of the Mapoon people ... it would be bad stewardship of public money obtained from taxation.'[2]

Indeed the Mapoon Aborigines were showing signs of becoming a strong militant community and it was indeed going to be difficult to assimilate them. The Government determined that somehow or other, the community was to be broken up.

The Government eventually explained to the Aborigines just why they were to be evicted.

Visits by the Deputy Director of Native Affairs [Killoran] and the Deputy Director of Health and Medical Services were made to advise the people that, in their own interests and in the interests of their children, Mapoon was a hopeless proposition if their children were to succeed

The Ward Memorial Mission Church, Mapoon, prior to its destruction by the police.

as assimilated members of the community.[3]

This was not a particular ambition of the Mapoon people for their children so the Deputy Director's plea fell on deaf ears. Rather they wanted their children to inherit their lands and culture.

Threats were employed too. The Mapoon Aborigines remember that they were told by missionaries and Government 'that Comalco would come and turn our homes over with the bulldozers, and they would dig holes all over our hunting grounds.'[4]

The missionaries tried to re-exert their control over the mission. The story of the brutal crushing of a strike has been told above. A missionary said that trouble was caused 'by immorality and having too much their own way,' so they exiled all those regarded as ringleaders. They stood down a much respected tribal elder for 'taking too much into his own hands.' They refused permission for Aborigines to leave the mission to contact Aboriginal organisations to gain support for their struggle to remain on their land.[5]

Mapoon people refuse to leave their land

The Mapoon Aborigines, like the Weipa Aborigines, absolutely refused to leave their ancestral and sacred land.

The official report of the Assistant Director Killoran on a joint visit to Mapoon with church officials, 22 September 1960, stated: 'it was apparent that the people had discussed any suggestion of a transfer from Mapoon prior to our arrival and determined on a complete negation of any such proposal'. However they went on to tell the people that they had to leave their land.

A Mapoon Aborigine, Mr Jack Callope, stated in 1961: 'The mission said "if you don't make up your minds to leave, we'll close the store, close everything." The people said: "That's all right, we'll manage. We'll stay here." '[6] Jubilee Woodley added: 'The church stated there was no money to keep up the mission, but the people are independent. They don't have to close up because there was no money. You people want too much money.'[7]

The tactics used by the church were described in an undated church memo:

From every point of view they must go voluntarily. We know that they will be better off in the future if they move. Our problem is to get them to recognise this and act upon it with good will. When the mission closes there will be no ongoing basis for a livelihood or for living standards for the people. They may not believe this now, it is our duty in love to lead them to see it.

Considerations will be:

They will have no legal right to remain on the area.

The Department of Native Affairs would be legally entitled to get them to move but would be unlikely to do so.

If they elect not to accept the Government offer they may wander in the bush around Mapoon for a time but without school, store, communications, health service or steady earning opportunity.

Moreover it would involve neglect of their children and the Government could not stand by and permit this.[8]

Other tactics were to be used too. 'If a wife goes up to the hospital on Thursday Island to have her baby, she isn't allowed to return home.'[9] If a man was to go off the reserve to find work, he wasn't allowed back. If a girl was expelled as a punishment, she was not allowed back. Family reunions were only possible if the rest of the family left their tribal lands for good.

Eventually the missionaries packed up and went. In 1963 they closed down, as they had threatened, all the community facilities provided by the church, Government and Aborigines, the health service, school, communications. But over seventy Aborigines still remained, determined not to be driven off their tribal land. They began to live off the bush, and to fetch other needed supplies by boat from Weipa. They still had their cattle, too.

But this was the last straw for the Government. Independent Aboriginal communities could not be tolerated. On 15 November

1963 an armed party of police landed after dark and arrested the whole community, putting them under armed guard. In the morning the police set fire to and burnt down the homes of senior Elders, the church, the school, the stores and shops. They then removed leading Elders and took them to a reserve one hundred miles away. Those who remained kept on for another six months, but eventually were forced off their land.

Some of the Aborigines pined for their land so much that they died, others became seriously ill. These things are all recorded in the words of the Mapoon people in the First Mapoon Book.

Thus the Mapoon lands were left empty for Comalco to mine. In 1965 Alcan took a 532 square mile lease over much of the remainder of the Mapoon land until the year 2070. It paid no compensation to, nor negotiated with the Mapoon people in exile. It had applied for this lease in 1962, the year before the people were evicted.

The Mapoon people return

In 1974 a group of Mapoon Aborigines decided that they were not going to accept their eviction from their tribal land, that they would return once again to assert their claim. Although by now two-thirds of the mining was on their land, the mining operation had not yet reached within thirty miles of the site of the old Mission. They would reclaim this land and claim damages and compensation for the land that had already been destroyed.

An elected chairman of their community, Jerry Hudson, declared:
Comalco is mining on our country today. Alcan, they have got another mining place. We have to crawl on our hands and knees to get a piece of land, maybe just enough to put a bed or a tub on. Why when we own this land in the first place through our great-grandparents . . . taking it right back before any European came here? . . . No compensation, nothing at all.[10]

Another elder, Mrs Jimmy, wrote:
We want our land back because the land is most

Jerry Hudson at Mapoon, 1975 (B. Russell).
Mrs Jimmy speaking for her land, Cairns 'Development Without Destruction' Conference, 1980 (Jan Roberts).

important to we Aborigines. It is sacred to us in our customs. We still carry our sacred customs. I think most white people do not understand us very much, but there comes a time when they must understand our Aboriginal ways which we think are sacred. We live by nature because God made our ancestors civilised in our own way—by nature . . . We live by nature.[11]

So they went back to establish a camp not far from the old mission on the mining lease. However it proved very difficult to continuously occupy the new camp. The Queensland Government continually harassed them, especially after the publication in 1976 of *The Mapoon Books*, documenting their fight for their land.

Comalco returned the site of the people's camp to the Queensland Government, enabling the Government to try to close the camp down.

The community had its bank account closed and vehicle taken away. Social benefits were denied and the Federal Government refused to honour the promise of the previous Whitlam Government to return tribal land to the Mapoon people.

However, in September 1977, they wrote a letter to CIMRA in which they said:

We are in the process of issuing a writ on the Queensland Government to have the case heard in the High Court, for we are demanding our land back unconditionally, to be self-supporting, and to be able to run our own affairs our way, and not to be under state control, to be free people.'

They are also taking legal action against Comalco.

In 1981, the Mapoon people still maintain their settlement on their own ancestral lands. They are still appealing for funds and support. They still need a school so they can bring their children back.

Comalco has now released from their mining lease the site of the old Mapoon mission and the area where the Mapoon people have their settlement. Comalco had previously said that they were considering using this area for a future port, when they got round to mining the northern side of their enormous lease.

Possibly, this was released because of the embarrassment for the company of the international highlighting of their role in taking Mapoon land. Certainly this release was used by RTZ in London when they recently (1979 AGM) denied that they had interests in Mapoon. What they did not say was that they are now taking 80% of their bauxite from the Andoom mine on the former Mapoon Aboriginal Reserve, and that they still hold vast areas of this reserve. Most of what they do not hold is held by Alcan.

The coastal strip released by Comalco has reverted to the status of Aboriginal reserve under the repressive Queensland Aborigines Act. The Mapoon settlement is thus 'officially' under the white manager of the Weipa South Reserve.

Evictions of other Cape York Aboriginal People

The story of the Mapoon people is by no means unique in northern Queensland.

Bamaga, and the nearby settlements of New Mapoon and Umagico, at the northern extremity of the Cape, were seen by the Queensland Government as an assimilation staging post and collection centre for the entire Aboriginal population north and east of Weipa.

Port Stewart Aborigines, whose traditional country is on Princess Charlotte Bay, were removed by the police and sent to Bamaga in 1958. The reason given was that station owners had complained that they were interfering with the cattle.[12]

The Lockhart River people were also to be shifted by the Government. They were to go to Umagico near Bamaga. But very strong community opposition prevented this taking place. Nevertheless, once the Government had taken over control from the Anglicans, they were compelled to shift 40 km to Iron Range—where presumably the presence of a mine would assist assimilation.

Footnotes

1. J. Roberts (ed.), *The Mapoon Books,* Book One, Book Two, pp. 85-112. A basic reference for this chapter.
2. Queensland Presbyterian Mission Board, press statement, 6 December 1962. *Mapoon Book Two,* p. 97.
3. Press statement, June 1962, in *Mapoon Book Two,* p. 100.
4. Mrs Rachel Peter, February 1975, in *Mapoon Book One,* p. 9.
5. Rev. G. Filmer, letter to Brisbane Mission Board, 24 September 1960, in *Mapoon Book Two,* p. 87.
6. *Mapoon Presbyterian Mission 1891-1961,* Federal Council of Australian Aborigines and Torres Strait Islanders (FCAATSI), in *Mapoon Book Two,* p. 90.
7. ibid, p. 91.
8. Mission Authority's memo (undated) in *Mapoon Book Two,* p. 89.
9. Rachel Peter, quoted in *Mapoon Book One,* p. 8.
10. *Mapoon Book One,* p.1.
11. ibid, p. 24.
12. B. Rigsby, *Aboriginal People, Land Rights and Wilderness on Cape York Peninsula,* Presidential Address, Royal Society of Queensland (Brisbane, 1980).

20 AURUKUN BETRAYED

Just fifty miles to the south of Weipa and the Comalco mine is the land of the Aurukun Aborigines. This is one of the strongest tribal communities left in Australia. They retain their languages and their culture. They still dance their sacred dances and hunt and gather on their ancestral lands.

The mining companies have several times looked over their lands but they have always been warned off by the Aborigines.[1]

When a small Texas oil company secured a 1,000 square mile prospecting lease, they were made to promise in writing that they would not proceed to mine without first negotiating with the Presbyterian missionaries, the Aboriginal inhabitants and tribal owners.

But the American company, Tipperary, sold part (20%) of their interest to the largest aluminium concern in Europe, Pechiney of France, to get bauxite know-how and markets. Another 40% was sold to Billiton, a wholly owned subsidiary of one of the richest companies in the world, the Anglo-Dutch company Shell. Shell promptly took over the management role. Tipperary had found 1,000 million tonnes of bauxite which could be strip-mined from some 736 square miles in the centre of the Aboriginal reserve.

In 1980 Tipperary agreed to sell most of its share to Billiton and Pechiney, retaining royalty rights and probably a minor equity interest.

The consortium is known as 'Aurukun Associates'. Under current Federal rules, before starting to mine they must offer Australian companies a 50% share or be refused an export licence.

The Presbyterian missionaries at Aurukun were not overly concerned for they had a written promise that the company would not mine without discussing it with them first. The Whitlam Government, elected in 1973, was against wholly foreign controlled consortia taking Australian resources, and had promised to protect tribal lands.

The Queensland Government had backed these promises.[2]

A promise to be broken

*Office of the Minister for
Conservation, Marine and
Aboriginal Affairs,
BRISBANE*

26th January, 1972

*Rev. J. R. Sweet,
Director,
Division of Mission Education
and Community Action
Box 1465, G.P.O.
BRISBANE, Q. 4001*

Dear Rev. Sweet,

I write further to your letter of 6th September and pursuant to subsequent discussions relative to the Tipperary Land Exploration Corporation and negotiations with regard to the Aurukun Reserve.

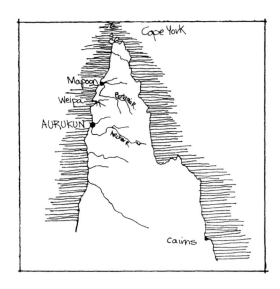

I can now advise that the Premier has indicated to the solicitors of the consortium who have assumed negotiations with regard to the development of the bauxite deposits embracing the Aurukun Reserve, that the Government requires the negotiation of a firm agreement by representatives of the companies with representatives of the Aurukun Aborigines and the Presbyterian Church of Queensland regarding the payment by the companies, in addition to royalties, of an amount to be credited to the Aborigines Welfare Fund. As Trustee of the Reserve, the Director of Aboriginal and Island Affairs will, of course, require to be present at such discussions.

No response is yet to hand from the Solicitors.

Yours faithfully
(signed) N.T.E. Hewitt
Minister for Conservation,
Marine and Aboriginal Affairs

Whitlam falls and Shell moves in

Within ten days of the overthrow of the Whitlam Government in November 1975, the consortium moved in. They ignored the vehement telegrams of protest from the Aborigines, one of which, sent from a meeting of all the Elders and community, said: 'We the people of Aurukun say no mining at Aurukun. We the people say no.'

The consortium secured without any agreement by the company or government with the Aborigines, a mining lease from the Queensland Government over the whole of the 736 square miles. They were given this lease to hold at least until the year 2038. The Aboriginal community are to be given no compensation for the devastation of their lands.

The consortium was given total rights to mine coral reefs for calcium, to mine coal or fluorine, to control the company town, and all the shops in it, to build and run a harbour, to control the areas over which the Aborigines can hunt or graze cattle, to build the township where they choose.

They are merely 'to cause as little inconvenience as possible to the Aborigines' and to employ those the company considers 'employable'. They have to restore after mining, but only 'to the satisfaction of the minister.' No standards are laid down; the Company alone shall ascertain whether or not any vegetation has any intrinsic value.

For all this, the company has merely to pay a rent of $3 per square km for the first five years, increasing to up to $20 after 15 years, and a royalty of up to $1 a ton, (less than one-eighth of the Jamaican royalties). After three years of mining they are annually to pay a sum to be determined by the company ('three per cent of net profits on which figure the company's word is to be final') into the revenues of the Government Department of Aboriginal Advancement, for departmental expenses.

For this they have been given mineral deposits worth a conservative $14 billion. The legislation granting the lease even exempted the company from all stamp duty 'in order to encourage and assist the company'.

They have been given the lands of one of the last surviving Australian tribal communities to bulldoze and strip-mine. It is at the virtual cost of this people's culture that the company will move in and tear their way of life to shreds.

What do the Aurukun people have to say?

Every responsible Elder has said that there would be no mining on their land, if only they could stop it happening.

Geraldine Kawangka, one of the responsible Elders, said to the Aurukun community and to church representatives: 'Give the answer back so that they know we are Aurukun people. Do not let the mining company in to destroy Aurukun for it is a beautiful place. Never never let the mining companies destroy and make a red wilderness through this country' (Dec. 1975).

Frank Yunkaporta said: 'I say I won't change my mind. There will be no mining around here and that's that.'

Violet Yunkaporta, another important Elder responsible for land now in the heart of the mining lease, stated: 'This is my place. I am responsible for up the Watson River. This is our tribal land and we don't want to see the miners come in.' She said firmly 'No!', when asked if she would sell the land.

Albert Chevathun, an Elder responsible for the land wanted for a mining port (land officially taken by Comalco back in 1957, but not yet used), said: 'Comalco never asked for this land. This is our forefather's land . . . we cannot give away our land. It is not well for the country to be destroyed and given away . . . we are trying to save this land for our children to help them stand firm and strong . . . No, we don't want the money, we don't want the jobs, we don't want the companies to take our land. All our children look very healthy here. They don't just live on store tucker—we have our own food out in the bush. If our country is destroyed, there will be no hunting places left just like Weipa. We don't want any mining. No, we don't want any refinery, I speak on behalf of all my people's land.'

Mabel Pamulkan, another Elder who has lost land to Comalco, added: 'From generation to generation it will be our land—God has given it to us. We thank those who stand behind us for our land—God has given it to us. We thank those who stand behind us for our land.'

Aborigines try to stop the mining of Aurukun

The Aurukun people did not only say they did not want the mining: they acted to try to stop it. Immediately the mining legislation was proposed, one of the Elders, Frank Yunkaporta went to contact Australian trade unionists to see if they could win support. Eventually the unions agreed there would be no mining without the agreement of the Aurukun people. They also attended a North Queensland Aboriginal Land Rights Conference to appeal for help.

When the mining legislation was passed the Aurukun Aborigines went up to the prospecting camp to expel the miners but found the staff had flown out. The Aborigines then put up signs at the mining camp and their settlement saying there should be no mining without their permission, and sent out a lengthy press statement denouncing the mining proposals.

Six of the Aurukun tribes have also moved back on to the parts of the Aurukun Reserve that are their own tribal lands. Some had only left these lands for the mission settlement in the late 1950s. They were brought in by the missionaries 'to protect them from the miners'. They now returned to protect their land from the miners and to protect their culture.

One of the Elders from one of the more distant tribal lands, Wallamby, when told that Shell, one of the mining companies, was partly Dutch, said that his people had defeated the Dutch before at Cape Keerweer and they would do so again. He then told the story, as if it had happened yesterday, of how the Dutch had landed and built a settlement on his people's

Frank Yunkaporta and some of his relatives at Aurukun, 1975 (Jan Roberts).

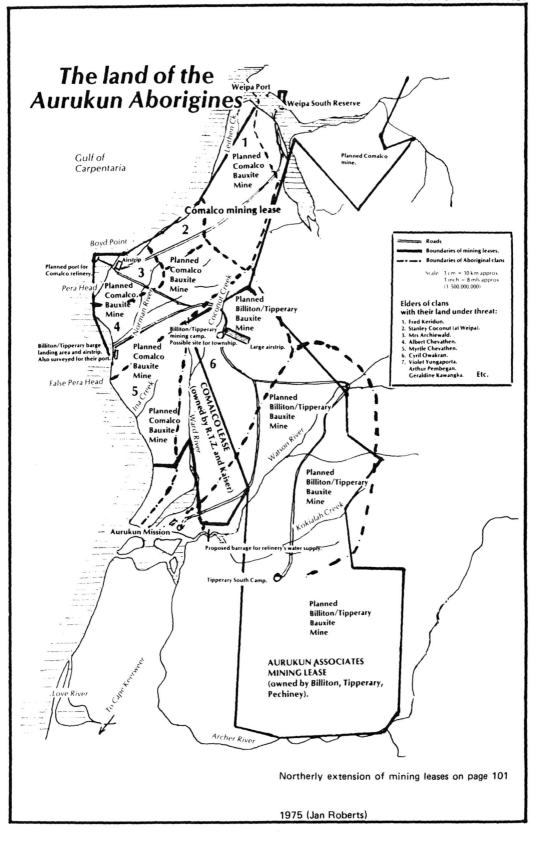

The land of the Aurukun Aborigines

Weipa Port

Weipa South Reserve

Gulf of Carpentaria

1
Planned Comalco Bauxite Mine

Leithen Ck.

Planned Comalco mine.

Comalco mining lease

2

Boyd Point

Airstrip

Planned port for Comalco refinery.

Pera Head

3
Planned Comalco Bauxite Mine

Planned Comalco Bauxite Mine

Coconut Creek

Planned Billiton/Tipperary Bauxite Mine

Norman River

4
Planned Comalco Bauxite Mine

Billiton/Tipperary mining camp. Possible site for township.

Large airstrip.

Billiton/Tipperary barge landing area and airstrip. Also surveyed for their port.

False Pera Head

5
Planned Comalco Bauxite Mine

Ina Creek

6
COMALCO LEASE (owned by R.T.Z. and Kaiser)

Ward River

Planned Billiton/Tipperary Bauxite Mine

Watson River

Planned Billiton/Tipperary Bauxite Mine

Kokialah Creek

Aurukun Mission

Proposed barrage for refinery's water supply.

Tipperary South Camp.

Planned Billiton/Tipperary Bauxite Mine

AURUKUN ASSOCIATES MINING LEASE (owned by Billiton, Tipperary, Pechiney).

Love River

To Cape Keerweer

Archer River

- - - - - Roads
━━━━━ Boundaries of mining leases.
— • — • — Boundaries of Aboriginal clans

Scale 1 cm = 10 km approx
1 inch = 8 mls approx
(1 500,000,000)

Elders of clans with their land under threat:

1. Fred Keridun.
2. Stanley Coconut (at Weipa).
3. Mrs Archiewald.
4. Albert Chevathen.
5. Myrtle Chevathen.
6. Cyril Owakran.
7. Violet Yungaporta.
   Arthur Pembegan.
   Geraldine Kawangka. Etc.

Northerly extension of mining leases on page 101

1975 (Jan Roberts)

land. At first his people had allowed this, but then the Dutch had made them work and work and took their women.[3]

Eventually they came to fight. Many Aborigines were killed, but finally the Aborigines, by setting their boats on fire, forced the Dutch to evacuate their settlement and leave. This happened in 1606. It was the first European settlement in Australia. The invading ship, the *Duyfken,* was the first European vessel to reach Australia of which we have records.[4]

The Aurukun Aborigines then, with support and encouragement from the missionaries, legally challenged the mining legislation. The church authorities helped them get legal aid, obtaining for them as a lawyer Frank Purcell, a man who stood recently for the conservative Liberal party. He also represented the Yirrkala people in their abortive attempts to find legal justice. The Aboriginal Legal Services paid legal costs.

The Aurukun people were advised that their best legal tactic was not to oppose all mining on their land, as the whole community had

---

'We Aurukun people will not allow any mining at all on our land.
We will not accept any money for our land.
Our land is sacred to us.
We hunt on it and have our Sacred Places on it.
We want Comalco, Billiton, Pechiney and Tipperary to leave our land alone.
We must protect our culture.'

Signed
Donald Peinkinna — Chairman
Frank Yunkaporta — Adviser (Former Chairman)
Eric Koo-oila — Adviser (Former Chairman)
Bruce Yunkaporta — Councillor
Fred Kerindun — Councillor (belongs to land which is major part of souther Comalco lease)

Albert Chevathun — (of Norman River) — where the mining port and refinery may well go.
Myrtle Chevathun — (of Ina Creek) — adjacent to Albert's land
Archiewald — (also of land in Comalco lease)
Violet Yunkaporta — (of the Watson River — in the centre of the mining lease)

Press statement made by the Aurukun people, 6/12/75

Aurukun people at Billiton's mining camp, 1975
(Jan Roberts).

Aurukun people, including some Elders and police, on their way to ask the miners to leave, 1975 (Jan Roberts).

emphatically decided at the time of the mining legislation being passed. Little legal hope could be seen for this. But they should press for financial compensation instead. The missionaries advised them that they could *not* properly say no to the mining since they had agreed to 'negotiate' some years earlier. They were told that they should keep their word even if the company had broken its word (Queensland Ombudsman Report).

They were advised that, as the Director of Aboriginal Advancement was called a 'trustee' in the Aborigines Act, they could challenge his authorisation of mining on their land without consulting them or negotiating a share in the profits for them.

Aurukun won its case in the Queensland Supreme Court in 1976 with a ruling that gave the Aborigines the right to challenge any agreement on the reserves entered into without their consent. But the Queensland Government appealed to the Privy Council in London, where their case was heard in October 1977. A delegation of five Aurukun Aboriginal Elders and councillors attended the hearing. These were Donald Peinkinna, Geraldine Kawangka, Fred Keridun, Bruce Yunkaporta and John Koowarta.

The appeal judges were Lords Salmon, Scarman, Edmund Davis, Russell of Killowen plus Sir Henry Gibbs of the High Court of Australia.

The Queensland Government argued that the Aurukun Aboriginal Reserve was a mere temporary Reserve for public purposes and that 'a mere temporary setting aside does not create a trust or give enforceable rights to any member of the public.'

The Privy Council, in January 1977, just before Australia Day, ruled against the Aborigines and for the Queensland Government.

On 8 May 1978, two of the senior Abo-

riginal Elders toured Australian cities appealing for public support. They said: 'We are making noise now because it is our last hope. Our case looks hopeless—but it is not completely lost. We will not go down without a fight.' That same day they tried to give a letter for President Carter to the U.S.A. Vice-President, Mondale, who was then visiting Australia.

This letter read:
We have heard that you are a strong man and keen to see that different human beings in the world get justice and basic rights . . . we hear that you are prepared to help the weak peoples of the world when they are not treated justly and we, therefore, ask for your help . . . as President of the U.S.A. as one of the reasons we are losing control of our land is because the Tipperary Company—an American company— means to mine bauxite at Aurukun. We think you would consider it wrong if Aboriginals were to lose their land so that an American company can make money.'

However, Mr Mondale refused to accept, or to pass on, this letter.

Since the Queensland Government was angered by the church support given to both the Aurukun legal challenge to the mining legislation and the movement of Aborigines back to tribal lands, the Government decided to take direct control over Aurukun and to throw out the church. (See Chapter 9.)

The Aurukun people refused to agree to this. They stated that although they wanted self-management they wanted the church to carry on with its administration of Aurukun for a transitional period. Under no circumstances did they want to come under the direct control of the Queensland Government.

When the Queensland Government tried to send in its administrators in May 1978, the Aborigines refused to allow them to leave the airfield and enter the settlement. The Aborigines occupied all key community facilities as a demonstration of their determination to control their own affairs.

The Queensland Minister for Local Government, Mr Hinze, came up on 7th July to explain the takeover. He was accompanied by eight police and threatened an Aborigine, who publicly disagreed with him, with arrest and expulsion. He ordered missionary staff to leave Aurukun so that their houses could be given to the police. Mr Hinze was responsible for the new Queensland legislation imposed on Aurukun in 1978—as described in a previous chapter.

Late in 1978 the North Queensland Land Council sent a delegation to Europe to raise international support and to meet with mining company executives.

One of the delegation was Jacob Wolmby who represented his people at Aurukun. They went to Le Hague in Holland to meet the Managing Director of Billiton. Their board room meeting was televised and the Dutch public saw the Managing Director hand over a written promise not to mine at Aurukun until the Aboriginal people agreed. The news of this agreement was telexed to and released by an Aurukun delegation then in Canberra. For the first time a mining company operating in

Queensland had promised to respect Aboriginal land rights.

Yet despite this promise, the Aurukun Associates have undertaken to the Queensland Government to start construction by 1983 to be in production by 1987.

The Billiton Metals Manager in Australia, Bernard Wheelahu, said in 1980,

I prefer not to give land rights to the Aborigines. It is a complex issue. When we give land rights to the Aboriginal people it means that they will be in the same position as the other white Australians. I don't like it. It is a very big problem and it is dangerous to the mining industries.[5]

In December 1980 the Aurukun consortium was in negotiation with Comalco over the commencement of co-ordinated mining operations on Aurukun Aboriginal Land. Comalco by now has developed plans to mine areas between Pera Head and the Coconut Creek Aurukun Associates camp. Included are areas for which they had not yet applied for permission from the Queensland Government although they are within their mining lease.

Yet the Aurukun people have not yet agreed to any mining. The Aurukun Community remains under immense pressure. They are hoping against hope that they might still retain the use of their tribal lands.

Aboriginal Delegates arrive at Billiton H.Q. in Le Hague, 1978 (Jan Roberts).

Delegates receive written pledge from managing director of Billiton not to mine without Aboriginal consent, 1978 (Jan Roberts).

Footnotes

1. With the exception of Comalco who, in 1957, secured without consultation or compensation some 200 square miles of Aurukun coastal land including many sacred areas as a southern extension of their Weipa-Mapoon lease. This lease practically surrounds the Aurukun mission on two sides, the other sides being sea and river. The Shell, Pechiney and Tipperary lease is inland of the Comalco lease.
2. J. Roberts (ed.), *Mapoon Book Three*, chapters 9 and 10. These are a basic reference for this chapter.
3. Wallamby, oral history recorded by J. Roberts in Aurukun, 1975.
4. East India Company Records, in *Mapoon Book Two*, p. 17.
5. Interview by Dutch researcher, 1980 (unpublished).

21 RANGER URANIUM AND ABORIGINAL LAND

The first uranium mines were all operated on land previously occupied by Aboriginal people without any consideration of Aboriginal title. Australia's first uranium mine was at Radium Hill, 140 kms north-west of Broken Hill in outback South Australia. This was very small. It was abandoned before the First World War, then restarted by the South Australian government after the Second World War and the discovery of atomic power. It was abandoned in 1961. It is now surrounded by many rich uranium finds.

Several small uranium mines were also developed for the Federal Government in the Northern Territory after the Second World War. The largest of these was Rum Jungle. These mines were the source of the uranium used for the first British atomic bombs. Rum Jungle was managed by Conzinc, now part of CRA and Rio Tinto Zinc.

It was a small mine, producing just 5,000 tonnes. The Fox Commission reported:

About 100 square kilometres of the Finniss River flood plain have been affected by contaminants (heavy metals, uranium, radium and sulphur.) In the ten kilometres of the Finniss River downstream from the mine, fish and other aquatic fauna have been almost eliminated with the effect reducing over the next 15 kilometres downstream.

. . . has killed pandanus palms, eliminated reeds, water lilies and other rooted aquatic plants . . .[1]

Rio Tinto, a British company, then purchased in 1954 its own uranium deposit at Mary Kathleen, near Mount Isa in Queensland. It closed this down when its ten year tax holiday ended. Rio Tinto Zinc, for Rio Tinto had by then merged with Conzinc, decided to shift production to other deposits it owned in Canada. In the late 1970s it decided to reopen its Australian mine. This was not a large mine by comparison with what was to come.

But in the 1970s many mining companies started investigating the Aboriginal lands of northern Australia. They were given easy entry by the Federal Government. On this land they found vast rich deposits of uranium. The Federal Government estimated that they found over 20% of the known western world uranium deposits by the end of 1977.

Most of this uranium was either on the major Arnhemland Aboriginal Reserve, or else on land nearby used mostly by its traditional owners, the Aborigines. These lands were to be returned to Aboriginal ownership by the Labor Government of 1972–75. While procedures were worked out for returning this land, all new mining developments were suspended by the Government.

This put the uranium companies, and the State Governments wanting uranium, into immediate conflict with the Aboriginal call for recognition of their land rights.

The idea of granting Aborigines ownership rights and of giving them a veto over mining developments was greeted with horror by the mining companies. They launched a major campaign against the proposed legislation.

A leading role was initially taken by an Australian company, Queensland Mines, which

Australian uranium reserves

(August 1981)

Name	Aboriginal consent	Company	Reserves
NORTHERN TERRITORY Ranger (Jabiru)	Fraudulent claim. Only 4 out of over 30 required signatures	Energy Resources of Australia, owned by Peko-Wallsend 30.8% EZ Industries 30.8% Overseas Interests 24.2% Australian Public 14.2%	110,900 tonnes in first 2 of 6 deposits. Others not published
Jabiluka	Negotiating	Pancontinental 65% Getty Oil (USA) 35% (Getty Oil is said to dominate) Pancontinental has high 'nominee' interests, possibly foreign	207,400 tonnes plus
Koongarra	Stalled negotiations	Denison (Canada) 100%	18,000 tonnes but in 1980 much more discovered. No figures as yet
Nabarlek	Yes (but divided local community)	Queensland Mines—controlled by Pioneer Concrete	12,000 tonnes
WESTERN AUSTRALIA Yeelirrie	None. Strong Aboriginal protest	WMC 75% Esso (USA) 15% Urangesellschaft (German) 10% Esso (USA) pays half bills and takes 50% of uranium. Urangesellschaft pays and takes 10%	33,800 tonnes
Lake Way (many deposits nearby)	None	Delhi, Vam	6,800 tonnes
SOUTH AUSTRALIA Olympic Dam (Roxby Downs)	None	WMC 51% BP (UK) 49% (BP paying all costs)	340,000 tonnes
Honeymoon (many others nearby)	None	Carpentaria 49%, AAR 21.7% IOL 3.8%, Teton 15.5%	2,400 tonnes
QUEENSLAND Mary Kathleen	None	CRA (UK) 51%	Producing but nearly exhausted 2000 tons
Ben Lomond	None	Minatome (French) owned by Pechiney 50%, Total 50%	1,700 tonnes plus
Westmoreland	None	Urangesellschaft (German management control) 37.5% Queensland Mines 40% AAR 12.75% IOL 9.75%	10,700 tonnes

Sources: 'Register of Australian Mining' 1980, 'Financial Times' 8th March 1978 and 8th August 1978.
Note 1: Pancontinental and Queensland mines are quoted as Australian-owned companies and, as such, escape the restrictions imposed on foreign uranium companies in Australia. However their true ownership is not fully known. Getty Oil is said to dominate. Pancontinental is dominated very much by the chairman, Tony Grey, a Canadian corporate lawyer. Over half of its top twenty shareholders are 'nominee companies' and cannot be investigated. (Australian nominee companies can be formed by foreign investors.) Getty Oil is providing all necessary finance apart from the first $3m. and effectively controls the company. Queensland Mines is owned 50% by 'Kathleen Investments' of which five of the top ten shareholders are 'nominee companies'. Noranda of Canada is the second largest shareholder in both companies.
Note 2: The 'Mining Journal', 10th February 1978, reported that: 'sources have been speculating' that new discoveries just north of Ranger at Ormac and Barote could contain up to one million tons of U308 —ten times the declared value of the Ranger mine. This speculation is based on the very high readings found on initial test bores.
It should be noted that local geological staff attached to the Pancontinental mine stated in 1978 that there was probably twenty times as much uranium in Arnhemland as had already been discovered and announced.

had 'found' an extremely rich uranium deposit on the Arnhemland Aboriginal Reserve near Oenpelli, an Anglican mission. This was purchased from a private leaseholder.

The offers this company made the Aborigines were called 'contemptuous' in the offical *Woodward Report* and were turned down by the Aborigines. The company then tried to pressurise the Aborigines and, although at one stage they gleefully announced they had secured Aboriginal consent, this so-called 'consent' was to be disallowed by the subsequent Fox Commission.

Queensland Mines were angered by having to wait until after Aboriginal land rights legislation:

The uranium cannot be mined because a small group of Aborigines now say they don't want it mined . . . Has someone told them they might get the land and the uranium—and be able to sell to the highest bidder?

Arnhemland Aborigines and uranium —The land endangered

The region where most of the uranium has been found has great sandstone escarpments rising abruptly out of forested plains. It is a land where, in the dry season, water is found in the few rivers that have carved deep gorges through the plateau, out through the cliffs on to the wide plains; in springs that run from the escarpments into the thirsty land to be drunk up by the ancient forest; or in some of the deeper billabongs and rock pools left by seasonal rivers. But in the wet season the rivers spread themselves luxuriantly over the plains, covering the land with flowing water, home to thousands of migrating water birds.

It is a land of rich life, full of animals, birds and plands that have made this their home for countless ages, evolving into their own kinds— one of the very richest parts of all Australia. Europeans might term it a true wilderness, but it is not wild for the people who have for over 30,000 years lived on and with the land, caring for it, loving it but never changing it.

Until now, the majority of the people living here are Aborigines. They outnumber whites four to one. They are among the most re-

nowned Aboriginal people in Australia for their art, for their culture and for the way in which they have preserved their way of life. Their land is vital to their survival, and extremely important for the survival of the Aboriginal race.

Aborigines say no

The Aborigines do not want this mining. The Aboriginal chairman of the Northern Aboriginal Land Council, Galarrwuy Yunupingu, stated at a Canberra Press Conference, 10th November 1977:

Now people are trying to force us to accept that mining, uranium mining, will go ahead. But we insist that we don't want uranium mining.'

The chairman of the Oenpelli Council, Silas Maralngurra, spokesman for the first Aboriginal community to be affected by the proposed mining, stated:

Balanda [white man] *push, push, push,—soon pubs everywhere and they will kill the race—look at the Larrakia. Darwin is their country, and they are living on the rubbish tip . . . This place will look real ugly and bad, just like Rum Jungle* (the former uranium mine nearer to Darwin).

Little Dolly, an Aboriginal woman from the community, spoke out for her land before the BBC *Panorama* crew in 1977. She said:

We don't want money—money is not important for us. We are in our ceremonial ground, and our culture is more important than money. Money is for the white man. He made it up, and he gave it to us. We don't know how to handle money . . . We know how to use our own culture . . . we know how to use our ceremonial grounds, which were handed down to our ancestors.

An Aboriginal man added:

White people are playing tricks on us. We can understand their tricks. They just want to get away with our inheritance, our country. We've got to hold it hard. We don't let our land go. If we do, we just lose it just like people from the southern States . . . a hundred years ago.

Government reports

Justice Woodward, in his commission's second report on Aboriginal land rights, recognised the determined opposition of the Aborigines to the Nabarlek uranium mine. He stated:

It is to my mind unthinkable that a completely new scheme of Aboriginal land rights should begin with the imposition of an open-cut mine right alongside a sacred site.[2]

The Fox Commission reported in 1977:

It was established to the satisfaction of the Commission that the Aboriginal people concerned were opposed to mining on their land . . . While royalties and other payments . . . are not unimportant to the Aboriginal people . . . Our impression is that they would happily forego the lot in exchange for an assurance that mining would not proceed . . . The reasons for the opposition would extend to any uranium mine in the region . . . The arrival of a large number of white people in the region will potentially be very damaging to the welfare and interests of the Aboriginal people there . . . It is not likely that the mining venture will add appreciably to the number of Aborigines employed.

But the Fox Commission concluded
in the end, we formed the conclusion that their opposition should not be allowed to prevail.

The Ranger negotiations

Once the Fox Commission had reported in 1977, the Government announced that the Arnhemland uranium mines would proceed. The Aborigines were given the right to negotiate royalties and mining conditions but *not* the right to say no. If they refused, the Government could appoint an Arbitrator who would conclude the negotiations so that the mine could go ahead. This was rather like telling workers they can negotiate working conditions but cannot refuse to go to work.

The Aborigines were told that *if* they agreed to Ranger they would get back their tribal lands around the uranium mines (if they

agreed to these lands being given back to the Government for 99 years to run as a national park).

If they did not agree, they were threatened not only with the loss of these lands, but the possible loss of the Land Rights Act and the destruction of the Northern Land Council.

Under these threats, ultimately powerless in law, the Northern Land Council conducted negotiations. However they did have some negotiating strength in the great support given to them in the southern cities. The Fraser Government felt that it had to produce an Aboriginal 'agreement' to defuse public opposition to the mines.

The negotiations took a year. In September 1978, Yunupingu, the chairman of the land council, presented the negotiated terms of the land council delegates. He told them that they had to sign because the Prime Minister had told him he could stop Aborigines going back onto tribal lands. The members very unhappily agreed.[3]

But, when the Aborigines who traditionally owned the land wanted for the mines heard of this, they applied for an injunction to stop the land council signing the proposed agreement. A thousand Aborigines converged on Darwin in protest. However this application was dropped when Yunupingu agreed to an out-of-court settlement. He undertook that no agreement would be made until the traditional owners had the proposed agreement explained to them, had discussed it to their satisfaction and had told the land council that they were ready to have a meeting to sign or reject the agreement. He agreed that those with a traditional interest in this land, but not living at Oenpelli, should also have a say in the decision. Translators were arranged at the various settlements to assist with explaining the proposed agreement.

But only one month later a secret meeting was called by Yunupingu. The delegates were not told where the meeting was to be held until after they had boarded their plane. A police guard was mounted on the meeting. The delegates were told that this was to stop white outside influences getting to them, but the white Government was not to be excluded. Yunupingu had arranged for the Minister for Aboriginal Affairs to be there on the second day of the two day meeting.

By this stage none of the consultation agreed to by Yunupingu had been carried out. Instead he had been angrily thrown out of one of the key communities, Goulburn Island, without even giving them the proposed agreement. He had been to Oenpelli too where they had told him they remained opposed to signing.

The meeting was at Bamyili. This is what happened. The following is from the transcript of the meeting.

Gerry Blitner, the vice-chairman, asked why this meeting? 'The motion was that traditional owners will tell us when they are ready and I thought we were all happy with that—and now we have this mysterious meeting with police outside guarding us . . . we could blame you for giving in, Mr Chairman.'

Yunupingu explained he thought that what the Oenpelli people had said changed the situation: 'they don't want the uranium, right—we don't want it all of us, right . . . One of the things that they ask of you is give them back the land in the form of a national park so they can go back.'

Yunupingu tried to reassure the delegates: 'I have a bad feeling . . . that you blokes are frightened of the government . . . don't be frightened of them.'

Yunupingu explained that they would only get Kakadu back if they agreed to give it back again to the Government to use as a national park for tourists. 'It was a deal that the Government would give that land to the Aboriginal people as long as the Aboriginal people would agree to make that land a Parks and Wildlife . . . The land is being given back to the Government for one hundred years.'

Gerry Blitner commented: 'That is why they give it to the Aboriginal people—because they want it back again.'

Leo Finlay added: 'It is more or less playing tricks on us, isn't it?

Gerry Blitner: 'No, it's going to the rich man.'

Women at Oenpelli

Toby Gangali, Oenpelli delegate, stressed, 'It must be the park first' (before the agreement to the uranium mine).

Yunupingu then recommended passing a motion 'strong enough to hit the Government right in the face.'

A motion was finally passed at the end of the first day of the meeting. This read:

That the NLC strongly supports the Oenpelli people in its requests that the Government deal separately with the National Park Agreement from the Ranger Agreement and that the National Park be established with outstations before any approval is given for uranium mining to go ahead.

Yunupingu next day came back with Mr Viner, the Minister for Aboriginal Affairs.

Mr Viner addressed them at great length. Among other things, he said: 'I have been a bit worried to see what has been happening over the Ranger agreement . . . So I was worried . . . that people would start to say land rights is a bad thing, that it shouldn't have been given to the Aboriginal people . . . I was very worried at what might be the end of it all.'

After this, which could be seen as an implicit threat, Viner went on to say: 'Isn't it time we settled up all this business over Ranger?'

'I want to emphasise to you . . . that the question has always been for you, what are the terms and conditions under which mining can be carried out, not whether Ranger will be mined or not, because that decision was made by the Government in August of last year.'

'We have to think about the future of the Northern Land Council and the future of Aboriginal land rights ... That is life—you never get everything you want ... we know you don't like the idea of mining, any mining, we know that you would prefer that no mining is carried out.'

'Now for your resolution (from yesterday's meeting), I would like to put that to one side for the moment because ... the two things come together, you know, ... it is very much part of the whole Ranger agreement.'

Yunupingu then reminded him of what they had undertaken in order to have the injunctions dropped. 'We are not signing this paper until such time when everyone is happy.'

Leo Finlay stated, 'I, for one, don't agree with the agreement.'

The representative from Milingimbi, Joe Mawundjil, said then that he could not agree without consulting his people: 'I don't know how many communities heard about the agreement.'

John Gawadbu for Goulburn Island, one of the key communities which Oenpelli had just nominated as essential to an agreement since they had a traditional interest in the Ranger area, then spoke: 'There are a lot of people back there who don't know anything about this agreement ... So my feeling is that I can't make my decision myself.'

Yunupingu disagreed with both the last two speakers. He told them that he didn't feel he needed to consult those who elected him at Yirrkala: 'You are like a Government person in Parliament, in the House, running the show.'

As the meeting went on, people started sounding more dispirited. Dick Malwagu of Oenpelli said: 'We have been talking too long. I don't want to talk about it more.'

Yunupingu agreed and added his own comment: 'I say, who is interested in Ranger? I would rather forget about it and give it back to the Government. If I was a traditional owner,

you know, if uranium was found at my place, this is what I would say.'

Leo Finlay expressed strongly his fears of the damage the mines will bring: 'You are going to crowd that country with mining companies.'

Gerry Blitner expressed their general feeling of unease: 'because we as a crowd have got to decide about other people's spiritual land.' He criticised the Land Rights Bill for this.

Dick Malagu said that they did not even finish their meeting at Oenpelli: 'We were going to send a telegram to stop this meeting here so we could finish our meeting first ... People say, can't sign, it is too rushed.'

Yunupingu finally said: 'The Aboriginal people know that the Government is going to mine anyway, isn't it, so what is the bloody point, what are we arguing about?'

Dick Malagu of Oenpelli agreed.

The lawyers then produced a motion that they had prepared. Yunupingu read it out:

Having heard from the delegates from Oenpelli and Goulburn and Croker and Toby Gangali, the Northern Land Council repeats that it is satisfied with the terms of the Ranger Agreement and will sign it as soon as it can lawfully do so.

One of the lawyers, Eric Pratt, explained that 'lawfully do so' meant that they had to *first obtain* the agreement of 'the traditional owners as a group.'

One delegate, Harry Wilson, interjected: 'Wait a minute—what about them people, that thing that we have got written down there, we are supposed to send the lawyers out ... ' He wanted to know if the previous agreement to send out four lawyers to advise all the communities still held, if the agreement made to have the threat of injunctions lifted still held.

Eric Pratt assured him that it did. 'Yes that is right and that comes in too, and they have to understand the nature and purpose of the agreement.'

With these reassurances the resolution was carried. Leo Finlay and Gordon Lansen were the only ones who voted against it.

Viner then announced that he would go to

Oenpelli next day to see if the traditional owners would agree. Yunupingu announced that 'the traditional owners are there . . . the field officers have got all the people together and they are waiting for us . . . We have had a successful day—one of the best meetings we have ever had.'

Next day at Oenpelli, Viner repeated the long speech he had delivered the day before, but to only four out of the thirty or more traditional owners. Others refused to come. The Oenpelli chairman, Silas Maralngurra, walked out of the meeting in disgust and watched the farce from his car.

Viner appears to have attempted to mislead them. He said: 'All the communities have been advised of what is in the agreement. They have had the opportunity to talk about it, and we heard yesterday from Dick [Malagu] how his community had talked about it and we heard yesterday from John [Gawadbu] of Goulburn Island.' Both of them had said that their communities had not had time to talk about it.

Viner added: 'We know, the Commonwealth knows, that in your heart you would prefer that mining didn't come.'

Yunupingu then told them that John Gawadbu had told the land council meeting that the Goulburn Island people had said, 'We give up.' (Nothing of this kind is in the transcript.)

Yunupingu then told them that when they agreed they would get their land and outstations and, within seven days, $200,000. He added that they 'represented' the other traditional owners (they did not) and said: 'Today, I

Yunupingu turns the first sod at Nabarlek to the applause of Deputy PM Anthony (N.T. News).

fly in here and find that everyone has gone simply because they are sick and tired of me.'

Finally he said: 'It is good that you have made your decision in a quiet way.' The four elders were then given the paper to sign and they did. They afterwards said that they did this because it seemed they had no choice. Viner then flew out to Darwin to triumphantly announce 'The Aborigines have agreed to uranium mining.'

In all this, Viner and Yunupingu never once asked the very few Oenpelli people present if they understood the agreement. They never discussed with them any of the terms of the agreement. They did not allow them any time to consult with the other traditional owners at Oenpelli or on the Islands. Yet these other owners had legally the right to be consulted. Their consent, too, was legally required.

The announcement of this 'agreement' caused consternation among the people around Australia who had been supporting the struggle of the Oenpelli people. Many could not understand how the 'agreement' could have been signed. Many felt totally impotent now that the Government had its legal bit of paper. If the Aborigines had agreed, how could Ranger be fought any more?

Even those who understood just how the Fraser Government had fraudulently acquired its 'agreement' felt impotent in the face of such bare-faced governmental lies. The Oenpelli people, who had borne the brunt of years of unremitting pressure from Government, companies and the media, were by now totally exhausted and disillusioned.

Some supporters were taken in by the Government announcement and felt there was no need for further support for the Oenpelli people. Others, who were more against uranium mining than for Aboriginal land rights, ceased their active support for land rights.

Ranger and the environment

What will this development mean for the land? It will mean not just the invasion of one of the few remaining Aboriginal lands, it will also involve enormous environmental dangers. These include the construction of the largest earth-wall dam in Australia with each of its four walls over a kilometre long and up to 40 metres in height to hold the tailings, the waste from the first two pits on the Ranger site.

This will be lined with clay to reduce seep-age, for it will be filled with thousands of tonnes of radioactive sludge from the concentration plant, covered by two metres of water to prevent the escape of radioactive gases. This dam has to survive 'for ever' according to the resident company engineer. If it breaks, it will certainly destroy for thousands of years the unspoilt, rich, wildlife-filled Alligator River Valley among whose headwaters both the Ranger and Pancontinental mine will be situated. This river is renowned throughout Australia for its magnificent untouched splendour.

The enormity of the risk can be seen if one remembers that this is a land of violent monsoon rains and of devastating cyclones. It only needs the earthen walls of the unsupported dam to be eroded for a deluge of lethal poison to sweep across the land.

The dam is eventually to hold up to 40 million cubic metres of contaminated sludge and water. It only needs the first winds of a cyclone like that which devastated Darwin, and such cyclones are not so rare, for the two metres of lethal water covering the radioactive sludge to be swept away leaving the sludge itself to be carried up into the air to poison all living things over vast areas. This is admittedly the worst possible scenario but it is possible.

It is not only one such dam that is being planned. Ranger itself may well need two or three. Pancontinental will also need a dam twice the size of Ranger's. Ranger admitted that it would not be able to stop normal rain run-off from its dam, let alone that from a violent storm.

The Fox Commission concluded that this normal run-off would necessarily entail the poisoning of all creeks near the mine. The Fox Commission reported concerning the nearby creeks:

Releases from the Ranger site will increase the amount of uranium in Magela Creek water by 360% (plus heavy metals). The effect cannot be predicted. Changes in the relative abundances of some species could occur.

Evidence suggests that contaminant concentrations (in Georgetown Creek) could reach some ten to twenty times the 'safe levels' (of heavy metals etc.).

Jabiluka (Pancontinental's mine) is downstream from Jabiru (Ranger's) and so any contaminants will be additive to those from Jabiru.

Finally, the Australian Council of Churches published in late 1977 a report on what this pollution would do to the traditional foods of the Aborigines. It concluded that the contamination would cause long-term illnesses among the Aborigines.[4]

A 60 million tonne plus waste-heap will also rise over 100 metres high next to the mine composed of the waste of the first of the pits. The other pits will multiply its size. The pits themselves will be vast. The first will be 700 metres wide and some 175 metres deep, the next will be 190 metres deep and sit on top of an underground mine. These will both emit poisonous radon gases. These are only two of the possible eight pits. Extraordinarily, the Fox Commission, charged to investigate and evaluate 'all the environmental matters' of the Ranger mine, confined themselves to just the first two of the pits. The Commission merely noted in passing that 'there are six other' deposits on the Ranger lease, which were 'not tested in detail' and which 'were not considered during this inquiry'.[5]

Nabarlek — the fight goes on

As previously quoted, Woodward said about the Queensland Mines 'development' at Oenpelli:

It is to my mind unthinkable that a completely new scheme of Aboriginal land rights should begin with the imposition of an open cut mine right alongside a sacred site.

The uranium deposit is by the site of 'Gabo Djang' (Green Ant) dreaming sacred place.

The Aborigines traditionally believe that the desecration of this place by disturbing the large boulders and environs will bring terrible consequences to humankind.

However, Queensland Mines has now built a yellow-cake concentration plant and a 300 metre long mine right by this sacred place.

The Nabarlet uranium mine deeply disturbed many of the people in Oenpelli and split the community. Most remained opposed, but one of the principal Nabarlek elders was eventually persuaded to agree to the mine going ahead.

It particularly worried people at Oenpelli because it was close to the settlement and inside the reserve. All the trucks going to the mine had to thunder up the road the Aborigines had built to Oenpelli and past it to the mine-site. The mining company, Queensland Mines, also wanted to use a road to the coast. This the Aborigines may have allowed, but the company mainly used the Oenpelli road.

Right through the 1979 dry season and into 1980 the trucks roared up, sometimes more than twenty road-trains a day. They went through the lands of Aboriginal clans that had not given permission for the company to use their land and their road. These Aborigines had repeatedly told the Northern Land Council that they refused permission for this. They had a right to do so under the Northern Territory Aboriginal Land Rights Act. The trucks were ripping up the road, disturbing the animals, making the area dangerous for children.

So the Aborigines decided to take legal action to stop the trucks. They believed they had a cast-iron case. It came up in court on February 11th, 1980.

Then, in an unprecedented move with scant respect for the law, just as the court began its sitting, the Fraser Government announced that, in the next session of Parliament, they were going to introduce legislation to *retrospectively* change the law. If the court found in the Aborigines' favour, the court decision would be overthrown.

Senator Chaney announced:

The proposed amendment will protect mining agreements from legal challenges from a third party. As the Act stands at the moment an agreement is open to challenge at any time after it has been made and acted upon on the grounds that the land council failed to obtain the consent of every traditional owner or failed to consult adequately with every community affected by the particular proposal.

Since the Northern Land Council was bound in law to obtain the consent of every traditional owner and consult adequately with the affected communities, this amendment effectively means that the Aborigines have no way of keeping the Northern Land Council to its obligations.

The account above of the Ranger Agreement showed that the land council only obtained the agreement of four out of thirty traditional owners and did not consult with key communities in any adequate way. This amendment effectively prevented the traditional owners challenging this in law to protect their rights. Thus the Government retrospectively covered its tracks in order to protect the illegal Ranger Agreement, as well as Queensland Mines' use of an Aboriginal road.

In 1979, Queensland Mines conducted a virtual mining blitz on their deposit. In one dry season they completely mined out their deposit and stockpiled the ore. This blitz involved 200 workers who worked ten hours a day, seven days a week. The miners complained they were bathed in dust. They worried over their health. One miner said, 'This is not coal, or sand or something like that—we don't know what the effect will be on our health in another twenty years or so.'[6] The Minister for Science and the Environment, Senator Webster, reported that radiation levels were 'five to ten times higher than predicted.'[7] Yet reporters saw many of the workers disdaining 'obligatory' face-masks or even singlets as they tore up the ore.

In late 1980, Queensland Mines produced their first 'yellow-cake' (uranium oxide). They flew it out from the mine site in order to avoid using the disputed road which the Aborigines had threatened to block. But, at the time of writing, they were having difficulties finding workers willing to ship it from Darwin.

In 1981 they announced that they wished to extend their drilling and mining operations to other nearby deposits on Arnhemland Aboriginal land. They only await the unfreezing of their earlier leases. Those acquired before the Land Rights Act are not subject to Aboriginal veto.

The Northern Territory Government has said that it hopes to have the many exploration leases unfrozen as soon as possible.

Other uranium deposits

There are many uranium deposits outside of Arnhemland of great concern to Aborigines. But apart from the Northern Territory and the Pitjantjatjara lands of South Australia Aboriginal land rights are not recognised.

Still, on the 1978 North Queensland Land Council speaking tour of Europe, Mick Miller, Joyce Hall and Jacob Wolmby went to Germany to visit the head office of Urangesellschaft, a company with uranium interests in north east Queensland and at Yeelirrie in Western Australia.

Mick Miller, the land council chairman, told the managing director of this company that his interests at Westmoreland in north east Queensland were on Aboriginal land, and that they wanted them out. He also spoke, at the request of West Australian Aborigines, about Yeelirrie, and how the Aborigines there were deeply distressed at the company's operations. The managing director said in reply, 'Mining is part of civilisation, and Aborigines have to be part of civilisation.'

This response was widely reported in German media—and today active German groups have adopted the cause of Australian Aborigines and are keeping pressure on this company.

What do the Aborigines who own the land that the Yeelirrie mine will destroy have to say?

Peter Hogarth, whose tribal name is Yambilli, Roley Hill, whose tribal name is Nulli and Croydon Beaman, Aboriginal tribesmen living near Leonora, said:

We been fight for Yeelirrie. The sacred ground is each side of Yeelirrie. 'Yeelirrie' is white

man's way of saying. Right way is 'Youlirrie'. Youlirrie means 'death', Wongi (Aboriginal) way. Anything been shifted from there means death. People been finished from there, early days, all dead, but white fella can't see it.

Uranium, they say uranium they make anything from it, invent anything, yet during the war when Americans flew over, what happened to Hiroshima? And that'll happen here too if they're messing about with that thing. They never learn.

Jackson Stevens, Chairman of the Nnanggannawili Community at Wiluna said:

Uranium mine. We got one up here. We trying to put a block to it. It's Aboriginal sacred site. If they, the Government and the mining companies come in here, we'll be pushed away from our own country, own place, to the town, Wiluna. No work there.[8]

Government approval for this mine has been given. Production is to start in 1985. The initial output of 2,500 tonnes has already been sold. Japan is taking 1,000 tonnes a year and Esso and Urangesellschaft the rest.

Betrayal 1981

No sooner had the first stage of the Kakadu National Park been proclaimed than the Federal Government was rushing through legislation to change its boundaries to allow more uranium mining.

This was occasioned by the discovery by Canadian-owned Denison Ltd of a vast uranium deposit in land adjacent to their Koongarra lease and inside the national park. Because mining is forbidden in such parks, the Federal Government pushed legislation through in June 1981 on the last day before they lost control of the Senate. This changed the boundaries of the national park so Denison could have the deposit they coveted.

However, because the previous 'owners' of the deposit, Noranda, did not apply in time before the coming into force of the Land Rights Act, the Aborigines retained the right to veto the mining of this deposit.

The Federal action greatly angered the

THE ABORIGINES ARE BEING MANIPULATED BY OUTSIDE SOURCES!

(AN OUTSIDE SOURCE IN A HURRY TO SUPPLY URANIUM, TO AS MANY OUTSIDE SOURCES AS HE CAN)

Aborigines who had given their land for the national park on the understanding that this would help protect their land. On 1st May 1981, a meeting of the Aborigines owning the land stated:

How can it be that the minister can give our land away to a mining company without asking what we think? This is not self-determination; this is the same as always, white fellahs making their own decisions about what is good for Aborigines.

They then decided to break off all negotiations with Denison Ltd.

The mining of this deposit had already been condemned on environmental grounds by the Fox Commission because it could poison a major river system. The Commission stated the region 'is so valuable ecologically we would oppose in principle any mining development upstream of it.'

In the so-called 'Razor Gang' report at the end of April 1981 the Federal Government decided to hand over as many formerly Federal responsibilities as possible to the States in order to cut the Federal budget. This would include giving the Northern Territory Government administrative control over the Kakadu National Park and environmental control over the Alligator River uranium mines. The Aboriginal traditional owners were aghast. The Northern Territory Government has shown itself unremittingly hostile to Aboriginal land rights and to Aboriginal control over the national park. It was actively pushing for the opening of more uranium mines. The Aborigines saw Federal control over the park and mines as an essential part of their agreement to make their re-won land into a national park. They fear what may happen now.

Kakadu Park is as yet only half complete. It is planned to have it extend to the north up to the coast. This will happen as soon as the Aboriginal claim to this traditional land is formally acknowledged.

However their claim to this 'second-stage' Kakadu land has been heavily opposed by the mining industry. Major deposits of uranium are already known to exist at Barote and Ormac (see p.126). The mining companies are maintaining pressure on the Oenpelli people and the related communities. A report tabled in the Federal Parliament by the Uranium Advisory Council on 18th September 1980 proposed that stage two of the Kakadu National Park should be explored for uranium as there are 'clear indications' that there is much more there. It also stated, 'most members are inclined to favour early resumption of uranium exploration in stage one as well.' In mid-1981, Aboriginal title to their ancestral lands in stage two was only partly recognised, despite Pancontinental dropping its legal objections to this Aboriginal claim in return for the Northern Land Council agreeing to the opening of negotiations on the Jabiluka uranium deposit.

How much at Ranger?

Even on the Ranger lease much more uranium could exist than in the six deposits so far indicated. John Elliston, Peko-Wallsend director and geologist, as stated that 'even a thin layer of sand or alluvium' can obscure 'most or all of the radio-metric character'—making the uranium ore undetectable on the surface. Since much of the Ranger uranium lease was covered by such a layer, it could be fairly predicted that more uranium may well be found.

An article in the December 1977 *Mining Magazine* stated that Ranger's six known deposits 'almost certainly contain additional recoverable uranium' over and above the 100,350 tonnes reported to the Commission for two deposits alone. They are therefore certain to be mined. We have no way of knowing how big these pits will be. All we know is that the Ranger company, according to the above mentioned article, suspended drilling on these deposits 'while the Fox inquiry was at work.' This they did not have to do from legal or investment considerations, for they at the same time carried out a A$4 million exploration programme on adjacent areas and a A$12 million development programme on other aspects of the Ranger lease.

Could it be that Ranger which then included the Australian Atomic Energy Authority, suspended the investigation of these deposits so as to limit the information that they had to supply to the Fox Commission? They were hard put to find ways to safeguard the enormous waste produced by just the first two pits. To include that produced by all the pits might well have stretched the credibility of their assurances just too far for the Commission to swallow.

In any case, it is rather astonishing that the Fox Commission could reach a conclusion based on such strikingly inadequate information. We may therefore have to multiply all the figures given for pollution at the Ranger mine by several times. We already have to multiply these figures to account for the four or more other mines planned for the same region.

The price to be paid

The total result could be the poisoning of parts of Arnhemland and elsewhere with much radioactive waste for thousands of years as well as the destruction of Aboriginal culture and land. The national park proposed by the Aborigines, and now authorised by the Government, may in future be used for the study of mutations caused by radiation, rather than of virgin bush in pristine condition containing life that has remained unchanged for thousands of years.

This is the price extracted by the atomic power programmes of the affluent Western nations and of Japan; programmes that are extracting a further price from the consumers themselves in terms of the tremendous pollution risks and the expenditures involve. But for the Aborigines, the price is beyond all this. It is ethnocide.

We could now have the establishment of a uranium enrichment industry and State-based nuclear power station programs in Australia. The Fraser Government in April 1981 handed over to the States responsibility for all nuclear issues as part of his 'Razor Gang' programme of cutting Federal responsibilities. Several of the State Governments are enthusiastic about having such 'developments' in their States despite the environmental hazards. Ironically, because these hazards have led to a massive cut in nuclear power station programmes in America and Europe it seems some now want to stimulate a domestic market for uranium in Australia to replace lost foreign markets even at the cost of bringing these hazards to Australia,

Bjelke-Petersen exemplified this 'development at any cost' mentality when he called on the Federal Government to drop its insistence on safeguards for the disposal of nuclear waste and the non-miliary use of Australian uranium exports because these safeguards 'don't mean much' and were cutting Australian exports.

In every way the proposed uranium mines are a disaster. The words of a Dene Indian of Canada, whose lands were threatened by a pipe-line, come to mind: 'Do you really expect us to give up our life, our lands, so that those few people who are the richest and most powerful in the world today can maintain and defend their own immoral position of privilege? That is not our way.'[9]

Footnotes

1. Fox Commission, *Ranger Uranium Environmental Inquiry, Second Report*, 1977, p. 75.
2. Woodward Commission, *Second Report*, 1974, par. 685.
3. In the 1980 Northern Land Council elections, Yunupingu ran for re-election as chairman. However Gerry Blitner was elected chairman and Leo Finlay vice-chairman.
4. *Age*, 10 December 1977.
5. Fox Commission, p. 75.
6. *Northern Territory News*, 25 May 1979.
7. *Northern Territory News*, 5 June 1979.
8. From their statement made in support of Noonkanbah, 22 June 1980.
9. *Akwesasne Notes*, newspaper of the Mohawk Nation (U.S.A.), Spring, 1974.

Aboriginal Elders in the Kimberleys saw and still remember the terror killings of their people that accompanied the establishment of the cattle stations on their land. Many lost parents and other members of their families.

The Kimberleys, despite the incursion of white pastoralists, police, missionaries and government officials, has remained in 1981 still very much Aboriginal country. But with its 15,000 Aboriginal people ruled by some 4,000 whites, the racial atmosphere is very similar to that of South Africa.

In the 1970s, some mining companies with South African experience began to see another likeness to South Africa. The Kimberleys, they found, had a strong geological resemblance to the diamond rich Kimberley region of South Africa.

Among the first to see this were Tanganyika Concessions (now known as Tanks) and Stockdale. The latter is named after Stockdale Street in Johannesburg, South Africa, where its owners, De Beers, the world's dominant diamond company, resides. These two companies soon realised that the Australian Kimberleys could be the world's largest diamond source outside South Africa.

Tanganyika, then operating on Oombulgurri Aboriginal Reserve in the Kimberleys, merged its operations with CRA as other companies joined the diamond hunt. Amax came in, too, but with wider interests including bauxite deposits in the north and oil exploration leases in the south.

The rush was on. The Aboriginal peoples of the Kimberleys, living in their widely separated communities realised that they would have to unite if they were to have any hope of getting their voice heard, so, in 1978, one thousand two hundred of them gathered from all over the Kimberleys for a cultural and land rights meeting on Noonkanbah Station.

Across the Northern Territory border, their fellow Aborigines were uniting in land councils and obtaining back their land. In north Queensland, the Aborigines had taken the initiative to establish their own land council so the Kimberleys' people resolved to do the same. Thus was born the Kimberley Land Council representing the many Aboriginal nations of the Kimberleys.

Noonkanbah

The Aboriginal community walked off Noonkanbah Station in 1971 because of the way the management maltreated and exploited them. But they sought ways of regaining their land. Noonkanbah had been badly managed by its white owners. At one time it had been the largest sheep station in the southern hemisphere, but it was so grossly over-stocked that its desert-edge grasslands were eaten out. With its Aboriginal workforce on strike, it became more and more neglected, and eventually the management decided to sell out. Before they did, they authorised West Australian Petroleum to drill for oil. The Aborigines were not asked. No oil was found, but the Aborigines believe that it was this drilling program that drove the kangaroo from the region.

Around this time, the Federal Labor Government set up an Aboriginal Lands Fund Commission to purchase properties to restore to

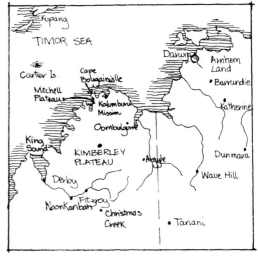

Aboriginal people the opportunity to live again on their own land and to run their own enterprises.

The exiled Noonkanbah Aboriginal community applied to this fund for assistance and asked them to purchase Noonkanbah for them for it was large enough to support many Aboriginal people and contained many sacred areas of great importance to them.

This station stretches north from the edge of the desert across hill ranges to the permanent water holes of the Fitzroy River. The homestead is near this river. The flat plain of the northern part of the station is broken by small rocky hills—the remains of ancient volcanoes—standing among the seemingly delicate desert scrub and the majestic fat-trunked boab trees.

In 1976, their application succeeded. They regained Noonkanbah and set out to restore it to running order. (This was not helped by station facilities being smashed by out-going staff because it was being taken over by Aborigines. Only one of the thirty windmills was left in running order.) Today, this is a very successful cattle station supporting a community of about 200–270 Aborigines. They call their community 'Yungngora' which means 'the land is everything to us'.

They built up community facilities with minimal help. Dickie Skinner, community spokesman, said:

We look after our old people. We have 56 children and they all go to school. I never had any education. When I grew up on Noonkanbah I had to work the stock.

It is much more than the usual Australian school. It is part of a revival of Aboriginal culture. Dickie Skinner said:

We decided the children should learn the language. We fought for our community school, but the Government wouldn't listen. There were promises but nothing. We paid our own teachers, black and white, for one year from a community chuck-in. Our children began to learn the language; to belong to the land.

THE SACRED RIGHTS BATTLE.

Help also came from other Aboriginal communities, particularly from the Strelley Aboriginal Station in the Pilbara where the Aborigines had already established a similar community school.

When the Government insisted that they accept a white manager, they threatened to walk off once more. They were not going back to the system of having a white boss. Eventually, they agreed to accept two friendly neighbouring station owners as advisers on their management committee, and the Government backed down.

They have strictly barred alcohol from the station and are planning to establish a special camp for the old people.

Above all, they are happy to be back on their own land and in control once more of their own lives.

The miners invade

When the Yungngora community returned to Noonkanbah, they were shocked to find that mining companies had practically simultaneously taken out new leases over their land.

Amax secured its petroleum exploration licence over Noonkanbah in 1976. This was a major licence also extending over other neighbouring lands.

Then came the diamond prospectors. CRA was one of the very first of many. Between 1977–78, some 500 mineral claims were pegged on Noonkanbah. The prospectors were particularly interested in the rocky, ancient volcanic plugs rising as low hills on Noonkanbah. These surround the station homestead to the north-west, north and east. They are all potential diamond sources, and the gravels surrounding them, covering much of the northern half of the station, are all potentially diamond-bearing. Such gravels would be strip-mined if they did contain enough diamonds. The ancient volcanic pipes, if rich in diamonds, would be turned into vast pits reaching down perhaps 300 metres or more. Of course, at that stage, it was not known if diamonds or oil existed on Noonkanbah. But it was because of favourable indications that the miners were flocking.

The miners' presence on Noonkanbah became blatantly obvious, 'evidenced as it was by Toyotas, helicopters, bulldozers, white-tipped pegs, trenches and camps of loud-mouthed, alcohol-imbibing, uncouth Europeans'.[1]

Everything the people were working for was clearly threatened by this intrusion.

One of the first places desecrated was Djada Hill where the people kept their most sacred ceremonial boards. A prospecting team found these boards, took twenty of them back to Melbourne and smashed six of them. Fortunately the community recovered the other twenty.

In 1978, the Yungngora community took legal action in the local Mining Warden's Court against the CRA mining tenements. The action failed—although CRA had to await a museum survey to identify sacred sites on two of its leases. Once these were protected, all the rest of the leases were CRA's. In 1980, CRA held 30 square km of Noonkanbah.

The people of Noonkanbah then called Kimberley Aborigines together to celebrate their culture and plan united action to protect their lands. This was the meeting that brought 1200 Aborigines together to form their own Kimberley Land Council. But right in the midst of this meeting, Amax blithely went ahead to bulldoze out its seismic survey lines, and sent a bulldozer through two burial grounds and a sacred birthplace belonging to one of the Noonkanbah elders. Great anger was caused. A petition was sent down to the State Parliament. It was sent in Walmajeri, their language, and on wood. In translation it read:

We are sending this letter to you important people who can speak and who are now sitting

The drilling rig at Ellendale, just north of Noonkanbah, 1979 (Jan Roberts).

down talking in the big house.

We, Aboriginal people of Noonkanbah Station, are sending you this letter. We truthfully beg you important people that you stop these people, namely CRA and AMAX, who are going into our land, which is at Noonkanbah.

These people have already made the place no good with their bulldozers. Our sacred places they have made no good.

They mess up our land. They expose our sacred objects. This breaks our spirit. We lose ourselves as a people. What will we as a people do if these people continue to make all our land no good?

Today we beg you that you truly stop them.

CRA on Noonkanbah

The Yungngora community had lost their court action against CRA so they had no way of legally stopping CRA from prospecting their land. But they have made many efforts to persuade CRA to leave them alone.

Friday Mullamulla said, pointing to the plain,

That's all CRA mob . . . they bring bulldozer about two miles back down that way, down west. They cut all the way around all dead bodies. All around that place where we been taking bones of the old people. And that's nearly all sacred ground through there too.[2]

Dickie Skinner said:

My law say that he can ask white man a question. If it's CRA's–if that diamond or mineral inside under the ground, if he's got the name CRA written on the gold, he allowed to go down and get him. If he got no CRA written in mineral–well, that mean there's nobody owning–it's for the tribal people.

In 1979, CRA tried another approach to the community. They said that if they prospected on Noonkanbah, they would employ an Elder to make sure they did not trespass on any sacred site. This, by comparison with Amax, seemed good. Some of their advisers thought that the Federal Government might support

Noonkanbah against Amax's plans to drill Pea Hill if the Aborigines allowed CRA to prospect large non-sacred areas in the north of their station. This was a 'more reasonable' position which the Federal Government could support. But it would mean giving up the attempt to protect their land as a whole.

This would indeed have fitted in with the evident Federal policy of trying to restrict talk of land rights outside the Northern Territory to sacred site rights.

The community were not sure. Initially they gave permission to CRA. But a week later, after a joint meeting between the Kimberley Land Council and a delegation from North Queensland Land Council, and the presenting of information on both diamond and uranium mining (the two minerals CRA was reported as seeking), the community came to another conclusion. Senior Elders sent the following letter to CRA in October 1979.

CRA, we have been thinking about you looking on our land. You say you only look at one part of our station and go away again after three weeks.

But we, after talking more between ourselves, say we don't want you because, if you find something up there, you may come more and more onto our land and we don't want that.

Also, you didn't tell us you looking for uranium–that stuff dangerous for everyone.

We have been born out of the ground and we have to stay in that bit of ground–so we don't want the mining companies to come.

We only say one thing–get out, we don't want mining companies on our land.

Nipper Tabagee, a very senior Elder on Noonkanbah, brought this letter into Derby and gave it to the land council and to the legal service. It was accepted by the Kimberley Land Council as the voice of the people of Noonkanbah and sent with the KLC delegate to Europe.

The Aboriginal community had up until then little idea of what a diamond mine would be like. They were concerned primarily about the damage done in prospecting. They heard the north Queensland delegates describe the Weipa bauxite mine. When they also learnt that most diamond mines in South Africa are vast pits of enormous depth with great waste heaps, often together with large areas strip-mined of gravel or sand, they were horrified at the possibility of this being done to the land on which they lived and for which they had fought.

Senator Chaney, Federal Minister for Aboriginal Affairs, expressed disappointment at this rejection of CRA. At a follow-up meeting two weeks later, the Federal Government sent its own representative; but, after this meeting Dickie Skinner, Noonkanbah spokesman, said the decision still stood, and that they would see what they could do about it again in 1980.

CRA ignored this, and the people did not feel able to enforce their will. The prospecting went ahead and CRA respected three areas pcinted out to them as sacred. By the end of 1979, fifteen pipes had been examined by CRA and they had found the first few small diamonds.

Many other companies are now claiming parts of Noonkanbah. These include Selection Trust (owned by BP Oil), Dampier (owned by BHP), Samantha and many others.

(But CRA's attention was distracted while it was on Noonkanbah, for over in the East Kimberleys, another of its exploration teams then discovered its biggest diamond strike yet—on a major Aboriginal sacred place near Lake Argyle.)

AMAX on Noonkanbah

Amax has been looking for both diamonds and oil on Noonkanbah. In doing this, they claimed two very important hills near to the homestead, Djada Hill and Pea Hill.

Djada is to the south of the Fitzroy River. This sacred hill is neatly pegged in each corner by Amax, and the *Register of Australian Mining 1980* says that this hill is a potential diamond pipe. In this hill are some of the burial caves of those who were killed earlier by the police. It is here, as mentioned before, the people used to keep their most sacred cere-

monial boards. It has been, even from the Dreaming, a big gathering place of the people—right across the river from the Goanna Dreaming Hill—Pea Hill, where Amax had wanted to drill for oil. It was to this oil drilling programme that Amax gave its first priority.

On March 12, 1980, the Jungngora Community publically explained for the first time just why Pea Hill was sacred to them. Dickie Skinner said:

I have been given permission to tell you that a sacred story concerns the goanna that lived under the hill. The goanna's spirit will be disturbed by drilling. Our people are concerned that if the spirit of the goanna is disturbed, the next season will not replenish goanna stocks at Noonkanbah.

The people maintain that the absence of kangaroos, once plentiful at Noonkanbah, is because earlier drilling activities disturbed them.

The drill site by the side of the hill is on sacred land joined to Pea Hill for it is, the people stated, on a site used to prepare initiates for the sacred rituals.

Amax did not relish their place in the lime-light. The President of Amax Petroleum said from Houston, Texas:

I run an oil business and we never had these problems before—not with Indians . . . The Aborigines won't talk with us. If they want to talk to me, I am in my office, anytime, in Houston.

AMAX and American Indians

Amax does in fact have problems with American Indians. In 1980, it faced at least three legal actions brought by different tribes.

American Indians share with Aboriginal people both a strong attachment to their ancestral lands and a recent history of being herded into reservations and deprived of their rights. (See Chapter 15.) They too have great difficulties with mining companies that had located mineral resources in their remaining lands.

Amax obtained a coal mining lease to 16,000 acres of Crow Reservation land and 71,000 acres of Northern Cheyenne Reservation land in Montana. On this land it located two billion tonnes of coal which it planned to strip-mine. However, the Indians took action to cancel these leases when they discovered they had been sold out very cheap by the Bureau of Indian Affairs (BIA).[3]

By 1980, the northern Cheyenne had won from the Department of the Interior a ruling that Amax would not receive a lease until it came to an agreement with the tribe; however negotiations remain at an impasse at the time of writing. The Cheyenne also won an anti-pollution classification for their lands as a 'class one air quality area'. Amax is taking legal action to get this classification declared invalid.

The Crow Indians won a court ruling that the BIA had not properly negotiated the Amax lease. Legal action was still proceeding in 1980.

The Papago Indian Tribe in Arizona, with US Government support, is suing Amax for taking their water supply. If this action is successful, Amax may have to close its operation in that State. Local farmers are also claiming $35 million damages from Amax over this water issue.

Amax is facing more legal action from American Indians than from any other group in the United States.

Jimmie Durham, of the International Indian Treaty Council, said of these leases:

They speak of our land as National Sacrifice Land (a term coined by President Carter for the coal-mining lands of the mid-west), land which can be destroyed so the great American nation can be energy self-sufficient. But that land is our land, and it's the only land we have got left. We have no other place to go.

We do not want Amax on our land at all. We do not want any of these coal companies or lumber companies or uranium companies on our land at all.

We are not against economic development.

WHO EATS OUR LAND?

Nobody wants to live in poverty. But we want to control the development of our land. We want to raise cattle, we want to raise buffalo, even some herds of antelope, and we want industries that go with those activities; fertilizers, bone meal, leather factories, things that make sense to us. Things that don't destroy our culture and our land, and still give us economic development. And so we want those coal companies forever off our land.[4]

Also there were bitter protests by the Nishga tribal council in British Columbia, on the west coast of Canada. They were angered by Amax being given a special permit to dump 100 million tonnes of waste from its Kitsault mine into Alice Arm, 130 km north of Prince Rupert. These waters are traditional fishing grounds for the Indians. The tailings to be dumped included arsenic, lead, radium 266 and other dangerous pollutants, at levels 10,000 times that allowed under the *Fisheries Act*. The Acting President of the Nishga Tribal Council, Rod Robinson, said: 'The company has offered us a share in the mine—our share is death!'

The State Government intervenes at Noonkanbah

The West Australian Government went to much trouble to reassure Amax. In April 1980, they sent the Minister for Mines, Mr Jones, to Amax's home town, Houston in Texas. When he spoke to the Houston Chamber of Commerce he said:

Certain activists have got among them [the Aborigines] and persuaded them to claim the land they lease is the land they own. The West Australian Government is quite firm that no-one can claim land rights this way . . . [The Noonkanbah drilling] will go ahead, because there is no way that lawful government can allow its laws to be overridden by pressure groups.

Early in 1980, the Noonkanbah community decided on a policy of calling for a three year moratorium on all mining company activities on Noonkanbah. This would, they hoped, give them the chance to build up their community and station, and do all the work that was being neglected while they were under such daily pressure. They hoped that this was a realistic target that the Government might accept to defuse the situation. But it was rejected.

Then, in August 1980, the West Australian Government decided to move against Noonkanbah. They organised a massive police escort to bring a drilling rig two thousand miles onto Noonkanbah Station. Aborigines, clergy, unionists and other supporters who tried to block its path, were arrested. When unionists refused to work the rig, the State Government took control of the rig and began drilling in sight of the Aboriginal camp.

The drilling rig was to find no gas worth testing and only a trace of oil in a formation too tight to permit any flow. The well was abandoned in November 1980. However, companies participating in the drilling consortium with Amax said that they remained very interested in further drill-holes in the area.

Since this operation had essentially been mounted just to drill a wild-cat with little chance of finding oil, why did the West Australian Government insist on the company going ahead in the face of so much public support for the Noonkanbah people? Sir Charles Court, the State Premier, saw the issue as a stand by his Government against Aboriginal claims of 'sovereignty' over State lands. He attacked the Federal Government for the pretence that only sacred site protection was involved. He said:

Senator Chaney and Mr Viner dismiss the land rights issue out of hand with the statement: 'The allegation (that the dispute is a cloak for land rights) is as unfair to the Aborigines at Noonkanbah as it is false'.

The Federal Government was indeed trying to direct the dispute away from land rights and to confine it to the protection of the Pea Hill sacred site. While the protection of this site was of enormous importance to the Noonkanbah people (and still is), Court was right in stating that it was basically a land rights issue.

He proved his point easily by quoting a letter sent to him by the Noonkanbah community on June 9th 1980.

You assumed that we recognise the State Government's ownership of the land. Instead of this you should have recognised us, the Elders who hold the law for this country, as the real owners of the land.

After establishing that the Aborigines are indeed claiming the land *as if they had a right to it* Charles Court went on to try to discredit this assertion of the Aborigines by saying that the Aborigines at Noonkanbah did not themselves believe it!

In fairness to the Aboriginal people living on Noonkanbah and as a guarantee that the Government is still willing to talk with them, I will repeat what I have often stated in public, namely, that I do not believe that such radical and unlawful views are really theirs.

The State Government is well aware that the doctrine of a separate law for Aborigines is being fed to them and expressed for them by outsiders. He went on to say, *the failure of negotiations at Noonkanbah is no fault of the company or the Government . . . It must be emphasised that the community at Noonkanbah was guaranteed protection of its **genuine** identified sacred sites . . .*

These things were known, understood and accepted by the community before the extremist agitation began which led the community to make absurd claims amounting to sovereignty over the crown land they occupy as pastoral leaseholders.[5]

The State Premier saw that it was because the Aborigines saw Noonkanbah as their own by an ancestral title, that they were fighting so hard to protect it. For Court, such an assertion had to be discredited. Recognition of it would have led to an opening for the recog- nition of Aboriginal land rights in Western Australia. Thus he had to force the drilling to go ahead on Noonkanbah.

In addition, he appointed himself an expert on Aboriginal religious beliefs and denied the drill site was on 'genuine' sacred ground. This was despite a report from his own official advisory body, the WA Museum, stating:

The whole area within which any drill hole could be located by the company falls under the influence of the special sites shown to me by the Aborigines of the clan descent group for that area.

Dickie Skinner, Chairman of the Yungngora community, and Wadgie Thirkall, Chairman of the Kurnangi community at Fitzroy Crossing, said on 7 March 1980:

Statement of Coppindale and Mick Lee, Tribal Representatives of the Pilbara District.

The Government and mining companies should keep away from that sacred ground there at Noonkanbah.

What's happening at Noonkanbah at sacred ground and burial ground, the Government people should not put a hole down on that sacred ground and disturb burial ground. In that burial ground is bad, that's really bad.

Poor people up there at Noonkanbah they try to fight for it and we, the Aborig- inal people of the Pilbara district, we sup- port them. White people are against us all the way, against Aboriginal people all over Australia.

We like to see it give us a fair go, white people. They just want to come on the land here and take everywhere. White people they just take everywhere. We got nothing off white people for our country.

Some Aboriginal people got shot, poor fellows, and some got put inside prisoner.

What we like to see, give us a fair go, if we want to keep our sacred sites from early days, hundreds of years ago, thou- sands of years. The law's been made by the white man that sacred sites be protected and now the law's being broken by the law. Why are they on the sacred ground? We go out in the bush on our sacred cere- mony grounds; we sing for them, we dance for them.

Coppindale
Roebourne, W.A., Friday, 4th July 1980

Statement of Freddy Johnson, Tribal Spokesman and Chairman of the Looma Tribes, and of the Tribal Lawmen of Looma.

What's been speaking now at Looma, all Looma elders, law people they are, and they hold their sacred site and open sacred sites, and women sacred sites, they keep this. They under law.

We tribal lawmen like to see all sacred sites left alone, we can't give it to him, gardia (white man), we can't let him go, white fella, he can't take him, white fella, and we, the community of Looma every time support Noonkanbah, the same as all the communities in the north-west of Australia support Noonkanbah in their fight to save their sacred sites, and we like to see these fellas to keep their sacred sites and women's sacred sites, all got it, and that's all I can say. I'm a lawman myself.

Freddy Johnson, Tribal Spokesman and Chair- man, and
Tommy Mukadi, Gibber Peter, Billy Layman, Davy Crockett, Rober. Tribal Lawmen of Looma.
Looma. W.A., 28th June 1980.

We know the land. We were born by this earth and that is why we know. We want our kids to live the same way, . . . by the sacred sites, by the law, by the land. . . The Government says they own the land. We say the Government is not owning any land. The land belongs to the Aboriginal people.

First national meeting of the land councils

Despite the drilling, the Noonkanbah people did not give up; instead, they summoned a meeting of all the land councils of Australia. People came from throughout the north and centre. Six land councils were represented.

At this meeting, it was resolved to form a National Federation of Land Councils to unite all Australian Aboriginal people, to give them a stronger national and international voice. It was resolved too not to start any new negotiations with mining companies until such time as the dispute with Amax and the West Australian Government was settled to the satisfaction of the Yungngora community.

The Kimberley Land Council, the Noonkanbah community and the National Aboriginal Conference resolved to send a delegation to the United Nations. Prime Minister Fraser intervened to try to persuade the delegates not to go, but failed. Instead Fraser secretly sent his personal Adviser, Alan Griffith, after them to help counter what the Aborigines were to say in Geneva.

Jim Hagen, one of the Aboriginal delegates, told the United Nations sub-committee on Discrimination: 'We are a people without hope and without a future unless discrimination ends.'

The Aboriginal delegates spoke strongly about the desecration of Aboriginal land at Noonkanbah.

But the Federal Government told the sub-committee that there had been no drilling on a sacred site at Noonkanbah, that Noonkanbah was an exception to the rule. They assured the sub-committee that all that was needed in Australia was more talk.

The diamond pipe at Argyle on the Barramundi dreaming track.

CRA, diamonds and the Barramundi Dreaming Place at Argyle

When CRA obtained diamonds in gravels near Lake Argyle in the East Kimberley in October 1979, the hollowness of the pledge that they had just given to respect Aboriginal sacred places became very plain.[6]

Initially, CRA kept its movements secret from all, including the Aborigines. However, the company's road improvements gave away their presence to Aborigines on the nearby Aboriginal cattle station, Doon Doon Station, formerly Dunham Station. A month after CRA had set up camp, the Aborigines hired a plane to see if these roads were being used by cattle thieves. Instead they found what was, in their law, a diamond thief trespassing on their ancestral land—CRA.

The traditional Aboriginal owners and guardians of the area were immediately alarmed. They knew that in the rugged hills where CRA was working were more than one important dreaming place. The gravels where CRA had found the first diamonds were along Smoke Creek. The area of Smoke Creek is very sacred and of the highest ritual importance to the senior Elders of the highest degree in the northeast Kimberley. It descends to the lake, the former Ord River, from a basin ringed by steep hills. CRA were moving into this basin searching for the source of the diamonds. This basin was, and is, the very ancient and sacred Barramundi Dreaming Place. This sacred place is of particular importance to Aboriginal women. It is also an ancient volcanic pipe, the source, CRA ascertained, of the diamonds.

The Aboriginal Elders immediately contacted the Kimberley Land Council and asked them to ask CRA to respect the dreaming place. After a day of negotiations, CRA stopped work on the dreaming site and paid for a survey by the WA Museum. In West Australian law, the Museum could register a site as of great significance. If it did this, disturbing the site would be illegal without a State Government permit.

On January 15th, 1980, the Museum notified CRA that its works affected several important sacred dreaming places, and that CRA should not work this area without a permit. They found CRA had already bulldozed one sacred site at Devil Devil Springs. CRA then announced that they were suspending operations. They applied for this permit with justifiable confidence that the State Government, enthusiastic about this 'development', would not hesitate in granting it.

However, the Aboriginal community soon discovered what they believed to be violations by CRA of its standstill agreement. The CRA Aboriginal Research Officer, Michael Bell, admitted on May 23rd, 1980, that CRA had done more work on the sacred site area after meeting with the community on April 22nd. Photographs were taken that seemed to show clearly that CRA was breaking the *Aboriginal Heritage Act* by commencing operations before the State Government issued the permit. The Elders warned Michael Bell, telling him of the area that CRA should not enter.

In the meantime, in the belief that no mining would proceed while he was away, one of the leading Aboriginal spokesmen, John Toby, came south to raise support for his people. He was to address the International Land Rights Symposium arranged by the Institute of Aboriginal Studies in Canberra, and while there, to his horror, he was notified that CRA appeared to have again broken the *Heritage Act,* and had done excavations on the Barramundi sacred site.

The Symposium, packed with representatives of all Land Councils and many of the most eminent anthropologists in the country, passed the following resolution without one contrary vote:

This, the 1980 Aboriginal Land Rights Symposium at the Australian Institute of Aboriginal Studies, having listened to the representatives of the Kimberley Aborigines, deplores the entry of CRA onto known Aboriginal sacred sites in the Smoke Creek region of the East Kimberleys and requests CRA to immediately leave these areas.

Furthermore, requests CRA to respect the call by the Noonkanbah people for a three year moratorium on all mining and prospecting activity on Noonkanbah Station. This motion is to be communicated to CRA, the Press and the Council of the Institute. [7]

John Toby then went to Melbourne, where he was met at the airport by Mike Bell and another CRA representative (a meeting arranged unknown to John Toby by the Department of Aboriginal Affairs). They asked him to get his community to drop their legal action against the company for violating the *Aboriginal Heritage Act*. He refused and returned immediately to his country in the Kimberleys and tried to press his legal action against CRA. Much to his dismay, he received legal advice that it would be hard to win anything from such an action.

He was told that the Aborigines had erred in trusting CRA. They should not have relied on the spoken word. They needed documentary proof that they had told CRA where the sacred sites were, and firm dates for the alleged CRA violations of these sites. The Aborigines needed properly surveyed and witnessed accounts. The photos the people had were deemed insufficient.

The promises of CRA's Aboriginal Research Officer had been all oral; his confession that CRA had broken the conditions by building a helipad had been oral and legally insufficient.

CRA could thus plead official ignorance as a defence against charges of desecrating the sacred sites. They could say they did not know their works were within the sacred area. CRA could have employed an Aboriginal Elder to mark the limits of the sacred site. CRA had

done this elsewhere and the Museum had requested them to do this here too. But CRA ignored this request.

The Aboriginal community then accepted advice that they should drop their legal action so that the WA Museum could proceed against CRA. The Museum would be legally able to demand from CRA access to official company records and use these to determine if the company had indeed carried out works on the sacred area after it had been warned not to do so. But the Museum failed to take legal action.

By this stage, John Toby and others in his immediate family group were exhausted by the unequal fight and became persuaded that there was nothing they could do to stop CRA. The Barramundi sacred site could not be saved. Further protest seemed pointless and likely to lose them any return from the mining venture. However most of the Aborigines who were responsible for this land and its sacred places maintained their opposition. There was no meeting between most of these Aborigines and CRA. CRA instead seized on the weakening opposition of John Toby and his clan to split them from the others. John Toby was not a senior elder and may not have known the full importance of the sacred places.

CRA, for the Ashton Consortium, met with about 15 of the nearly 50 Aborigines responsible for the area. CRA had its lawyers there. The people had none. The Kimberley Land Council intervened to recommend that they got legal advice and this was agreed to. But John Toby and about three others of his clan were persuaded to give their consent to the mining in exchange for some community facilities for their outstation at Glen Hill.

CRA immediately flew them down to Perth to conclude an agreement away from the other responsible Elders and from the Kimberley Land Council. They ignored a telegram from their community asking them to come home and not sign. The price they obtained from CRA was just $200,000 worth of community facilities plus $100,000 a year for the community while the mine was operating.

What will CRA and the rest of the Ashton

Consortium get for this? The Chairman of one of the consortium companies, Northern Mining Corporation, at first estimated at their 1980 Annual General Meeting that there was at the very minimum two billion dollars worth of diamonds in the Argyle deposit. But, on February 23rd, 1981, he stated that he had learnt that his estimate was far too low. He stated that the diamonds were worth over $20 a carat and that the Argyle diamond deposit could well contain as many carats as the total world reserves outside Russia before Argyle was discovered—1,100 million carats. Even at $20 a carat, this would make the pipe worth $22 billion. About $300 million worth of diamonds will be dug out each year, according to CRA which more conservatively values the diamonds at $13.28 a carat. The yield of diamonds per tonne mined will be about ten times that of the typical South African mine—and thus considerably cheaper to mine.[8]

Mining company plans include bringing in over 1,200 workers to construct the mine, strip mining over ten kilometres of land along Smoke Creek as well as digging out a vast pit that will be, according to Michael O'Leary, the managing director, 'the same size as the two largest South African mines put together.'

No wonder that Phillip Adams called the agreement with CRA 'pitiful barter of pocket knives, mirrors and beads for perhaps the richest piece of real estate on earth'.[9]

The rest of the Aboriginal community responsible for the Barramundi Dreaming Place reacted with absolute horror and dismay. On 30 June 1980, forty members of this community (known as the Warnum Community) met and unanimously agreed that this agreement with CRA was invalid in their law. They too were responsible for the sacred places and they had not agreed.

One of the Elders, Mr George Evans, said that the signatories had put aside Aboriginal law and were therefore in danger. 'They will be punished.' They contacted CRA and told them of their disgust and of their repudiation of the agreement. Nevertheless, CRA, for the Ashton Consortium, pressed ahead.

The Kimberley Land Council was horrified too. To secure a settlement CRA had side-stepped recognised procedures and had sought to isolate and negotiate with individuals rather than the community. This left these individuals very exposed, without access to expert advice and at a very great disadvantage in having to negotiate with a company as rich as CRA. It also left out the rest of the Aboriginal community responsible for the land in question.

One of the Aborigines, David Mowaljarlai, said on 14 May, 1980:

Disturbing sacred sites and land is agony for our people. Land and mountains and spring water—the heart of the sacred sites—is really our body. Grader, bulldozer are pressing down on our body, liver, kidney bleeding. The spirit of the landowners is sickened. Graders are scraping the skin off our flesh—a sore that will not heal up: in my language, wilu, *killing us.*[10]

It should be remembered that in these negotiations the Aborigines knew they were on frail ground in whiteman's law. Legally, CRA did not require Aboriginal consent to mine this deposit. Nor did the State Government have to obtain Aboriginal consent before it gave CRA a permit to mine a registered Aboriginal sacred site.

The only hope the Aborigines had in legal action was in proving CRA had moved onto their registered sacred sites before the permit was issued. Even if successful, this case would

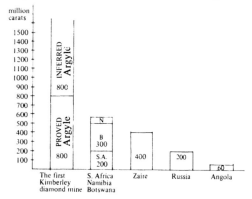

World Diamond Reserves

not necessarily have done more than embarrass and delay the company. But it *could* have meant the forfeiture of the diamond mining leases. The possibility of this penalty had made the company take the community's legal action as a serious threat. CRA also needed the Aboriginal 'agreement' for an appearance of justice for public relations sake, because of the support Aboriginal people have won among the general public in Australia and overseas.

The people of Oombulgurri

On the north-eastern coast of the Kimberleys is the largest of the Kimberley Aboriginal reserves. Once named Forrest River, it was an Anglican Mission, but when it closed down, the Aborigines were moved off their tribal lands to the town camps behind Wyndham.

In 1972, they decided to move back and re-establish themselves on their own land. They came back, rebuilt the old settlement under the cross erected in memory of Aborigines massacred by the police in 1928, and renamed it 'Oombulgurri'. But when they returned, they found that a mining company had entered its land looking for diamonds. It was ensconced some 70 km from the settlement. Its name was Tanganyika Concessions, now known as Tanks. The people did not feel they could ask this company to leave since it had come when they were not there, but they decided to keep out any other companies that should try to enter their tribal lands.

Later, this company merged its Kimberley operations with CRA so CRA inherited control over the diamond leases on Oombulgurri. By 1980, CRA had two camps there, one named 'Mumbo Jumbo' and the other 'Geebung'.

In the meantime, Dampier (owned by BHP) and Stockdale (owned by De Beers of South Africa) applied to enter the reserve, but the community, with the support of the Aboriginal Land Trust, succeeded in keeping them out by denying them an entry permit.

This angered the Court State Government so, in 1978, they gazetted new regulations under which only the State Minister for Community

Welfare could authorise an entry permit, thus leaving the Aboriginal residents powerless.

In 1980, Dampier Mining took advantage of these new regulations to take possession of a large exploration lease in the heart of the Oombulgurri Reserve. This BHP-owned company had previously promised in writing not to do this without Aboriginal permission.[11]

In August 1980, the Oombulgurri Community despite this change, refused to authorise a renewal of CRA's exploration agreement with the community because of the way CRA had treated the Warnum Community over the Argyle diamond find. In response, CRA offered to give the people a much needed decent water supply. (Water supply normally being a governmental responsibility.)

The community has drawn up a list of requirements for any new exploration permits. These include recognition of the Kimberley Land Council as the negotiating body for Oombulgurri Council, at least three months notice of intended activities, negotiated compensation payments, training and employment, improvements to community facilities and protection of sacred sites.

They have also agreed to record where their sacred sites are and have asked CRA to finance an ethnographical survey by a person of the community's choice.

The bauxite of the North Kimberleys

Another major battle now looms on the horizon for the people of the Kimberleys. They are to be given no peace, no rest in the fight for their land.

Up in the far north of the Kimberleys, massive bauxite deposits are located on Aboriginal reserve land, and on traditional Aboriginal land with many sacred places.

So far, the mining companies have defined at least 200 million tonnes of bauxite on the Mitchell Plateau and a thousand million tonnes on Cape Bougainville nearby. These are close to the Kalumburu Aboriginal Mission.

Amax first took possession of these deposits back in 1965. In 1968, they built a pilot beneficiation plant there and tested bulk samples.

In 1969, the State Government gave them 1,500 square miles to exploit for a minimum of 42 years. The company planned to build a town, a deep-water port and an alumina refinery, using money lent to them at cheap rates by the Government for, said Charles Court, then Minister for Mines, 'alumina production on its own is not regarded throughout the world as being a highly profitable operation.'[12]

He went on to say:

Overall, this project is of great importance to the state and, in particular, to the Kimberley region, as it could be the initial breakthrough for the establishment of large-scale industry in this area . . . It must be realised that this is a location where there is literally nothing else. (This would not have been the view of the Aboriginal inhabitants.)

Twenty-seven square miles were also excised from the Cape Bougainville Aboriginal Reserve. In all this, there was no consultation with traditional owners and no compensation for Aborigines.[13]

At that time, the State Government was expecting to start operations immediately. But Amax failed to get together the consortium it needed to finance the project. Anaconda joined, but then dropped out when its properties in Chile were nationalised by President Allende.

Amax sold half their aluminium business to Mitsui, and formed Alumax with them. The West Australian Government extended their lease over the Mitchell Plateau to 1980 with a possible extension to 1984. Alumax in the meantime contracted to purchase the large amounts of alumina it needed from Alcoa, 400,000 tonnes per year.

In 1980, the project started moving once more. CRA conducted an appraisal of the deposit, and then bought a dominant 52.5% of the prospect. Alcoa also purchased 17.5% of the Mitchell River deposit and 22.5% of the Cape Bougainville deposit.

The Alumax plans included a township for 3,000 people on Port Warrender and a large reservoir west of the town. The alumina refinery would probably go on Walsh Point in the Admiralty Gulf with an adjacent deep water port. The initial alumina production planned was 1,200,000 tonnes.

A mobile crusher plant would be needed to crush the bauxite after it has been blasted and bulldozed loose. From this the bauxite would go to a beneficiation plant to remove some of the waste. Out of every 100 tonnes treated here, 35 would be waste. It would then go to the refinery where, for every tonne of alumina produced, well over two tonnes of caustic soda-treated poisonous red mud would have to be dumped. Thus, over 2,400 million tonnes of this waste would have to be disposed of. This is usually dumped in mangrove swamps—as it is in Gove and Gladstone—producing a sterile wasteland in what were very food-rich Aboriginal hunting grounds.

At the time this book was being written, CRA was studying whether the refinery should be located in the Kimberleys and what size it should be.

Such an operation would change the face of Aboriginal North Kimberleys. Such developments were bitterly opposed by the peoples of Yirrkala and Weipa in the 1960s. This could well be a repeat of those disasters. The only hope is that the growing strength of the Kimberley Land Council will eventually force the companies to the negotiation table.

CRA at Christmas Creek

While attention has been focussed on Argyle, CRA's actions on Christmas Creek have escaped public attention. Here they did not wait in 1980 until a requested survey of sacred places was completed but went ahead with drilling to evaluate a coal deposit. They succeeded in putting their drill right into a main sacred place, or Tjilla, called Kurungal.[14]

This area is also a traditional Aboriginal gathering ground where very sacred objects were stored and a burial ground—just as is Djada Hill at Noonkanbah. CRA's action greatly upset the Aboriginal community living on this station.

A meeting was held with CRA's Field Geologist who promised to move the drilling rig as soon as possible—but the drill stuck in its hole and CRA had great difficulty and expense in removing it.

Mobil and Esso have fortunately shown more respect for Aboriginal rights in recent negotiations with Aborigines concerning drilling programmes around Beagle Bay and Balgo. But oil drilling need not destroy the land like mining, if sensitively handled. It is therefore less of a threat to Aboriginal communities than bauxite strip-mining or diamond pits.

But until the State or Federal Government recognises the Aboriginal right to own their Kimberley lands, the mining companies will

Press Release: from the Chairman of the Kimberley Land Council

TED: Friday 5 June 1981

The Kimberley Land Council (an independent organisation representing Kimberley Aboriginal Communities) believes the Ashton Joint Venture at Argyle continues to demonstrate callous disregard for the rights, customs and integrity of Aboriginal communities in the East Kimberley.

The Ashton Joint Venture has strong corporate links with South Africa and is believed to be negotiating to enter the South African dominated Central Selling Organisation. Much of the expertise to be used at Argyle will also be South African. But the comparison goes further still. The AJV refuses to recognise the Kimberley Land Council despite its three years independent existence and instead operates on the principle of divide and rule. The effect of its policies is to ensure the separate development of the European economy in the Kimberley, while ignoring the desperate situation of Aboriginal communities unless they sign 'agreements' limiting their rights to oppose any aspects of the development.

The terms of the first Argle agreement involve an annual payment of $100,000 to the small family group at Glen Hill. While the Joint Venturers have thereby tacitly *admitted traditional Aboriginal ownership of land in the Kimberley, the financial terms are pathetically inadequate even by Australian standards. The annual operating turnover of the Argyle development will be $400,000,000 (based on annual production figures of 20 million carats). * On this basis the terms of the Argyle agreement amount to 0.05% of annual operating turnover. At Ranger in the Northern Territory royalties to Aborigines amount to 4.25% of annual operating turnover.*

On the question of Aboriginal sites of significance the Ashton Joint Venture has an atrocious record. At least two sites were desecrated in full knowledge that they were of significance in the rush to prove up the deposit.

We believe that the Argyle development is potentially compatible with Aboriginal interests. But until the mining industry and State and Federal Governments come to terms with the basic issue of human rights involved, recognition of our cultural integrity and of our spiritual link to the land and of our rights to equal access to law and justice, Australia will remain different only in degree to the blatant racism so evident in South Africa.

Part of a Press Release from the Co-Chairman of the Kimberley Land Council, Mr Darryl Kickett, 5 June 1981.
* A conservative estimate. In excess of 35 million carats per year could be mined.

continue to take advantage of the law to dispossess the Aborigines. With the discoveries of bauxite, of diamonds, of off-shore gas (off the Oombulgurri Aboriginal Reserve) and of coal deposits near Broome, the fight for survival for the Aboriginal communities in the Kimberleys is sure to intensify.

Ironically, despite the Federal push for some Australian share in the ownership of Australian resources, Australian Aboriginal ownership of resources has been totally ruled out and foreign companies preferred—despite these same resources being owned by Aborigines for thousands of years. In practice, Aborigines are still not recognised as citizens of Australia.

Instead, by offical policy and mining company actions, we have the Kimberleys continuing in the South African direction of 'separate development'. There are two Kimberley economies—one for the dispossessed based on government and company handouts, the other for the whites.

CRA is pushing for the direct linking of the Kimberley diamond industry with that of South Africa. This is not surprising as Oppenheimer is represented on the board of CRA's parent company, RTZ.[15]

Currently CRA is advertising in South Africa for staff for its diamond mines, offering top technical staff around $100,000 a year. It is also engaging South African mining engineers Van Ecke and Lurie to help design the mine. They are also employing Australian labourers for around $750 for a 60 hour week. They are building a Kimberley society of rich whites living in enclaves among impoverished blacks.

This is currently the established 'Australian' way of 'developing' the north. It seems it is the way of the future too.

In desperation, the Kimberley Land Council has started to look for support from abroad to help them put pressure on the Australian Government and on the companies. In 1979, they sent their chairman to the USA and a delegate to the World Conference of Indigenous Peoples on Uranium Mining. In 1980, they sent delegates to the United Nations and to the Bertrand Russell Tribunal on Violations of the Rights of Indigenous Peoples.

They are getting their voice heard. But it promises to be a long fight before they win back their land.

Footnotes

1. Philip Vincent, legal representative for Noonkanbah community, in *Noonkanbah*, a paper prepared for the AIAS Biennial Meeting, 21-22 May 1980.
2. As told to Steve Hawke, unpublished document, 1978.
3. The Bureau of Indian Affairs is the U.S. equivalent of the Department of Aboriginal Affairs in Canberra.
4. *The Amax War against Humanity*, People's Grand Jury, Washington, 1977.
   It is interesting to contrast what Amax were to pay the Indians with what they offered the Yungngora community.
   Amax had rented the Indian land for $US9 an acre and were to pay 17.5 cents a ton royalty. Another company offered the Indians, two years after the Amax agreement, $US35 an acre and 24 cents a ton royalty, plus a $1.5 million community health centre.
   Amax were to offer the Aborigines at Noonkanbah two dams, a ford and some help with fencing. (Aboriginal Mining Information Centre Newsletters Nos. 1 and 2, October 1980 and March 1981).
5. *West Australian*, 8 August 1980.
6. In their 1979 *Annual Report*.
7. Motion passed 23 May 1980.
8. For fuller details, see *Age, Sydney Morning Herald* or *Adelaide Advertiser*, 22 August 1980, feature article on diamonds by J. Roberts.
9. *Age*, 11 October 1980.
10. David Mowalharlai, recorded at Argyle.
11. Mr R. M. Williams, BHP Manager, wrote to a concerned shareholder, Ms Elaine Bruen, to say that Dampier Mining 'has not and will not enter the Aboriginal land in question until it has obtained permission to do so from the Oombulgurri people.'
12. West Australian parliamentary debate on *Mitchell Plateau Bill*, 26-27 March 1969.
13. Stan Davey, letter published in the *Age*, 20 May 1969.
14. *Kimberley Land Council Newsletter*, mid-1981.
15. 'The Oppenheimer Links', a chart in the *Age*, 22 August 1981.

23 CRA AND THE INTERNATIONAL STRUGGLE FOR ABORIGINAL LAND

It is difficult for the curious to locate CRA in Melbourne. The sky-scraper block on Collins Street that bore CRA's name now bears the name 'Comalco'. CRA has moved to the upper floors of the tall twin-pronged Collins Place further up the street, with its own name modestly concealed behind the security guards in the lobby.

Yet this 'modest' company dominates the Australian mining industry. True, BHP is listed as bigger in its own name. But when all CRA's substantial interests in other well-known companies are added, we find that it controls many mining enterprises and much mining capital, ahead of BHP which makes only a minor part of its income from minerals and which does not have a controlling interest over its major income-earning projects. CRA's net profit after tax in 1979 was $135 million, in 1980 it was a record $195 million.[1]

While BHP makes most of its money from its half share in the Bass Strait oil and gas field, and secondarily from its steel, iron and alloy minerals operations, CRA's interests spread all over Australia and involve nearly every mineral. Wherever a dollar can be dug out of the earth, there probably you'll find CRA. If you can't find CRA, then it's most probably at the door trying to buy its way in. Currently CRA has major interests in aluminium, iron, coal, lead, zinc, gold, uranium and diamonds. In August 1981, it had under lease 54% of Victoria alone.[2]

CRA is now expanding around the Pacific rim and into the Pacific islands—into Chile, Philippines, Niugini, Hong Kong, Malaysia, Fiji, New Zealand—for this is the part of the world allotted to it by its masters in England. CRA is indeed the largest and most profitable jewel in the crown of the major British mining company, Rio Tinto Zinc (RTZ). RTZ currently owns 61% of CRA—the rest being divided among a host of small investors, insurance and superannuation funds. Even if RTZ reduces its holding in CRA to under 50%, as it has said it will one day, RTZ will still control CRA.

How Rio Tinto Zinc came to invade Australia

It all started in Australia with the formation of a British-based company called the 'Zinc Corporation', which made its money from mines at Broken Hill in New South Wales. In 1949, this became 'Consolidated Zinc' (Conzinc)

with headquarters in London. In 1953, they obtained their first operation in northern Australia—the management of the Rum Jungle uranium mine for the Australian Government. In 1955, they found that the Aboriginal reserves along the western coast of Cape York in north east Australia contained the world's biggest bauxite deposit and in 1956 they formed Comalco to exploit this deposit, much to the dismay of the local Aborigines.[3]

In the meantime, another British company entered Australia by purchasing a newly discovered uranium deposit near Mt Isa in Queensland. This was Rio Tinto. The deposit was named Mary Kathleen, ironically after a woman who had just died of cancer, the disease to which uranium miners are most vulnerable. Rio Tinto then recruited its first Australian managing director from Conzinc.

Both companies ran uranium mines in northern Australia, and since Conzinc was flush with valuable mineral deposits, and Rio Tinto flush with money from its Canadian and Australian uranium operations, it was not surprising when the companies merged in 1962 to form the London-based Rio Tinto Zinc, with Conzinc Riotinto of Australia (CRA) as the manager of all their Australian operations. (In that year too CRA found iron in the Pilbara.)

CRA thus became a target for Aborigines protesting over the lands stolen by Conzinc and Comalco at Weipa, Mapoon and Aurukun in Queensland. What happened at these Aboriginal settlements is described in earlier chapters.

By 1976, CRA had begun a rapid expansion into even the remotest parts of Australia. The company regarded Aboriginal reserves as potential targets—and even drew up a list of what it regarded as 'prime targets'.

CRA targets thirty-nine Aboriginal reserves

CRA, in complete confidence that Aboriginal reserves were suitable targets for continual exploitation, commissioned a report on *all* the large Aboriginal reserves in Australia from

Harry Evans, the geologist who had brought the Weipa bauxite deposits to the attention of Conzinc. This report, made in 1976, listed the reserves in order of importance as 'exploration targets'. Out of some thirty nine investigated in some detail eight reserves were described as 'prime targets which should be given top priority in our future programmes.' These were eight of the largest Aboriginal reserves in the country, all of vital importance to the survival of Aboriginal communities and culture.[4]

The Arnhemland Reserve was given top priority, with zinc, lead and copper possibilities listed as well as uranium. The next seven were Groote Eylandt (Northern Territory), Forrest River (Oombulgurri, Western Australia), Northwest Reserve (Pitjantjatjara lands in South Australia), Petermann Range Reserve (Northern Territory), Warburton Mission Reserve (central Western Australia), the Central Australian Reserve (Western Australia) and the Daly River Reserve (Northern Territory).

It then listed nine reserves with 'fairly good mineral potential', including nearly all the Kimberley and Northern Territory reserves. It then mentioned ten reserves with low potential and, finally, twelve 'with little or no mineral potential.'

International pressure bites

RTZ, the London boss of CRA, had followed a policy of allowing CRA to be managed by Australians in most matters. It was happy at the quiet way CRA was making RTZ richer and richer.

Continual pressure has been applied to RTZ over its uranium mine in Namibia, established in defiance of United Nations sanctions, but it never had much pressure applied to it over its Australian involvements. RTZ thus reacted with shock when, in May 1978, a very active campaign was launched in London against the activities of its subsidiary, CRA, in Australia. CRA's 'targeting' of Aboriginal reserves was widely reported. The company was particularly concerned at the wide backing this attack received. The prestigious 'Survival International' organisation gave the criticism its full backing

Geographical Analysis of RTZ Income
(In Million Australian Dollars)

	Profit to RTZ Shareholders	Group Profit before Tax	Group Assets
Australia (CRA)	$65m (26.3%)	$250m (30.8%)	$1,754m (37.3%)
Niugini (CRA)	$20m (8%)	$126m (15.6%)	$ 661m (14.1%)
USA	$50m (20.1%)	$ 82m (10.1%)	$ 327m (6.9%)
Namibia	$34m (13.6%)	$ 87m (10.7%)	$ 268m (5.7%)
South Africa	$16m (6.4%)	$ 71m (8.8%)	$ 211m (4.5%)
UK	$28m (11.2%)	$ 54m (6.7%)	$ 690m (14.6%)
Canada	$23m (9.1%)	$109m (13.5%)	$ 575m (12.2%)
Others	$13m (5.3%)	$ 31m (3.8%)	$ 222m (4.7%)

(From 1980 RTZ Annual Report, converted into Australian Dollars at $1.60 equals one pound).

as did the well-known British charity War on Want and the environmental group Greenpeace.

The protest had been initiated by CIMRA—an educational group established in consultation with the North Queensland Land Council and other Aboriginal groups and individuals—to help get the voice of Aborigines and other colonised tribal peoples heard. CIMRA had a web of supporting and co-operating groups organised across Europe. Some of these groups were already in touch with American Indians but knew little of the situation in Australia; others were established specifically to support Australian Aborigines.

In the May 1978 protest, CIMRA and War on Want, with the full support of Survival International and Greenpeace (London), went to the Rio Tinto Zinc annual general meeting in London. The author of this book asked the RTZ Chairman, Sir Mark Turner, the following questions:

... We ask not what you are doing out of charity for Aborigines. No, Aborigines do not need charity but justice. When will RTZ recognise the natural rights of Aborigines to own and control their tribal lands, rights that are already recognised by such international bodies as the ILO?

In a recent report, the Chairman of Comalco reassured the public that the company worked in harmony with the Queensland Government on Aboriginal issues—at Weipa, Mapoon and Aurukun. The Queensland Government is internationally infamous for its treatment of Aborigines—especially recently at Aurukun. RTZ has taken 200 square miles of Aurukun tribal land for a future mine. Albert Chevalthun, an Aboriginal elder responsible for this land, said: 'Comalco never asked for this land ... part of this land is mine. It is our forefathers' land. We cannot give it away ... No, we don't want the money. We don't want the jobs. We don't want the company to take our land ... I still stand up. I am fighting for my land.'

Mr Chairman, do you intend to continue to support the infamous Queensland Government in your policies and to destroy this Aurukun land?

Would you and your executive be prepared to discuss the issues involved with Australian Aborigines if such a meeting were arranged by CIMRA and War on Want here in this country?

In response, Sir Mark Turner said that the document targeting Aboriginal reserves was confidential. He refused to answer the questions but denied that they had any basis in fact.

However, when he was further questioned by shareholders, he added that Lord Shackleton, the Vice-Chairman, would be going to Australia the next morning and would be asked to report back to him personally on these allegations. He further stated that Lord Shackleton could not be committed to meeting with Aboriginal leaders 'because they are so divided that it is difficult to know who are the leaders.'

Lord Shackleton did go to Australia. He avoided the waiting press and went for a one hour visit to Weipa accompanied by company personnel. At Weipa, he went on a guided tour of selected sights. He did not go to Mapoon or Aurukun. He found time only for a brief talk with a few Aborigines including the chairman of the Weipa South community and Mrs Joyce Hall, the Weipa delegate to the North Queensland Land Council.

The Aborigines were dismayed that they

Rio Tinto Zinc's well placed controllers

Rio Tinto Zinc, the owner of CRA, is one of the very largest diversified mining companies in the world. It has based its operation on the Anglo-Saxon settled former British colonies—such as Canada, Australia, United States and South Africa—and on Niugini and Namibia.

Its owners and controllers are represented in great part on its board of directors. In recent years these include:

a) International Financiers

The Oppenheimers South African multi-millionaires with wealth based on gold and diamond mines and who control De Beers, Stockdale, Anglo-American and Charter Consolidated. De Beers and its subsidiary Stockdale are very active in Australia.

The Rothschilds British and French multi-millionaires. The French branch controls the major supplies of French uranium, New Caledonian nickel mines and mines throughout Europe, Africa and Latin America. They have uranium interests in Queensland and in other parts of Australia. The British branch of the family has major interests throughout North America, in Amax and in Australian finance. Both branches of the family have interlocking interests with the Oppenheimers.

b) The British Establishment

The Queen is said to be a major shareholder, although her shareholdings are officially confidential.

The Conservative Party. The present Foreign Minister, *Lord Carrington*, was an RTZ director until he was appointed Minister. Former Prime Minister, *Anthony Eden*, was also a director.

Lord Assheton is a prominant Tory, as well as a director of Tanganyika Concessions—active in the Kimberleys and involved with the Argyle diamond mine with CRA.

Other political interests. Lord Shackleton, Vice-Chairman of RTZ, was also head of the Labour Party in the House of Lords. *Lord Byers* was head of the Liberal Party in the House of Lords. *Baron Green of Harrow Weald* was Chairman of the Trade Union Congress (the equivalent of the ACTU in Australia) and General Secretary of the National Union of Railwaymen.

Baron Guy de Rothschild with his wife, Marie-Helene de Rothschild, at the French Derby at Chantilly.

were only given a few minutes to talk to him, that they were not given notice of the meeting, and thus not allowed to arrange a proper meeting between Shackleton and the other dispossessed Aborigines. Mrs Hall said: 'I told Lord Shackleton that I wasn't happy with Comalco because our houses are no good and the wages too low.'

She told him that Comalco had caused many difficulties for them and that they needed royalties from the company, in order 'to fix up the mess'. Lord Shackleton told her, she said, to go and ask the Queensland Government, that it wasn't a company responsibility.

(Joyce Hall, a month later, addressed the National Aborigines' Day rally in Sydney. She declared: 'White people have taken too much from the blacks. We don't want money or riches, all we want is our land, we don't want it mined.')

Despite Sir Mark Turner's denial of any effective leadership among the Aborigines, in fact all the Aboriginal communities of North Queensland have united themselves into a land council with an elected executive. This land council has been empowered by the Aborigines to open negotiations with Comalco and other mining companies on Aboriginal lands to obtain, for the first time, a settlement between Queensland Aborigines and mining companies. (See Chapter 28.)

Sir Mark Turner in fact expressly stated that they would not recognise the North Queensland Land Council because it was not recognised by the Queensland Government. This is a stand also maintained by Comalco.

On hearing that Lord Shackleton was coming, the chairman of the North Queensland Land Council, Mick Miller, interviewed on the national ABC radio, 26th May 1978, stated:

If Lord Shackleton wants to come up and speak to me as chairman of the North Queensland Land Council, I would be very pleased to talk to him and take him to reserves where his mines have done a lot of damage to the Aboriginal culture, the Aboriginal style of life, and to show him the physical damage to houses and the land.

However, Lord Shackleton ignored this open invitation and did not meet with or contact the land council. He spent, indeed, far longer with the company 'experts' on Aborigines than with Aborigines.

On the basis of this trip, Lord Shackleton on his return to England denied there was any truth in the accusations made by CIMRA and War on Want against Rio Tinto Zinc.

First Aboriginal speaking tour of Europe

In October 1980, the North Queensland Land Council came to London to seek the meeting that Shackleton had not given them. They sent a delegation of three—Mick Miller, the council chairman, Joyce Hall representing Weipa, and Jacob Wolmby representing Aurukun. They sought a meeting of which a public record would be kept. At first RTZ would not agree but when the Aboriginal delegates toured Britain speaking on television, at public meetings and to RTZ workers, on what RTZ's companies were doing to Aboriginal people and their land, and when the delegation led a thirty-strong group of newsmen to the RTZ company office to present them with a bag of dirt ('for that is all they give our people') and to ask for a meeting, the company gave in.[5]

The meeting took place about three weeks later. In the meantime, the delegation carried out the first Aboriginal speaking tour of Europe which included a meeting with Billiton, which had mining interests on Aurukun, and Urange-

Mick Miller, Joyce Hall and Jacob Wolmby give the RTZ Secretary a bag of dirt and a notice of protest, London, 1978 (Jan Roberts).

sellschaft, which has mining interests near Doomadgee Aboriginal Reserve, on Westmoreland Station in North Queensland. Billiton undertook not to mine at Aurukun without Aboriginal consent.

At the RTZ meeting, the company invited along as its neutral observer the Dean of Windsor, —the private chaplain to the Queen. The Aboriginal delegation was accompanied by the director of the Anti-Slavery Society and by representatives of CIMRA and War on Want. Lord Shackleton was accompanied by another RTZ official and by two representatives of Comalco that it had had flown across from Australia.

Mick Miller informed them that they had been asked by the Weipa Aboriginal community to ask RTZ and Comalco to open negotiations with the Weipa community. Joyce Hall spoke strongly of the suffering that Comalco had brought her people.

But the two and a half hours of discussions were fruitless. Shackleton would admit that housing at Weipa was very poor, but nothing else. He maintained that it was not wrong for the company to take Aboriginal land if the State Government said that it was all right. They did, however, state that in the five weeks previous, they had doubled the money that they had committed for the welfare of the Weipa Aborigines over the previous ten years— one indication of the usefulness of such a campaign. He reiterated that they would not recognise the North Queensland Land Council as representing the Aborigines because the Queensland Government had not recognised it.

This meeting was valuable principally because it forced RTZ to treat Aboriginal objections seriously and helped provide a focus for the media. But it was only a breaking of the ground for a long campaign.

Strangers in their own land

The next stage in maintaining pressure on RTZ, and thus on CRA in Australia, was the preparation of a televised film, *Strangers in Their Own Land*, based on the first edition of this book, with much assistance from the Kimberley and North Queensland Land Councils. It was shot for Granada Television, under the direction of Chris Curling, maker of award-winning documentaries on apartheid such as *Last Grave at Dimbasa*. The film was made on location at Weipa, Aurukun, Oombulgurri and Noonkanbah. It was given national release in Britain in March 1979, and in Australia in May 1979. In England, it provoked an angry but ineffective response from RTZ that drew little publicity. In Australia, Comalco decided to prosecute the ABC for screening the film, even though the ABC had allowed Comalco the chance to defend itself in a debate immediately following the film, and had televised part of a Comalco film as well. Joyce Hall of Weipa, who had been featured in the British film and was one of the North Queensland Land Council delegates to RTZ in London, was at the studio to take part in the debate, but Comalco refused to take her part. Comalco have since been using the impending legal action to have the film withdrawn from public use in Australia.

Since then, in late 1979, a joint Kimberley and North Queensland Land Council delegation has been to Europe on a speaking tour, with a report on how CRA had entered Noonkanbah against Aboriginal wishes. Then again, in November-December 1980, a joint South Eastern and Kimberley delegation has been to Europe, again with much information on CRA, this time on how it has taken mineral exploration leases out on about 54% of Victoria including sacred sites, and on how in 1980, it took up Aboriginal lands at Argyle, Mitchell Plateau and Christmas Hill Station in the Kimberleys.

Reaction of CRA to national and international pressure

CRA showed obvious concern to mend their public image. The chairman, Sir Rod Carnegie, speaks often of the need for the company 'to be a good corporate citizen and a good neighbour.'[6]

He did this at the 1980 annual general meeting and, in the same speech, said that the company had made mistakes in the past but sought to learn from these in its Aboriginal policy. Senator Chaney, then Minister for Aboriginal Affairs, was much impressed. He called this speech 'a real step forward'.

In its exploration work, CRA developed new rules of consultation with Aborigines that showed more respect for Aboriginal culture than its earlier methods. On land claimed by Aborigines, it started to employ an Aboriginal Elder as a guide to make sure that sacred sites were not trespassed on or interfered with. It stated that it would consult before entering such lands.

The company's annual report for 1979, published in 1980, stated:

CRA's exploration in northern Australia often involves entering land in which Aborigines may have an interest. Aboriginal land holders are consulted before exploration is commenced on their land, and care is taken to safeguard sacred sites. The assistance of the relevant museum authority is also sought in order to avoid the unwitting disturbance of sacred sites.

CRA cite their 1979 exploration on Noonkanbah Station, where they employed an Elder and relinquished claims in three sacred areas. But what they do not say is that the Aborigines of Noonkanbah strongly objected in the Mining Warden's Court, to CRA securing exploration leases, and that they gave the Kimberley Land Council a message to send to CRA and to take to Europe in 1979: 'CRA get out. We don't want mining on our land' (for details of this and other CRA activities in the Kimberleys, see Chapter 22).

It is a small gain to have companies consult that would have previously ignored the Aborigines entirely. It does mean that sometimes sacred sites can be protected, even when they are not protected in State law.

But it seems that CRA is only prepared to follow this code of behaviour where it suits them. It did not suit them when they found their richest strike of diamonds right on top of a major Aboriginal sacred place at Argyle at the end of 1979. What happened is described in more detail in the chapter on the Kimberleys, but what concerns us here is the complete

violation by the company of its written pledge to respect Aboriginal sacred sites. Indeed Carnegie was pushed on this very point at the 1980 CRA annual general meeting. He was asked if he would respect Aboriginal sacred sites and he answered: 'I am not prepared to say that we will never mine in areas where there is controversy.'[7]

When the desecration by CRA of the dreaming place at Argyle was made known at the 1980 biennial meeting of the Institute of Aboriginal studies the company was condemned.

At the 1980 CRA annual general meeting Carnegie questioned the meaning of 'sacred' and said it was often distorted and used too widely. However this attempt can scarcely excuse the mining of the Argyle dreaming place against the wishes of most of the Warnum Community Elders. Carnegie cannot pretend to be a greater authority on the Aboriginal religion than the Aborigines. Also at this annual general meeting, he stated that CRA had to press ahead with mining because of the needs of the poorer nations. Since when have such countries needed diamonds? Only industrial diamonds serve a real need, and today these are manufactured by the thousands.

Aborigines at RTZ's annual general meeting

In May 1981 yet another international campaign focussed on RTZ's disregard of the rights of colonised peoples. The action in Australia began with Aboriginal delegates attending the CRA annual general meeting in Melbourne and questioning the company chairman, Sir Rod Carnegie, on his company's policy towards Aborigines.

Then two delegates flew to London. These were Joyce Hall of the North Queensland Land Council and Les Russell of the Aboriginal Mining Information Centre and vice-chairman of the South Eastern Land Council. They gave evidence at an *International Tribunal on RTZ and Indigenous Peoples.* Also present were lawyers representing Latin American Indians. One result of the evidence given was that the County of London authority decided to divest itself of

370,000 of its 375,000 shares in RTZ. It retained 5,000 in order to remain able, as a shareholder, to raise social responsibility issues.

The Aboriginal delegates then went on a speaking tour. At the end of May they attended RTZ's annual general meeting. Never before had this meeting been attended by any Aborigines. They had a dramatic impact. Their questioning of the new RTZ chairman, Sir Anthony Tuke, and Sir Rod Carnegie and the answers given by these directors deeply upset the shareholders. Questions were also asked on behalf of Namibians and South American Indians. The *Times* reported, 28th May 1981:

The crescendo came when two Aborigines, whose land had been earmarked for mining by CRA . . . made impassioned speeches. Mrs Joyce Hall told Sir Anthony: 'Aborigines have no rights. You should be ashamed of yourselves. My land is ripped, and nothing is given to me, because of your greed. You take the riches from the land which is like our own mother. God gave us that land.' Les Russell said, 'We came here because we had got nowhere with CRA.'

The *Guardian* newspaper reported (28th May) that the 'RTZ chief was shouted down by shareholders'. One shareholder 'claimed that he had never seen such a display of lies and obfuscation by company directors'. Finally

the meeting came to a halt when one shareholder, not representing any of the pressure groups present, stormed out, yelling at Sir Anthony that he intended to sell his Rio Tinto shares because of the information that had come to light. 'I find it totally incompatible that you are trying to safeguard your profits by upsetting people around the world, by desecrating land and by violating international law' he shouted. As shareholders spilled into the aisles, yelling at the board, and in some instances at each other, Sir Anthony's attempts to push through resolutions to adopt the annual report and to approve the re-election of directors was obscured.

However under questioning from the Abo-

riginal delegates, Sir Anthony did make some important commitments. He stated that the company would not damage or desecrate by exploration or mining any Aboriginal sacred place, burial ground, site or significance or sacred object. He also stated that they would always obtain the agreement of the Aborigines recognised as traditional land owners by the West Australian Museum or other State authorities before carrying out mining or exploration works. It remains to be seen just how well these promises will be kept. Certainly at Argyle diamond mine company geologists have confirmed that mining works will totally destroy the Barramundi dreaming place.

CRA's public relations campaign

CRA also has been conducting in its own defence a major propaganda campaign. Vast numbers of publications have been distributed— many through the Australian Mining Industry Council. Of these, Carnegie stated at the 1980 annual general meeting, 'we sponsored (through the Australian Mining Industry Council) booklets which have been widely used in schools because of their balanced arrangements.' (No mention that they may have been used because they were free!)

CRA is also distributing free a leaflet mostly on Aboriginal land rights entitled *Mineral Exploration: Social Aspects in the 1980s*. This leaflet talks of the prejudices against Aborigines but puts no arguments forward to counter them. In particular, it does not say Aborigines have any right to their land. Instead it argues against full Aboriginal land rights. It states that: 'many see this (the land rights legislation) as posing a threat to the ideals of a multi-cultural Australia and suspect that it will exacerbate racial divisions.'

It does not put forward any other view. It is particularly concerned with combating the idea that Aborigines have a right to the minerals under the land. It baldly states that minerals belong to the Crown as if this were a law of nature; perhaps because it knows that the Crown, the State, is willing to give them to

CRA. But, in Australia, the Crown took these rights from the Aboriginal inhabitants by the raising of Captain Cook's flag. CRA would know too that most of the coal mineral rights in New South Wales are held privately and that rights to some minerals in Victoria are privately owned. Companies wishing to mine these minerals have to negotiate with and to pay royalties to private owners. The companies do not campaign against this as they do against Aboriginal claims.

The real concern of CRA is evident when it says:

If Aborigines are given effective control over exploration access, vast areas of land with mineral potential may be denied to the owners of the minerals.

This begs the question of just who are the 'owners'. CRA is obviously concerned that Aboriginal ownership may affect their future profits.

In 1979, RTZ also produced a leaflet entitled *The RTZ Group and Aborigines*. This stated that Comalco's policy was to create an environment that will help Aborigines 'choose the lifestyle they wish to adopt, and the locality in which they wish to live.'

This was an extraordinary thing to claim. Obviously, they will not allow Weipa Aborigines the option of living on the tribal lands that they are now mining. This document also says that Mapoon land was of no mineral value. Comalco today extract the greater part of the bauxite they mine from Andoom on the former Mapoon Reserve. It says that Mapoon was

closed primarily on grounds of health and economics; but the Aborigines deny this and say they were told it was to help them 'assimilate' and 'progress', and that Comalco was coming to mine their lands.

International campaigns

Finally, a leaked document from the Ashton Joint Venture (Kimberley Diamond Mines), 56.8% owned by CRA, clearly showed that their public relations programme is *primarily* aimed against Aboriginal land rights.

The document, titled 'Public Relations Programme 1981' and dated November 1980, was written by Greg Walker, the group's public affairs manager. It states:

The public relations programme for 1981 will be concerned principally with the following issues:
1. Sustaining the Argyle Agreement with the Glen Hill Aboriginal community and isolating this agreement from the general debate on Aboriginal land rights while encouraging community acceptance of the company's policy towards its Aboriginal neighbours.

Only one other specific objective for 1981 was listed. This was to lobby 'decision-makers' against the setting up of an Australian diamond cutting operation underwritten by the profits from Argyle. Instead the company (at least the CRA component—Northern Mining, one of the partners, disagrees but it only has a 5% interest) prefers to export the stones uncut to the Southern African controlled C.S.O. or 'syn-

dicate' founded and controlled by the Oppen-heimers who are represented on the RTZ board.

These two objectives have been officially adopted and are now guiding the company's programme. How do they hope to achieve these goals? The leaked document goes on to say:

There is general consensus that the Ashton Joint Venture (AJV) should:
1. Undertake a broad public relations pro-gramme designed to establish a strong corporate identity.
2. Undertake a vigorous lobbying programme in State and Federal circles with a view to ensuring that our position regarding the Aboriginal issue and downstream processing is fully appreciated among key decision-makers.
This is consistent with our view that the path to success is not via a high profile partici-pation in the broadscale public debating of the Aboriginal land rights issue.

It is obvious from this that the company does not feel it can win a public debate. Instead it is intensively and privately lobbying Govern-ment ministers with arguments that presumably would not stand up in public.

This public relations programme is cur-rently being handled by Eric White Associates. The document explains how this company was selected. Submissions were sought from 'the two largest and most respected firms in Aust-ralia—International Public Relations (IPR) and Eric White Associates.' IPR's submission how-ever was rejected. One reason for this was, states the document:

IPR believe that those dedicated to securing a larger share of mining revenues for Aboriginals will ultimately succeed and that our best policy is to position ourselves to conduct these negoti-ations . . . given this view, it is difficult to see how that agency could effectively work towards objectives which it does not believe are attain-able.

On the other hand, 'Eric White Associates perception of the scenario with regard to our continued interaction with Kimberley Abo-rigines is in accord with our own.'

Interestingly, IPR already has the CRA account. This could indicate a difference of view within CRA. CRA's public relations budget is three million dollars in 1981. The Argyle budget is separate from this and amounts to $279,000 including a fee of $35,000 to Eric White, $15,000 for 'government relations' and about $50,000 to take journalists to the mine.

Finally the policy document states:

The threat posed by these two issues demands action by the company . . . If Kimberley Diamond Mines Pty Ltd can resist moves to meet Aboriginal compensation/royalty claims and deflect pressure for the establishment of a subsidised cutting industry, its savings in the long-term will be substantially greater than the proposed expenditure on the company's public relations programme next year.

The managing director of IPR, Mr John Fitzgerald, said afterwards that in their rejected submission,

we argued that the mining industry as a whole would have to come to terms with the Abo-riginal people and that until it did there could be no hope of an eventual settlement of the mining-Aboriginal struggle.

The rejection of these views by the Argyle consortium does not auger well for the future of race relations in the Kimberleys.

The payment the company is making under its so-called 'good neighbours' policy to Kim-berley Aborigines amounts on company figures to less than 0.05% of the expected annual income of the mine—which compares favourably with the 4.25% at Ranger and the still far higher royalties won by North American Indians. The real level of Argyle profits is still a closely guarded secret.[8]According to some industry experts with South African experience, CRA is publicly under-valuing its find to less than one quarter of its real value.

Rio Tinto Zinc is now also under attack from other directions. In 1980, at the inter-national Black Hills gathering of indigenous peoples, it was agreed that an international

Les Russell speaks for his land at Cambridge University, 1981.

campaign would be waged against Amax and CRA. This has now been endorsed in Australia by the Kimberley, South-Eastern, and North Queensland Land Councils and by the Aboriginal Mining Information Centre.

Rio Tinto Zinc is under attack for its new venture in Panama as well as its operations in Australia. In Panama, RTZ is embarking on a feasibility study for the construction of one of the largest copper mines in the world. This, the Cerro Colorado Project, is in the heart of the Guaymi Indian Territory, land occupied by 24,000 Indians whose very survival will be put at risk. In two pastoral letters, the country's Catholic bishops have judged the project as *morally unacceptable*, unless the Indians have a real and effective say in the shaping of the project and in all decision making, with real compensation and a real chance to survive culturally.

CRA and its parent company have been continually held responsible for their actions against tribal people around the world. The company's defence is usually that 'we do but obey the law of the country'.

This attitude is virtually that *if Australian law permits theft from Aborigines, then theft is an acceptable company policy.* For Aborigines, confronted by the power and wealth of companies like CRA, such a policy is a terrifying reality. They have watched as CRA exploration teams tramp, fly and drive all over their country, but today the dispossessed are gaining a voice that can be heard around the world.

Footnotes

1. *CRA Annual Report*, 1980.
2. *Age*, 22 August 1981.
3. David McLean, *The History of Comalco*, in *Mapoon Book Three*, Chapter 1.
4. H. Evans, memo to J. Collier, *Summary of Aboriginal Reserves in Australia*, internal CRA Exploration document, 15 December 1976.
5. *From Massacres to Mining* (CIMRA and War on Want, London, 1978), the first edition of this book was launched during this campaign by the North Queensland Land Council as documentary support for the tour. Lord Shackleton, Vice Chairman of RTZ, stated to the author that he found it 'compulsive reading'!
6. CRA's track record as a 'good corporate citizen' includes Carnegie's telexes in October 1977 to Canberra in which he threatened the Federal Government with a $250,000 international campaign for refusing to allow them, as a foreign company, to take over an Australian coal company. (*Age*, 8 April 1980). Eventually Carnegie backed down.
   In 1981 CRA also had serious litigation against it in the US for allegedly violating US anti-trust laws by taking part in a cartel to raise the price of uranium, and litigation against it in Europe for allegedly violating ECC anti-cartel laws on zinc and lead.
7. *The Australian*, 7 May 1980.
8. J. Roberts, 'The Glittering Prize', *Age*, 22 August 1981.

24 ABORIGINES CHALLENGE THE WHITE MAN'S LAW (GOVE, AURUKUN AND PORTLAND)

Nabalco challenged at Gove

It was at Gove at the place called Nhulunbuy that the white man came and settled down to work. My people thought it was very bad because they came and pulled down our sacred trees that my father's father used for hunting and dancing place. The Riratjingu and Gomaitji own this country . . . before the mining there were animals everywhere and it was a pretty place. Now it is ruined. We only got a few animals, and there are lots of beer cans and grog and it's dusty everywhere.[1]

The Aboriginal counter-offensive to the onslaught by the mining companies first took a strong national shape in 1969 when Nabalco, a company 70% owned by Alusuisse, and 30% by Gove Aluminium (which, in its turn, is 51% owned by CSR, 12.6% by Peko-Wallsend, 12.1% by AMP and by other, smaller share-holders) was granted bauxite strip-mining rights over 20,000 hectares (80 square miles) of Arnhemland Reserve, and a further 1,800 hectares for a mining town and waste pits.

Nabalco was granted a large part of the land of the Yirrkala Aborigines all around the Aboriginal Mission settlement, on a lease that does not expire until the year 2053. (They took over a 1958 Comalco lease after Comalco had decided to concentrate on Weipa.)

Alusuisse was delighted with its 'find'. They had just lost their main source of supply, and this lease would provide them with a firm foundation for their profitable empire for the foreseeable future. On this lease they would build their mining town and refinery and call it Gove.[2]

The Aborigines were not so delighted. They were not even consulted. But this time the missionaries (Methodists) were willing to support the Aborigines by helping them see if they could establish their right to their land through the courts.

This became a nationally publicised court case. If it had succeeded, it could have allowed Aborigines to reclaim their land nationally.

However, Judge Blackburn ruled against them. He stated that, despite precedents from other former English ex-colonies, in Australia the law is 'without regard to any communal native title'. The Federal Government supported this decision, insisting that mining was 'good' for Aborigines.

Several other efforts to use the white man's law have followed the Yirrkala precedent, and to date they too have all been failures, except in that they have achieved some publicity for the appalling situation of Australian Aborigines.

Aurukun goes overseas

One recent case was that of the Aurukun Aborigines fighting a consortium of Shell, Pechiney and Tipperary to stop bauxite mining on their land. Again this was a mission-assisted approach.

The legal case was based on the Director of Aboriginal Advancement being called a 'trustee' in the Queensland *Aborigines Act*. It was said that he had violated his trusteeship in agreeing

How Nabalco protects a Sacred Tree.

to mining at Aurukun without consulting the Aborigines or arranging any financial return for them. If won, it would have established a legal recognition of Aboriginal ownership of reserves in Queensland, but with the Government as a 'trustee' for the Aboriginal land. It was won in the Australian court, but was finally lost in the Privy Council (see Chapter 20).

Alcoa and the State of Victoria versus the Gunditj-Mara

The next major legal battle over a specific case of Aboriginal dispossession began in the Victorian Courts in 1980 and is still continuing at the time of writing.

This is centred on the building of an Alcoa smelter on land of great importance to the local Aboriginal community. They are attempting to use a law framed principally to protect Aboriginal 'archaeological relics' for the use of non-Aboriginal archaeologists, to establish legal recognition of Aboriginal rights over such sites. Since the Victorian Government refuses to introduce land rights legislation for the State, this legal action is one of the few ways open to the Aboriginal people of Victoria to establish a claim to some of their traditional lands. This action, if successful, could help establish a precedent for other States where the Aborigines are in a similar position.

The presumption of Victorians that there were no Aboriginal 'tribes' left in Victoria was shattered when the Gunditj-Mara people of the western Portland region began their fight to stop their ancestral lands being taken by Alcoa for a giant aluminium smelter.

They maintained their camp on the smelter site for six months in 1980 despite police harassment and company pressure.

There were on that land, as Alcoa admitted, traces of over sixty Aboriginal campsites and workshop areas. The Gunditj-Mara still came there to camp, hunt and fish, and teach their children their culture.

More importantly there are sacred sites, including a burial ground and the paths the

The Mara camp on their land to try to protect it from Alcoa at Portland, 1980 (Jan Roberts).

Spirits take from their burial ground to Deen-mhrr (home of the Spirits after death).

But in November 1980, Alcoa moved in its bulldozers. The people managed to stop one by throwing themselves in front of its wheels. Supporting environmentalists climbed on others and were arrested. But a fleet of bulldozers roared through their bush and cleared fire-breaks. Soon it was in flames—and the Aboriginal people wept.

Some days later, the police came and, on Alcoa's request, charged the Aborigines with 'trespass'. They were released on bail—on condition that they did not re-enter 'Alcoa's' site. When this came to court, one of the Aborigines charged stated: 'If you find us guilty of trespass, then you find Captain Cook guilty. If you find Captain Cook guilty, then the law doesn't exist.'

The court's decision was that since the Aborigines had a 'reasonable belief' that they were not trespassing, the charges were to be dismissed. The court also stated that the land was Alcoa's. Victorian law does not recognise any Aboriginal title to ancestral lands.

But there was one Act that the people were advised they could try to use to protect their land—the *Archaeological and Aboriginal Relics Preservation Act (1972)*. This states:

A person who wilfully or negligently defaces or damages or otherwise interferes with a relic or

carries out an act likely to endanger a relic shall be guilty of an offence against this Act.

A 'relic' was defined as anything 'pertaining to the past occupation by the Aboriginal people of any part of Australia'.

But between November 1980 and January 1981, Sandra Onus and Christina Frankland, two spokespeople for the Gunditj-Mara, failed utterly in trying to use this provision to protect their land before a Supreme Court judge, before the Full Court of the Supreme Court and the High Court.

It became clear that the Act was not passed with any intention of helping Aboriginal people protect their culture.

Justice Jenkinson put it plainly. He said that the relationship between Aborigines and their 'relics' (a word that in itself suggests that the people are dead) was of no concern to the *Archaeological Relics Act:*

Which seems to me to manifest no legislative concern for such a relationship, but rather to be directed to facilitating the scholastic and educational activities of a Western European community planted on alien soil.[3]

The major reason given by the judges for dismissing the action was the narrow ruling that *no-one* has the right to claim their interests are being damaged unless these interests are expressable in terms of the dollar. One judge, Starke, said that returned servicemen would equally have no right to take action if the Trustees of the Australian War Memorial in Canberra were defacing and damaging war relics that the servicemen considered practically sacred! Such action could only be taken by the official guardian of the common good, the Attorney-General. Private individuals without a financial interest 'are no more than concerned bystanders.'

Judge Starke likewise ruled of the Aboriginal plaintiffs:

Their interest, in my opinion, is entirely emotional and intellectual. They will no doubt be grievously and most understandably offended by interference with these relics, but in my opinion they are no more than concerned bystanders.[4]

By this ruling, the Victorian Supreme Court decided, in effect, that Aborigines cannot use this law to protect objects of spiritual, cultural or historical importance to them.

But in late 1981 a High Court appeal finally ruled that the Gunditj-Mara *could* claim special interest under the Relics Act. The Victorian Government Minister for Minerals and Energy responded by suggesting a change in the law to prevent further Aboriginal action. The struggle continues.

The Paul Coe case—the Aboriginal nation versus the Governments of Australia and Britain

Between 1977–79, unnoticed by the Australian public, what could well have been the most important legal case ever considered by Australian courts, was pursued by Paul Coe, an Aboriginal solicitor with the New South Wales Aboriginal Legal Service.[5]

He charged the Governments of Australia and Britain, in the name of his tribe, the Wiradjeri, other tribes and the whole of the Aboriginal community and nation, with unlawfully dispossessing the Aboriginal people of their lands and rights.

He first argued that Captains Cook and Phillip *unlawfully claimed* Australia contrary to the rights of the Aboriginal inhabitants. He said they 'wrongfully treated the continent as *terra nullius* (unoccupied) whereas it was occupied by the sovereign Aboriginal nation.'

Therefore, he sought from the court an injunction restraining the Australian Government from further disposing of Aboriginal lands until 'internationally recognised arrangements were made'. He claimed, in the name of all Aborigines, proper compensation for the losses inflicted illegally on them.

However, if the courts were to decide to presume that Australia had been lawfully claimed from the Aborigines, Paul Coe presented two alternative claims.

First, that if Australia had been acquired by peaceful settlement and therefore came under

British common law, this law would have protected Aboriginal lands and other possessions. Therefore, Aborigines were illegally dispossessed of their lands.

Second, if Australia had been acquired by conquest of the Aboriginal inhabitants, then the Aborigines, while losing their sovereignty, would have retained their rights of occupancy 'unless these were taken away by specific acts of prerogative'. But no such specific acts of prerogative were ever exercised. Therefore the Government 'unlawfully and contrary to the common law dispossessed certain of the Aboriginal people' of their lands.

Finally, it was pleaded that Aborigines had taken possession of the United Kingdom when they 'planted their national flag on the territory of the second named defendant' on 2 November, 1976, and of Australia when they raised the Aboriginal flag on 9 April, 1977 at Kurnell on the site of Captain Cook's raising the British flag to claim Australia.

This last plea highly annoyed the judges. Murphy said that this in particular exhibited 'a degree of irresponsibility rarely found in a statement intended to be seriously entertained by a court'.

Despite this somewhat illogical outburst by Murphy, Coe won both Murphy and Jacobs to his case. But the other two judges, Gibbs and Aicken, found against him. This was sufficient to defeat his appeal.

Coe was asking them to overthrow a previous court decision that his case was not suitable for court consideration. He was also asking them to consider alternative arguments not put forward before. If he had won his appeal, his case would have then gone on to another court for a decision.

Gibbs, with Aicken's support, said in judgement:

The annexations of the east coast of Australia were acts of state whose validity cannot be questioned.[6] Jacob explained further, *These are not matters of municipal law but of the law of nations and not cognizable in a court exercising jurisdiction under that sovereignty which is . . . challenged.*[7]

This suggested that the only appropriate forum for a decision on whether or not the occupation of Australia was, and is, illegal, since it violated the rights of the Aboriginal nation, is an international forum such as the International Court at The Hague in the Netherlands. Action before this court is enormously expensive.

The Judges then went on to consider Coe's alternative arguments.

Gibbs and Aicken found that Australia was *not conquered!* They stated:

It is fundamental to our legal system that the Australian colonies became British possessions by settlement and not by conquest . . . For the purpose of deciding whether the common law was introduced into a newly acquired territory, a distinction was drawn between a colony acquired by conquest or cession, in which there was an established system of law of European type, and a colony acquired by settlement in a territory which, by European standards, had no civilised inhabitants or settled law. Australia has always been regarded as belonging to the latter class.[8]

They found too that, unlike the Cherokee Indians in the USA, Aborigines were not a nation.

They have no legislative, executive or judicial organs by which sovereignty might be exercised. If such organs existed, they would have no powers . . . The contention that there is in Australia an Aboriginal nation exercising sovereignty, even of a limited kind (over its own people) is quite impossible in law to maintain.[9]

Gibbs, with Aicken's support, then considered whether Paul Coe had a case to say that British common law should protect Aboriginal land rights and religious land needs. They decided that his claims were inadequately worded and too vague. They wanted definite areas of land indicated and specific cases described. They suggested another approach to the courts with the claims put:

dispassionately, lucidly and in proper form.

[They said] it should not be difficult to select particular areas of land as a subject of a test case if that is desired.[10]

But since Coe had not presented his case in such a form, they dismissed his appeal, awarding the substantial costs against him.

Jacobs did not agree, although he too wanted to avoid the issue of land rights.

I wish . . . to carefully avoid any discussion or consideration of the problem of Aboriginal land rights and I only say the problem is one which is difficult and complex.[11]

But both Murphy and Jacobs agreed that the legality of the dispossession of Aborigines was questionable in common law, and that it had never been definitively settled in court whether or not Australia was peacefully acquired or conquered. Therefore, they stated, these were legitimate issues for Coe to bring to court.

Jacobs asserted that Coe should be

entitled to rely on the alternative arguments when it comes to be determined whether the Aboriginal inhabitants of Australia had and have any rights to land.[12]

Murphy allowed that the Privy Council in 1883 said that New South Wales was not conquered but

practically unoccupied, without settled inhabitants or settled law at the time it was peacefully annexed. [But] that view is not binding on us . . . The statement by the Privy Council may be regarded either as having been said in ignorance or as a convenient falsehood to justify the taking of Aborigines' land . . . It was a cardinal condition of a valid 'occupation' that the territory be terra nullius*—a territory belonging to no-one.*

He then quoted Professor J. G. Starke:

Territory inhabited by tribes or peoples having a social and political organisation cannot be of the nature terra nullius.[13]

He continued:

The extent to which international law of

occupation is incorporated into Australian municipal law is a question which would arise for determination in the proceedings (of Coe's case).

He quoted a ruling in international law in favour of the nomadic tribes of the Western Sahara (after recognising that Aboriginal tribes had traditionally-defined territories). This stated that the Sahara tribes had a right to the lands they travelled over and used.

Finally, he described the settlement of Australia. It was not a 'peaceful annexation',

the Aborigines did not give up their lands peacefully; they were killed or removed forcibly in what amounted to attempted (and in Tasmania almost complete) genocide.[14]

Murphy concluded:

the Plaintiff is entitled to prove that the concept of terra nullius *has no application to Australia . . . Whether the territory is treated as having*

been acquired by conquest or peaceful settle-
ment, the plaintiff is entitled to argue that the
sovereignty acquired by the British Crown did
not extinguish 'ownership rights' in the Abo-
rigines and that they have certain proprietary
rights (at least in some lands) and are entitled
to declaration and enjoyment of their rights or
compensation.

Thus all four judges found that *even if* it
were presumed that Australia had been legally
acquired by Britain and 'peacefully settled'
(facts on which they by no means agreed),
the taking of Aboriginal-occupied lands was
possibly illegal in common law and Aborigines
possibly entitled to restitution of these rights or
compensation. They left the door open for
another court case to determine this.

But this process is nearly prohibitively
expensive. The legal battles fought to date by
Aboriginal people to try to gain recognition
of their rights has already cost a small fortune.

The end results could well be just more
frustration. After all, they are having to fight
their cases in the courts and under the laws of
those they regard as invaders. They must win
their rights under laws framed in great measure
to protect the interests of the colonists.

The only alternative to trying further action
in Australia and to approaching international
courts, is to obtain from State and Federal
parliaments a change in Australian law so that
it explicitly recognises and restores to the
Aboriginal people their right to their land.

Other recent legal actions have included
that of the Oenpelli people who opposed
Queensland Mines using their land. This action
had to be suspended when the Federal Government announced that it would introduce
legislation that would act retrospectively to
invalidate any court decision in favour of the
Aborigines! [15]

These attempts to utilise Australian or
British law have merely confirmed that there
was little hope in these quarters to achieve what
some might have thought to be natural justice.

The New South Wales Legal Service and
other Aboriginal organisations are hoping to
utilise international law to embarrass the

Australian Government. Possible conventions
that could be utilised would include:

I.L.O. Indigenous and Tribal Population
Convention 1957, part 2, Article II:

The right of ownership, collective or individual,
of the members of the populations concerned
over the lands which these populations tradit-
ionally occupy shall be recognised.

These moves may follow the precedent of
North American Indians in recent years seeking
recognition by the world community as nations
in their own right.

'Change Australian law'—the Tent Embassy

The failure of the Yirrkala people's legal battle
showed many Aborigines throughout Australia
that they had little or no hope under existing
law of ever achieving justice. Therefore, they
had to change the law. Thus, after the Federal
Government's endorsement of the Alusuisse-
Nabalco mining lease, Aboriginal people from
all over Australia converged on Canberra for a
series of public demonstrations to demand
'Land Rights Now.'

They put up a tent embassy on the lawn in
front of Parliament House. This became a focus
for a national campaign for the recognition of
Aboriginal land rights. It remained up for six
months, during which time the police came at
least twice in great numbers to tear down the
tent. Again and again it was re-erected to the
great public and overseas embarrassment of the
Liberal/Country Party conservative Government.

A statement was made in Parliament that

The Government is not prepared to see a
separate race within a race develop in Australia,
with an embassy from the Aborigines to the
Government of Australia as if they were a
foreign power . . . the Aborigines, these bewil-
dered gentle folk of another civilisation whose
land we share. Today the savage apostles of
race hatred and division try to fan their prob-

*lems into issues calculated to harm our society
... We have a long way to go to help these
ancient people into the twenty-first century.*[16]

Eventually the Aborigines won a commitment from Whitlam, then leader of the opposition Labor party, to recognise Aboriginal
land rights if they came into office. This they
did shortly afterwards, and, in February 1973,
they announced the *Woodward Commission* to
prepare land rights legislation—but only for the
Northern Territory, not, as they could have
done, for all Australia.

The Labor Government did not act on this
issue with any speed, and made no moves to
give the control of Aboriginal affairs to Aborigines. Thus the Aborigines found they had to
keep maintaining pressure by such actions as a
national Canberra demonstration, involving
over 1,000 Aborigines, on February 28th,
1974—at the same time as the Queen was
opening Parliament.

Establishment of the Northern Territory Land Councils

One of the first concrete results of the *Woodward Commission* was the establishment of two
democratically constituted Aboriginal land
councils in the Northern Territory: the Northern,
based in Darwin, and the Central, based in
Alice Springs. These councils represent all
Aboriginal communities in their region. Their
immediate purpose was to advise and assist
Aboriginal communities in their preparation
of land claims and to assist in negotiations
with mining interests. These regional councils,
with their access to independent legal advice,
have now become a major force in the Aboriginal campaign for land.

The second *Woodward Commission Report*,
released in April 1974, recommended that all
Aboriginal reserves be returned to Aboriginal
ownership and be held by Aboriginal land
trusts.

It also recommended that vacant Crown
land (i.e. land not used by whites) be returned
only if an Aboriginal community could prove
traditional ownership *or need* for this land,

and that land now held by whites could only
be returned if the whites wished to sell.

It has often been overlooked that the
Woodward Commission recommended that

*the only appropriate direct response for those
who have lost their traditional lands is other
land—together with finance to enable that
land to be used appropriately, either for housing
or for some economic purpose.*

This was deleted from the bill by the Fraser
Government.

Woodward also recommended that mineral
rights were not to be restored to the Aborigines, but that they should get royalties and
have a veto. This veto could only be overthrown by a joint decision of both Houses of
Parliament that mining was 'required' in the
national interest. This was only partially
accepted by Fraser. The final bill laid down
that several major mining projects could not be
vetoed including the Ranger uranium find, and
that the Governor-General rather than Parliament should decide whether or not other
mining projects were required in the national
interest.

The land councils fought strongly for the
retention of full rights to minerals found in
Aboriginal lands. The Northern Land Council
stated:

*We believe that any attempt to compromise
in relation of this question of mining or minerals may largely undo the benefits of granting
to Aborigines the ownership of their land.*

But Woodward decided this with a compromise, for he was trained within British law.

Justice Woodward said of his decision:

*What I set out to do was to find the best
possible alternative that was politically viable.
My judgement is that if I had said they should
get mineral rights, the proposal may well have
fallen through. I tried to avoid unrealistic
recommendations.*[17]

The two legal systems

Aboriginal people see land rights law differently
from whites. Whites see it as the granting of

land rights; Aborigines see it as the official recognition of Aboriginal law.[18]

Contrary to the popular idea that Aborigines live in an anarchic state, they do have a very clearly worked out and binding legal system.

Blackburn, in his judgement over the land claim of the Yirrkala people, who were trying to stop Nabalco at Gove, found:

a subtle and elaborate system highly adapted to the country in which some people led their lives, which provided a stable order of society and was remarkably free from the vagaries of personal whim or influence. If ever a system could be called 'a government of laws and not of men', it is that shown in the evidence before me.[19]

Under their law Aboriginal people have definite responsibilities for particular areas of land, not vague mystical ties. Similar responsibilities are the basis of land laws in other societies, but not in the current western materialistic system. This makes land a possession which can be used solely for individual profit.

For Aboriginal people, their law not only pre-dates the arrival of whites but is still in existence regulating their lives. Many have never conceded the superiority of white Australian law.

Therefore, for them, the *Northern Territory Land Rights Act* was a victory in which the Balanda, as they call whites, recognised their ownership of their land in their own law.

However, it was unfortunately not as clear cut as that. There were major areas of Aboriginal land law that were not recognised. Mineral rights were not recognised. Much Aboriginal land was omitted, for Aboriginal title was recognised only for those parts of the Northern Territory left over after whites had had their selection.

Also, this Act set up a colonialist way of 'returning' land. The bill could have simply said that all Crown lands were Aboriginal in virtue of their prior occupation. This would have been far simpler. The Aborigines could then have stated who were responsible for which areas of land according to their law.

After this, the Aboriginal owners could have negotiated with whites who wanted to use any of these lands.

But what did happen was that, to the very great profit of the legal and anthropological professions, a system of white experts was set up to allot the tribal lands, to make decisions on Aboriginal law. (In saying this, I am not personally criticising the several exceptional lawyers and anthropologists that have worked with the Aboriginal people in the Northern Territory to help them regain their lands.)

The system set up was that Aboriginal Elders had to tell non-Aboriginal anthropologists many of their sacred stories, who had then to summarise these to a non-Aboriginal judge in a European court situation. This judge had then to say whether or not the Aboriginal Elders had proved they owned the land in Aboriginal law (in which law this judge is not qualified). This process violated Aboriginal privacy and coerced them into revealing the location of sacred sites. It was a process that could naturally be resented by a proud people.

The Pitjantjatjara expressed their pleasure in not having to go through this process under their *South Australian Land Rights Bill.* They said, 'We don't want committees to map our land.'[20]

This process also set an anthropological stereotype for land claims that failed to take account of the wide variation in the way Aborigines hold their land and to allow the disruption and adaptation caused by colonisation.

In addition, the *Northern Territory Land Rights Bill* reserved many powers to the Federal Minister, including that of the final acceptance of the judge's recommendations. Several powers were given to the Northern Territory legislature in violation of Aboriginal law, such as the granting of sea rights to Aboriginal fishing grounds and coastal areas (which often contained sacred places); the declaration of public roads over Aboriginal lands; free entry to Aboriginal lands for government employees without Aboriginal permission; even regulations for sacred sites.

Even the very concept of 'traditional owner' was westernised with 'ownership' or 'responsibility rights' confined often to fewer people than had these responsibilities in Aboriginal law.[20]

Another distortion crept in because most of the anthropologists and lawyers were men. This meant that the land rights of the Aboriginal women were neglected and their testimony under-valued.

Finally, the Northern and Central Land Councils were also set up under this law in a form not fully in accordance with Aboriginal law. The tensions this caused can be seen in the report on the Ranger 'Agreement' in the chapter on uranium mining.

Aboriginal people have, in the case of these land councils, brought them rather more under their own law, but not without strains. These strains have been more evident in the north rather than in the centre. The Northern Council came under the greatest amount of pressure from Government sources in the Ranger negotiations, particularly from the Department of Aboriginal Affairs which tried to shape the council in its own image, taking away as much as possible its accountability to the Aboriginal Elders.

The Central Land Council came under similar strains earlier. Geoff Eames, a lawyer who worked with this land council, reported:

For six months the Lutheran Church waged an extraordinary campaign against the Bill. [The Church argued that] Land Councils meant that non-owners would dictate to owners of land. It would cause fights, even deaths. If a clan wished to negotiate with a mining giant, then they would do so direct without the interference of a Land Council.[21]

But this attack meant that the Central Land Council went out many times into the bush and justified itself to the Elders, re-affirming the primacy of the traditional owners, the primacy of Aboriginal law, and this helped forge a council that belonged to the Aboriginal people.

Thus Aboriginal people have been challenging white law in recent years, either by

trying to argue within this law for the recognition of principles of natural justice or by campaigning for new laws that explicitly recognise their rights.

There are still possibilities of arguing within the law—but this may yet require an approach to the International Court in the Hague. The campaign to have the law changed is sure to strengthen. Already some changes have been effected in the Northern Territory and (as will be seen in the next chapter) in South Australia. But it may be difficult to effect further changes without changes in government in the other States and in Canberra.

Footnotes

1. *Aboriginal Children's History of Australia* (Rigby, 1977).
2. The company's operations in 1977 caused chronic pollution of the sea water with heavy metals and caustic soda, so that the Aborigines could not safely fish within 50 kilometres of their settlement – and this is despite it being the open sea. They also completely destroyed a valuable source of food for the Aborigines in the swamps that were once full of fish and crabs, but are now sterile, deadly wastelands of caustic red mud.
3. Full Court Judgement, Melbourne, 19 December 1980.
4. High Court, Melbourne, 12 January 1981.
5. *Coe v. the Commonwealth of Australia and Another*, 5 April 1979, Sydney, in Australian
6 - Law Reports 118, pp. 118-138.
15. See also p. 133.
16. S. Stone, *Aborigines and White Australians* (Heineman Educational, 1974), p. 236.
17. Speech at AIAS Land Rights Symposium, 21 May 1980, Canberra.
18. An excellent as yet unpublished paper on this was delivered at the 1981 AIAS biennial
19. conference: *Two-fella law* by Mark Drefus, NLC Field officer.
    Milurrpumis Case, p.267.
    Rev. Downing, AIAS Land Rights Symposium,
20. Canberra, 1980.
21. Geof Eames in paper delivered at same symposium.

25 STATE GOVERNMENTS AND LAND RIGHTS

There is today a concerted campaign against land rights in both Queensland and Western Australia. Although the Northern Territory is officially committed, by Federal Government decision, to supporting land rights, in practice its Government shares many of the prejudices of its neighbours to the east and west, and has, in fact, opposed in court nearly all the land claims made under the *Northern Territory Land Rights Act.*

Tasmania and Victoria have not recognised Aboriginal land rights (apart from nominal areas at Framlingham and Lake Tyers in Victoria). Their Governments have turned a deaf ear to all Aboriginal requests for land rights. South Australia has recognised the land rights of the Pitjantjatjara peoples alone. New South Wales has committed itself to restoring Aboriginal land rights but so far has not passed any legislation to do so.

Queensland

The Queensland Government has declared a policy of speeding up assimilation by closing down all the reserves. They have stopped the Aboriginal Lands Fund Commission buying property for dispossessed Aborigines on the grounds that they are opposed to solely Aboriginal independent ventures. Bjelke-Petersen, the State Premier, wrote to the Prime Minister on 19th January 1977:

My Government's policies ... are specifically opposed to the permanent development of areas by Aborigines and Aboriginal groups in isolation.[1]

The Minister for Lands, Mr Tomkins, explained this refusal at the time:

If this programme extended to north Queensland, it would create a 'black state' across the whole of northern Australia—surely apartheid in the extreme and an introduction of the South African Bantustan policy to Australia, a situation the Queensland Government will not

tolerate ... It concerns me not because they are black but because this area would be allowed to become a burden on Australian generosity.[2]

He further said that it would be 'harmful' for the Archer River Aborigines to be allowed their own cattle station on their tribal lands although he allowed that they were 'good employees, good horsemen and musterers.'[3]

Premier Bjelke-Petersen explained in 1978 to the Aurukun Council that they had lost land rights through conquest:

Another thing I want to say ... in relation to when you say it's your land ... This sort of thing happens all over the world. There is no country without it. This country's been taken by this country. Germany has been taken by this country. Russia has taken this country. You can't claim it's yours.[4]

In other words; Give up! Don't you know you are conquered?!

The Queensland Land Minister, Mr Tomkins, said:

It's all very well to say Aborigines own Australia because they were here first, but we think that if they want to get hold of certain lands they should do it the same way as whites—work, make money, buy a block of land, and pay it off.[5]

In July 1976, the Queensland National Country Party held a conference in Cairns, at which the State Minister for Aboriginal Affairs, Mr Wharton, put the motion:

As the Aboriginal Land Rights (NT) Bill 1976 is a racial deterrent to investment and development and encourages Aboriginal enclaves to be established as permanent units, it constitutes a serious threat to Australia as well as the Northern Territory ... and should be withdrawn and abandoned.

This motion was easily carried.

Queensland also uses national parks, forestry reserves and 'wilderness areas' to thwart Aboriginal claims to land and to pit environmentalist against Aborigine.

For example they declared the Archer River pastoral property, that the Aborigines were trying to buy, a 'national park'. The *Forestry Act* that governs State Forests bans all normal Aboriginal living activities such as hunting, gathering, building huts. (The same happens in other States.)

Western Australia

On the 150th anniversary of the colonisation of Western Australia, Ken Colbung, as a traditional leader of the Bibelmun tribe and head of both the Aboriginal Lands Trust and Legal Service, gave the Governor of the State an eviction notice dated 31st December 1978.

This invited the Government to negotiate with the Aborigines of the State. It concluded:

This should not be seen as a threat to you but as a reminder of your living obligations at a time when you are celebrating a lifestyle born out of the dispossession of our land.[6]

Charles Court, on behalf of the Government, answered:

The Aboriginal people, whether as a race or as tribes or as individuals, do not have by reason of their Aboriginality any legal claim to the territoral land of Western Australia. Nor do they have any moral claim . . .[7]

An Aboriginal Lands Trust, set up by a previous Labor Government, controls and manages the Aboriginal reserves, but this is little more than an advisory body. The State Government retains final control in all important aspects such as permitting mining and issuing permits to enter reserves.[8]

The Western Australian Government indeed claims that the 'granting' of Aboriginal land rights to reserves would be morally wrong for it would create a South African apartheid and Bantustan situation.[9]

A senior Liberal Party member in Western Australia was quoted as saying: 'The fight for the north has begun. If we don't hold on, the

Statement of Reg. C. Johnston, Fullblood Tribal Spokesman for Menzies.

I'm really concerned about the Aboriginal sacred ground at Noonkanbah. I would like to ask Mr Charles Court what happened to the promise he made at Noonkanbah just recently to the Aboriginal people that our sacred ground would be protected, and yet he's allowed the mining companies to go on our sacred ground now. The sacred ground of the Aboriginal people is supernatural, supreme of God, supreme to the Aboriginal peopel in their belief.

The Aboriginal people and their sacred grounds and their burial grounds and their beliefs was here long before any anthropologists ever came to this continent. I challenge and I ask the anthropologists, did the Aboriginal people and their sacred beliefs and their sacred grounds exist in the first place? I challenge them to come to me and ask me these questions. I'm not as educated as them but at least I'd be able to tell them where I existed from in the first place, through my ancestors in the past, right up to the present moment. Mr Court and his anthropologists are trying to imprison and destroy the Aboriginal people's sacred sites, not only at Noonkanbah but all over the State of Western Australia.

I know the Aboriginal law there at Noonkanbah. Over thousands of years the sacred sites there have been sacred to the Aboriginal people of Australia because the Aboriginal people of Australia communicated with all the people. They communicated with the rest of Australia and their parliamentarians before the white man came into existence. The white man doesn't know what Australia is. Australia is made of many names.

Part of a statement in support of Noonkanbah by Reg. C. Johnston, Tribal Lawman who speaks for the Menzies area, W.A. 20th June 1980.

blacks could take over right through the Territory and Queensland.'[10]

Western Australia has, if anything, more repressive laws than Queensland controlling access onto Aboriginal reserves. Since the Aborigines of Oombulgurri Reserve recently refused admittance to two mining companies onto their reserve (De Beers' Stockdale and

BHP's Dampier Mining), the State Government gazetted extremely repressive laws. These came into effect in 1979.

Under these laws, Aborigines have no legal right to give anyone permission to visit their communities on reserves or reserve lands, nor to refuse anyone entry. The issuing of entry permits can only be done by the Minister for Community Affairs in the Western Australian Government. This is despite Aboriginal affairs in this State being officially under the Federal Government.

What now happens in practice is that the Federal Minister for Aboriginal Affairs fully co-operates with the West Australian Government in policing the reserves. Normally a blind eye is turned to people going on and off Aboriginal reserves with Aboriginal council permission as before.

But the new regulation is being selectively used. In 1979, the Federal Minister for Aboriginal Affairs, Senator Chaney, personally ordered reluctant police to arrest two women who had gone to Oombulgurri with the Aboriginal council's permission to discuss mining matters with the community and to give them factual information on diamond mining. (CRA has a diamond exploration lease on Oombulgurri.) One of the women was the author of this book. There was no Aboriginal complaint against these women. However neither had the Minister's permit, only the permission of the Aboriginal people whose land it was. This was the first time this new regulation had been used against the guests of Aboriginal people.

In 1980, the Government used the new regulation to enable at least one of the companies previously excluded by the Aborigines to enter Oombulgurri Reserve without the people's permission. This was Dampier Mining, owned by BHP.

In self-defence, the Aboriginal people of the Kimberleys have organised their own land council to unite and strengthen their communities in the face of governmental intransigence.[11]

There are also moves to organise a land council in the Pilbara where, the 'Nomads' (as

they call themselves) of Strelley Station have long been at the centre of an Aboriginal movement uniting Aborigines from the many widely scattered communities centred around the Western Desert and Pilbara. (More of their story is told in the final chapter.) But nearly all the Pilbara is now the reserve of transnational mining companies.

Their struggle first started with walk-offs from the white-owned cattle stations after the Second World War. They joined together to support themselves through small-scale mining and to purchase their own cattle stations. This they did—to find the first they purchased made into an Aboriginal reserve under the control of the State Government. Thus was created the only Aboriginal reserve, Yandeyarra, in the heart of the Pilbara. They have had to counter every kind of Government obstruction and have overcome them.

Aboriginal people in the south do not yet have their own land council—but those of the centre are united in the Pitjantjatjara Land Council with others of their people in South Australia and the Northern Territory. The Pitjantjatjara Land Council represents the Pitjantjatjara, Yankunyatjara and Nggaanyatjarra peoples.

This land council sent deputations to Perth, but they were told: 'Look if we granted these rights, blacks all over the State would want the same'. Phillip Toyne, solicitor for the Council said: 'The mob in Perth are called 'The Cement Mob'—they are very hard.'[12]

The division of the Pitjantjatjara lands by State boundaries is meaningless in their law. But it means that they are subjected to three different sets of State laws and endless difficulties.

Northern Territory

The Northern Territory, up until 1978 governed from Canberra because it had too small a population, has now its own government. This is already regarding Aboriginal land rights as a test-case for exerting its control.

In 1977, Dr Letts, the Chief Secretary for the Territory, repeatedly used the threat of a white backlash to try to stop the *Land Rights Bill.* He told the Fox Inquiry that Aboriginal land rights, if granted, would 'invite massive demonstrations of civil disobedience . . . whites would invade the Aboriginal territories without asking the Aborigines'.[13]

Fox replied that he considered these remarks inflammatory.

Northern Territory Aborigines have also asked for rights over sea-waters off their land for two kilometres out to sea, for the coastal peoples have sacred stories in the sea and in the rocks and islands, and rely on fishing for much of their foods.

Again, the whites threatened a backlash. The chairman of the Northern Territory Fishermens Association said, 'We have racial harmony up here at the moment, but the whole Territory will be up in arms if Aborigines are given these rights.'

Robertson, a member of the Northern Territory Assembly, stated,

'the Aboriginal Land Rights (NT) Act . . . *is in my view a most destructive, derisive* [sic] *and unjust piece of legislation.*

*Just entitlements of **traditional** [his emphasis] Aboriginal people over **traditional** [his emphasis] Aboriginal land is one thing, deliberate apartheid is another . . . If we were already a State, there would be no Federal Aboriginal Land Rights Act. The longer we remain a colonial outpost of the Federal Government, the more such laws they will impose on us.*[14]

The Northern Territory Assembly secured from the Federal Government the right to pass supplementary legislation to the *Land Rights Bill.* So they immediately proposed ordinances controlling entry to Aboriginal land, providing for 'authorised Aborigines' who would be appointed by themselves to control entry, removing Aboriginal rights to use bore-water on pastoral properties, restricting in many ways the rights of Aborigines on their tribal lands.

Roger Vale, a right-wing Assembly member who, like Bjelke-Petersen, the Queensland Premier,[15] has interests in oil, natural gas and uranium, said that the land rights legislation

'places the heavy hand of stagnation on all sectors of development in the Territory; mining, pastoral activities and tourism.'

However, this was obviously an exaggeration. Aborigines did not have their rights restored to them over most of the Territory. Those living on cattle stations had no provision made for them to reclaim their land. There was no provision for those in towns. They are the forgotten people.

All the *Northern Territory Land Rights Act* allowed them to claim were the existing reserves the few Aboriginal-owned cattle stations, and the 'crumbs' that the whites had let fall from the table after they had divided up the Territory. Obviously, all the best lands were already taken by the pastoralists—and could not be legally reclaimed by the Aborigines. There is a possibility that Aborigines may be able to claim these cattle stations when their leases come up for renewal, but this is by no means a certainty.

The unremitting hostility of the Northern Territory Government to Aboriginal land rights has been clearly obvious in their recent actions. It has acted to exclude claims by Aborigines to areas near the major white settlements. It has vastly expanded the town boundaries of Darwin, Katherine, Tennant Creek and Alice Springs. Darwin is now officially three times the size of Greater London. It did this in the midst of the Kembi claim to tribal lands near Darwin, and effectively halted their claim.

In May 1981, the Northern Territory Government announced a freeze on providing special purpose leases to Aborigines until those already holding such leases make 'adequate and rational' use of them. It stated too that Aboriginal organisations will have to pay for them in future. In Alice Springs alone nine applications from the Tangentyere Council, representing the Aborigines living in and around the town, were frozen. Three of these were for sacred site protection, four for permanent housing and two for housing for transients.

While preventing about 200 Aborigines from benefiting from housing and from protecting

sacred sites, the Northern Territory Minister for
Lands, Mr Jim Robertson, sent a team to
demolish temporary Aboriginal housing and
lavatories on an 'illegal' camp outside town.
He stated that Aborigines had 'ring-barked'
the town with their camps and sacred sites and
that he would 'bring the full rigour of the
law to put an end to this nonsense.' It had
been reported that the town plans an arti-
ficial lake that will cover one of the Aboriginal sacred sites.

While all this was happening in Alice Springs,
at the other end of the Territory the Government announced plans to help mining companies
move into the Arnhemland Aboriginal lands
and onto Aboriginal lands elsewhere. All
exploration leases granted prior to the *Land
Rights Act* had been frozen but remained
exempt from Aboriginal veto. These leases
cover vast areas of Aboriginal land. They are
now threatening Aboriginal communities who
had thought themselves secure.

All this was summed up in a powerful letter
sent by the Central Land Council to the Prime
Minister on 17th June 1981.[16]

Ayers Rock, tourism and land rights

Tourism is scarcely being seriously held back
by Aboriginal land rights. Take, for example,
the scandal of the national parks. Tourism is a
major threat to Aboriginal people for it brings
many whites who do not know Aboriginal law
onto their land. These people can unwittingly
trespass on sacred sites, interrupt important
ceremonies, perhaps vandalise Aboriginal pain-
tings. Some believe that the Kakadu National
Park, forced on the Aboriginal community as a
condition of the return of their land,[17] may prove
as great a threat as the Ranger uranium mine in
the long run, for it allows most of this region to
be 'developed' for non-Aboriginal tourists.
Aborigines are also under pressure to agree that
Coburg Peninsula be declared a national park.

Perhaps the worst example of what this can
mean is Ayers Rock. Despite its well-known
sacredness to Aboriginal people, they failed
in their land claim for it. Mr Justice Toohey
said of this in his judgement:

*[Ayers Rock] and Katatjuta [Mt Olga] are both
places of enormous significance not only to
the local claimants generally but for a wide
range of Aboriginal peoples . . . the attachment
of all Aboriginal witnesses to both places was
obvious.[18]*

But he could not award it to them because
in 1958 it was removed from the local Aboriginal reserve and made into a national park as
a result of a long campaign to open it to the
tourist business. (Only unassigned crown land
can be claimed under the *Land Rights Act*).

In an appeal to the Prime Minister, two
traditional owners, Nipper Winmati and Peter
Bulla, said:

*Ayers Rock and Mount Olga has always been
ours. The National Park has been there only a
few years. We do not want to steal anything.
We are not greedy. We want everybody to know
that by Australian law as well as Aboriginal law,
Ayers Rock and Mount Olga is our land. We
appeal to Mr Fraser to do what is right. We ask
all Australians to help us.*

*If we have freehold title, we are happy for
there still to be a National Park, we can give our
word on that.[19]*

Needless to say, their appeal was ignored.[20]
The Northern Territory Government instead
announced a $35 million tourist development
scheme for the Rock. Qantas and Ansett are
advertising it widely. A major solar electricity
scheme has been proposed near the Rock. The
United Permanent Building Society is claiming
proprietary rights over the Rock as an advertising logo. So much for Aboriginal land rights
versus tourism!

South Australia

This State is the only one to enact its own significant land rights law, but it is confined to
only one of the many tribal groupings in the
State. The others still have nothing.

The *Pitjantjatjara Land Rights Bill* was
initiated by the Dunstan Labor Government
which fell from office before passing it into law.
After a vigorous campaign by the Pitjantjatjara,

including a protest convoy by 150 representatives who came from their desert lands to camp in the heart of Adelaide, the Liberal Government passed it into law nearly intact.

This bill has one great advantage over the Northern Territory's in the eyes of the Pitjantjatjara. It cedes their lands without them having to bare their secrets to anthropologists and courts. They say, 'We don't want committees to map our land. That bill is our true word.'[21] They are pleased too that they don't have to tell the mining companies exactly where all their sacred places are—as Aborigines have to in the Kimberleys and the Northern Territory if they are to have a hope of protecting these places. Instead a company has to submit to the Pitjantjatjara maps of proposed company works. The Aborigines then specify which areas the company may enter.

A woman delegate of the Pitjantjatjara Land Council spoke in her language at the International Land Rights Symposium held in Canberra 1980. In translation, what she said was:

We have been very sad about our land. Our dreaming has made this land. Our dreaming comes from our land. All this a long time ago.

Beforehand we were very happy in Australia. We had our word or dreaming, and we were very happy about that.

Other people came—they came on camels and they did bad things to us . . . because of this our fathers and mothers were very sad because others were hitting us and our law was broken by the confusion . . . because of this, things have been very bad all over Australia.

The Pitjantjatjara living in South Australia won recognition of their title to about 100,000 square kilometres of their desert tribal lands in October 1980. (This is about one tenth of the State.) The title to this is vested in the 'Anangu Pitjantjatjara', comprising all the Pitjantjatjara and Jankuntjatjara men, women and children.

Their title includes the right to have mining companies negotiate terms with them for entry onto their lands and for mining and royalties. However, they are not permitted to veto a mine. Their title to the minerals in their lands is not fully recognised.

If they cannot agree with the proposals of miners, then the Government will appoint an arbitrator, a judge, who has to weigh the survival of the people's culture against the economic benefits to the State.

This is a change from the bill proposed by the former Labor State Government. In that the Aborigines could veto a mine but could be over-ruled by a joint sitting of both Houses of Parliament.

The Pitjantjatjara have tribal lands further to the south which they have not yet recovered. Parts of this land have been permanently poisoned and devastated by their use as testing grounds for British atomic bombs. South of these testing grounds are the impoverished and landless Aboriginal communities of Yalata and Ceduna. To the east are many other Aboriginal communities, nearly all are landless.

The Mintubi opal field, despite being on traditional lands, will not go back to the people, but it will pay part of its royalties to the owners in Aboriginal law.

The Pitjantjatjara living in South Australia are united to their people in the Northern Territory and Western Australia through the Pitjantjatjara Land Council based in Alice Springs. This council in fact unites the Pitjantjatjara, Yankunyatjara and Ngganyatjarra peoples.

So far, most of the Northern Territory lands of the Pitjantjatjara and Ngganyatjarra have had their Aboriginal title recognised with the exception of Mt Olga and Ayers Rock. But they have got nowhere in Western Australia.

Neither have the Yankunyatjara had their rights restored. Their lands lie more to the east, and are taken by cattle stations which they cannot reclaim under the *Northern Territory Land Rights Act.*

New South Wales

Although a New South Wales Aboriginal Lands Trust was set up in 1973 to hold title to the reserves, this did not recognise the rights of local Aboriginal communities to hold their own titles to their own land but instead acted more like a landlord. Nor were the New South Wales Aborigines able to claim non-reserve lands even if these were their traditional lands.

In October 1977, over 200 community representatives met to form the New South Wales Aboriginal Land Council, and, meeting with the State Premier Mr Wran, they sought both recognition that New South Wales was their land in the first place and land for their communities.

A Legislative Assembly Select Committee has since reported. In July 1980, it recommended the recognition of Aboriginal claims based not only on 'traditional' but also on 'need' grounds, for freehold, crown and leasehold land. These recommendations are far more sweeping than the *Northern Territory Land Rights Bill* which only allowed traditional claims on crown land.

This report recognised that in New South Wales, the destruction and fragmentation of Aboriginal society had been so severe that the normal definition of traditional lands could not apply. They recommended that Aboriginal land rights should include mineral rights. Freehold titles should be given, to be held collectively by groups.

Finally, they suggested that the State set aside six to eight per cent of State tax revenues (about $10 million in 1980) to purchase the land that is to be returned.

However, in January 1981, there is concern that these recommendations will not be made law before the next elections.

Victoria

It has been generally presumed by the Victorian Government up until now that Aboriginal people in Victoria are 'assimilated' and have lost all real interest in their land. Yet in Victoria there are more Aborigines than there are in South Australia. The Aboriginal population is around 15–18,000, and there are at least as many Aborigines in Victoria for its area as in any part of northern Australia.

In 1980, the South-Eastern Land Council was formed by the Aborigines to actively pursue the restoration of Aboriginal rights in the Victorian region. (It utilises tribal boundaries rather than the State's.),

Official alienation of Aborigines from their own country is obvious in Victoria, where Aboriginal tools, even if made by living Aborigines, are classified as 'relics' and are officially crown property.

In those parts of the State that are as yet undisturbed, there still remain many Aboriginal sacred and archaeological sites. Aboriginal people in Victoria have become accustomed to keeping these places, and the surviving parts of their culture, secret in order to preserve what they have.

Aboriginal claims have often been voiced to such parts of the State as the Grampians. Yet the Aboriginal sites of the Grampians remain the preserve of the tourists and not of the Aborigines. Areas such as the Barmah Forest on the Murray are also of the greatest importance—and often claimed—but all their claims fall on the totally deaf ears of the State Government.

Aborigines officially only have their claims recognised to two small areas, at Lake Tyers and at Framlingham. Otherwise they have no land rights.

Part of the Grampians in Victoria where Aboriginal sacred places are threatened by CRA's drilling (L. Russell).

There is no legislation to protect sacred sites —only to protect 'archaeological relics'. Even these are not protected for Aboriginal people but for the study of white Australians. This was the ruling of a judge in 1980 during the determined fight of the Mara people against the siting of an Alcoa smelter on their land (see previous chapter).[22]

At the time of writing (June 1981), the Victorian Government remains determined not to recognise Aboriginal land rights. Two private members bills—one to give back a nearby forest to the Framlingham people, the other to initiate the study of an appropriate land rights bill for Victoria—were both defeated in 1980.

Tasmania

There are about 4,000 Tasmanian Aborigines, most descended from those who survived the massacres. They are still fighting for some recognition of the right to their land. They have won recognition from the State and Federal Governments who officially had termed them 'extinct', but not the return of any land excepting Trefoil Island, a small mutton-bird island, bought for them by the Aboriginal Land Fund Commission.

They are asking for the restoral of all the mutton-bird islands, crown lands and sacred sites.[23]

The Australian Capital Territory

The Australian Capital Territory has no land rights legislation. This is despite having a large Aboriginal settlement of about 160 people at Wreck Bay, part of the Jervis Bay Territory acquired to be a port for Canberra.

This was an Aboriginal reserve between 1954 and 1965. In 1971, all the 'non-residential' land of the former reserve was made into part of the Jervis Bay Nature Reserve mostly for the use of non-Aboriginal holiday-makers. Both of their beaches were taken and they were left with just the headland between them. White holiday makers stream through the main street of this Aboriginal community to get to these beaches. This invasion of Abo-riginal privacy is for them like tourists trampling through a white person's home without as much as a knock on the door.

There has been strong protest about this. The Aboriginal community has been continually pressing for the land they were using before 1954—only part of which was made into a reserve—as well as for the return of the land they lost in 1971.

In 1981, these Aborigines still do not have land rights. They have been treated like dirt swept under Canberra's carpet.

Footnotes

1. Bjelke-Petersen, letter to Prime Minister Fraser, 19 January 1977.
2. *Sunday Mail*, 6 March 1977.
3. *ibid.*
4. Speech of 11 August 1978, reported in *Sydney Morning Herald*, 23 August 1978.
5. *Courier-Mail*, 6 March 1977
6. *Notice to Quit*, Ken Colbung to Governor of Western Australia, 31 December 1978. Reprinted in *Natural People's News*, nos. 2, 3 (CIMRA).
7. Charles Court, letter to Ken Colbung, reprinted as above *Notice to Quit*.
8. See also p. 149.
9. *Age*, 22 August 1979.
10. *Daily News*, 28 March 1980.
11. See also pp. 139, 189-90.
12. Philip Toyne at Land Rights Symposium, AIAS, 1980.
13. *Central Australian Land Rights News*, February 1977.
14. *Central Australian Land Rights News*, July 1977.
15. *Under Investigation: the Business Empire of Bjelke-Petersen*, 1976.
16. See the *National Times*, June 28-July 4, 1981, p. 14.
17. See also page 129.
18. Justice Toohey, April 1979.
19. Statement dated 10 April 1979 in author's possession.
20. *Age*, 11 April 1979; *Sun*, 11 April 1979.
21. Reported by Rev. Downing to AIAS Land Rights Symposium, Canberra, 21-22 May 1980.
22. See Judgement of Jenkinson, p. 166 above.
23. Michael Mansell, *History of Land Claims by Tasmanian Aborigines* (1980).

**Statement of Darson Wumi,
Fullblood Aboriginal Tribal Elder
of Jigalong Community.**

*Me and my people of Jigalong, we put all
this letter down and who's going to help
us? We afraid what Government's doing
to our sacred sites and law at Noonkanbah.
The sacred law at Noonkanbah links up
with us. We afraid Government will come
along here, do same thing to us, our sacred
sites, the law here. We Aborigine people
try Australian Government, we try, Australian Government never help, and might be
who's going to help us? No-one. We just
about lose the Australia all over the place.
Australian Government should stand for
Australian people, Aborigine people. Why
we don't get help? We got all sort of Aborigine culture and law so why Government
say blackfella's law not true? He's there,
he's law there. This like we signed by the
Aborigine law, we, from grandfather, way
back, father, grandfather, old, right back
from the beginning. Who create 'em this
world, this law? This blackfella we under
the law so if we lose this, give it to white
men, mineral and something like that to
Government, I can see that we can lost
something, everything. So we got to stand
really hard against your Government. We
have tried Government of Australia good
enough, so please, we put 'em through
and make sure and ask Governments from
over sea he might be help us. Chinese
might help us, we just asking, and America,
and Russia, please. We're crying here for
our law. Break through in the law, please.
That's what we like, we're asking three
place, yes or no, please can you help us?
We just about push away from Australian
Government. We're asking good enough
here.*

Darson Wumi,
Tribal Elder, Jigalong Community, W.A.
24th June 1980.

legislation, because it is already being used by
white people.

This clause was a disaster for the Aboriginal
people living around Alice Springs. They were
the only Aboriginal people to have their claims
heard before Whitlam fell. Their claims were on
the basis of need and dispossession rather than
on a traditional basis. Since then they have
repeatedly asked Fraser on his visits to Alice
Springs for their land, but to no avail.

In addition, against the express recommendation of the Fox Inquiry, the Ranger
project area of 83 square km was placed under
the *Atomic Energy Act*. This act gives the
Atomic Energy Commission dictatorial powers
over the Ranger mining area, making it, among
other things, a serious criminal offence to
tamper with or hinder the proposed mine,
giving the Minister powers to expel anyone
from the site. It practically authorises martial
law. It is impossible to initiate proceedings
for unlawful arrest or detention if the security
forces abuse their power, without Government
permission.

Not only did the Fraser Government thus
amend the original proposals of the Woodward
Commission and Labor Government, it also
slashed funds to the Aboriginal bodies responsible for representing and assisting the isolated
communities wanting to reclaim their land.

Nevertheless, under this bill Aboriginal
people received legal recognition of their
right to own some of their tribal lands, for the
first time in Australian history since the arrival
of the British.

They also received recognition of their
right to control development of their tribal
lands, *if* these lands were already reserves or
crown land not already used by whites or did
not already have mining works planned for
them.

A major defect of the bill was that it 'forgot'
all those lands in the Northern Territory which
had already been given to Australian or foreign
cattle companies or other 'developers'. All it
restored to Aborigines were the leftovers.[2]

Many cases of Federal intervention have
been noted in earlier chapters. The following

26 THE FEDERAL GOVERNMENT AND LAND RIGHTS

In the early days of his Government Malcom Fraser succeeded in gaining an international reputation as a statesman by his efforts to bring about a solution in Zimbabwe in opposition to South African racism.

But inside Australia his Government shows no desire to do anything to restore Aboriginal rights. When he came to office, the Northern Territory land rights machinery was already effectively in place. He had committed his Government prior to the election not to scrap the Labor-prepared legislation. However, he immediately had it watered down as much as possible. Initially, nearly all powers were to be taken from the land councils, despite the Woodward recommendation that they be strong enough to resist pressures from the mining industry and others wanting Aboriginal land; also to be independent of the Government.) However, a strong campaign, particularly by central Australian Aborigines, forced the restoral of these powers.

He inserted in the *Northern Territory Land Rights Act* a number of clauses protecting the immediate interests of the mining industry.

Sub-clause 40 (5) stated that any company already granted a gas or oil exploration lease could now go ahead without Aboriginal permission.

Sub-clause 10 (3) stated that any mining lease granted before June 4th, 1976 could go ahead without Aboriginal permission. The mining companies were informed by the government of this clause well in advance of June 4th. Hence, Queensland Mines got their authorisation despite the Aboriginal veto and the strong earlier condemnation of the proposed mine by the Government Woodward Commission. Under this clause, Pancontinental got permission for their giant uranium mine despite an Aboriginal veto, so too did MIM get permission to start their giant lead, zinc and silver mine at Borroloola.

When the Fraser Government was asked in Parliament for the list of companies and mining

PSST. WANNA BUY A COUNTRY? VERY CHEEEP

SCHOFIELD

plans approved under this clause, the Government replied that the information was not available.[1]

Sub-clause 40 (6) specifically authorised the go-ahead of the Ranger mine without Aboriginal consent.

Sub-clause 40 (3) stated that if a company had an exploration lease before June 4th, then they could get a mining lease for this land without Aboriginal permission. (Several exploration leases for Arnhemland have been granted—Esso and others have been active.)

Sub-clause 40 (2) stated that when the Aborigines grant an exploration lease they must allow subsequent mining. Section 3 (5) excluded Aboriginal ownership of land on which there was a public road or right of way.

Sub-clause 11 (1) only allowed for Aboriginal trusts to be set up over 'traditional' land claims, and not for land to meet the chronic need of those who cannot reclaim their land under this is a summary of just a few of those by the Fraser Government.

—Fraser personally intervened to put pressure on Yunupingu, then chairman of the Northern Land Council. He reportedly threatened to substantially withdraw the Northern Territory land rights legislation.

— His government again intervened in February 1980 to protect the Ranger and Nabarlek mines by retrospectively taking away from traditional owners the right to object if the land council broke the law by agreeing to mining without securing the agreement of the traditional owers as a group.

—He refused to meet a delegation of Elders who wanted acknowledgement that Ayers Rock belonged to them even though they were prepared to leave it as a national park.

— Outside the Northern Territory, his Government has made absolutely no moves to restore land rights. Indeed, with Queensland and Western Australia, his Government has agreed not to support moves by the Aborigines to set up their own land councils and claim land.

— On Noonkanbah, Fraser twice intervened. Once he met personally with community representatives, who wasted their time coming to Derby to hear him tell them to allow Noonkanbah's sacred Pea Hill to be drilled. Another time, he tried to persuade Aboriginal delegates not to go to the United Nations in protest. When they did go, he sent word to the United Nations that the drilling was not on a sacred site.

—In his own electorate, he has refused the urgent requests of the Portland Aborigines to protect their sacred and historical sites from the Alcoa smelter. When the Aborigines went to his sheep station the first time, his wife met them to explain that her husband wasn't available— but 'Do go to meet him when he comes to his Portland office on his odd-grumbles day, next month'.

The Mara then sent a delegation to see him on Christmas day, 1980. Again he would not come out. So two of the delegation, Aboriginal flag flying high, walked up his long drive. They surprised Fraser sunbaking in his shirt-sleeves. He fled indoors calling for the police who shot

out of the house, wiping their mouths and with their guns in their hands! The delegation were escorted off the property.

Many Aboriginal people now feel that international pressure is essential if they are to ever have their rights recognised.

Mining industry comments on Fraser's electoral victory

The London *Mining Journal*, December 16th, 1977, commented:

The return to power of Mr Fraser's government is likely to result in more active efforts being made to encourage foreign investment. Although before the election most of the restrictions on foreign investment had been largely removed, the political uncertainties which existed prior to last Saturday's voting deterred any significant response for the majority of overseas mining groups. [But,] it is still clear that the government is not likely to be allowed to press ahead with its uranium programme without opposition from some unions and other groups within the community. Mr Fraser is unlikely to be deterred from pressing on.

Footnotes

1. The Fox Inquiry noted thirteen mineral leases had already been granted in the region the Inquiry was recommending to be a national park and in nearby parts of the adjacent Arnhemland Reserve. These included two for Ranger's first two pits, one for Queensland Mines, another one, like Queensland Mines, within the Arnhemland Reserve, three north-west of Ranger and six in the proposed southerly extension to the National Park. Also, thirteen exploration leases were authorised covering large areas. Fox also noted that, before the cut-off date of 4th June 1976 after which Aboriginal permission is necessary, about fifty other areas were applied for as mineral leases.
2. See also p. 176.

27 THE AUSTRALIAN MINING INDUSTRY COUNCIL – COUNTERING ABORIGINAL LAND CLAIMS

The policies of the Whitlam Government were strenuously opposed by the mining industry. Reports that at one stage Whitlam considered buying back Australian resources from CRA's parent company, RTZ in London, were not well received. Nor was his policy on Aboriginal land rights in the Northern Territory. The very idea of giving to the Aborigines a veto over mining developments was greeted with horror by the mining companies. They therefore launched a major campaign against the proposed legislation.

The mining industry contribute heavily to the opposition parties. CRA has admitted its own contributions went primarily in their direction and played a part in Whitlam's eventual defeat. A powerful Australian Free Enterprise Association was formed to lead what the *Age* newspaper called the 'capital counter-offensive'.[1]

The incoming Fraser Government, despite its immediate restoration of concessions to the mining companies, and its immediate cut in funds for Aboriginal organisations, was still committed by a pre-election promise to give Northern Territory Aborigines land rights.

Therefore, the campaign against Aboriginal land rights continued. The lead was taken by the Australian Mining Industry Council (AMIC) rather than by individual companies. (Despite its name, many of the companies it represents are foreign-owned.)

In 1976, AMIC fought against the *Land Rights Bill* being passed in any form. In their June 1976 newsletter, they based their arguments on the premise:

the special rights and interests of the Aboriginal people can be catered for most adequately through the present system, which protects citizens' rights generally . . . The legislation . . . will achieve a downgrading of the rights of the community as a whole to the detriment of everyone including the Aborigines . . .

The head of AMIC, a Mr Phillips, said that the legislation should be 'the number one priority' of the industry.[2]

Advertisements were placed by AMIC in the national press saying Aborigines should have no say at all in whether or not their land was mined. AMIC tried to justify this by saying that other Australians were not protected.

Senator Chaney replied that owners of land in Australia:

are given substantial protection against mining without the land owner's consent. The extent of protection varies from state to state, but in my state of Western Australia all developed and cultivated land is protected. Even pasture, including uncleared pasture, cannot be mined without the consent of the owner and occupier, if it is in bona fide and regular use.[3]

AMIC stated that to grant these powers to Aborigines:

would be divisive and would lead to long-term social problems because of the sense of discrimination engendered in other Territorians and Australians generally. It would also create a greater division between traditional Aborigines

and those who see land rights primarily in terms of financial gain. The granting of these exceptional powers to the Aboriginal people seems neither wise nor just.

Logically, AMIC should also have opposed any person or mining company having greater wealth than the average member of the population! This they did not do. Instead they advocated that Aborigines remain in their present ill-protected and exploited state, unable to protect their lands or culture from destruction. They used the threat of a white back-lash in the Northern Territory to argue against giving Aborigines any right to protect their land-based culture.

In 1978, before the Ranger Agreement was 'signed', AMIC produced a paper on land rights. This was attacked in the *Age* as a

cynical exercise to discredit attempts by Aborigines to protect what they see to be their rights. It paraded a spectre of racial violence, 'foreign' enclaves open only to blacks and a total halt to mining.[4]

An *Age* editorial two days later referred to AMIC's claim that there could be the emergence of

'a system of unauthorised totalitarian control by a minority within particular areas of Australia... To be blunt, the motivation for the attack on the Northern Land Council in such excessive and inflamatory language seems to come down to money. If Aborigines are trying to drive a hard bargain, that merely shows that they have learnt the ways of white men. They are operating within the framework of the law. They want to protect their land-based culture. They want generous compensation for the sacrifices they will have to make.[5]

In March 1979, AMIC issued another document on Aboriginal land rights, this time calling for revision both of the Northern Territory *Land Rights Bill* and of the South Australian *Pitjantjatjara Land Rights Bill*.

In this, they argued:

logic dictates that if the people as a whole own

what are termed Crown minerals, then a government elected by the people cannot give a selected few the privilege of either vetoing or extracting tribute from mining.

Leaving aside the Aboriginal claim to own the land as a birthright, this argument is a dangerous one for the mining industry. Logically it leads to the conclusion that the Government should not allot minerals to companies owned by a few for private profit, but instead set up public authorities to mine the deposits so the profits remain with the community.

Finally this paper stated:

While the Queensland and West Australian approach to the Aboriginal land rights question has been the subject of much criticism, they have in fact much to commend them.[6]

The approach of these Governments has been to deny all land rights to Aborigines; this then is the recommendation of the Australian Mining Industry Council.

Galarrwuy Yunupingu, the Aboriginal chairman of the Northern Land Council, answered the mining companies' claim that Aboriginal land rights cannot include sub-surface rights to minerals. He said:

The mining companies are always challenging Aboriginal people, they are always ignoring Aboriginal wishes... I think they say our land is just the top-soil... They don't know that the very core of the land itself, which is the mineral, is the very bone of the Aboriginal being. It is my bone. And when you go around and ask... every Aboriginal person about the mineral, that we don't have, [that instead] belongs to the Commonwealth Government, [they will say] that is taking the bone of the Aboriginal person and leaving him with just the skin and flesh... saying the Aboriginal person doesn't have mineral rights is like saying you got no bone... we just have to seek people within Australia or internationally for support on how we can stop uranium mining on Aboriginal land.[7]

The pressure on the mining companies from the Aboriginal communities and land councils, coupled with a frequently sympathetic media in the major cities of the south, has produced a more favourable response from some of the mining companies than from the State and Federal Governments.

One geologist explained this:

It's better to take Jackie for a ride in a helicopter or drive your scrapper around a particular clump of rock than upset him and find yourself in court for six months.[8]

Although Aborigines seem invariably to lose these court battles because their rights are not adequately recognised, public support for the Aboriginal underdog and the legal costs make these legal actions something for the companies to avoid.

Even so, the companies seem unprepared to recognise Aboriginal rights at all if by this they will lose substantial profits.

Current mining company tactics

Many companies have been notably disturbed by the level of both Aboriginal opposition to their activities and public support for the Aborigines.

This has occasioned top-level discussions between senior company officials, the Australian Mining Industry Council and the Department of Aboriginal Affairs to try to work out an appropriate code of conduct, including a policy on the hiring of Aboriginal workers.

Unfortunately, the adopted policy seems to have these aspects:

1. Ignore Aboriginal land councils wherever possible. Thus Comalco has expressly stated, as has RTZ in England, that it will not recognise the North Queensland Land Council. CRA did not consult the Kimberley Land Council before attempting an agreement to mine at Argyle. The grounds for this are purportedly that these land councils are not recognised by the State or Federal Governments. The Central Land Council was long ignored by Magellan Oil which hoped to stimulate Federal intervention. It did not, and

eventually negotiated terms.

2. Isolate any Aboriginal group or individual who is a 'traditional owner' and concentrate company pressure and offers on this person or group (e.g. Argyle in Kimberleys, Ranger, Nabarlek).

3. Attempt to discredit white advisers accepted and used by the Aborigines as 'outsiders', or 'stirrers' or 'manipulating the Aborigines' (as at Noonkanbah, Oenpelli etc.). Use the law to remove these advisers if possible (as at Oombulgurri).

4. Offer tangible community services rather than money. This is very much cheaper and often more appreciated by local Aboriginal communities because they are not money orientated but need to survive. Thus in 1980 CRA offered to restore a water supply at Oombulgurri in return for access; CRA offered $200,000 in community services at Argyle; Esso offered a sporting oval and changing rooms at Beagle Bay; Alcoa offered a $50,000 museum building at Portland and Amax offered two dams and some fencing at Noonkanbah. This is equivalent to offering beads and bangles. For the West Australian Government beads and bangles are too much. It says Aborigines have no special rights to compensation for loss of tribal land.

5. Invoke public pressure, using arguments that:
— it is racist to deny us access to Aboriginal lands;
— minerals belong to all Australians because the Crown claims them, therefore all Australians should benefit from them, therefore we should be allowed to claim the minerals (even if we operate for foreign interests);
— if we don't mine, Australia is in danger of invasion from a mineral hungry world. (Why shouldn't operating mines attract foreign interests more?)

— it is unfair to other Aboriginal groups if one group gets a financial return for the good fortune of having rich minerals, therefore no Aborigines should get any royalties (as said Comalco)

6. Offer to safeguard sacred sites. This offer may give access to most of the land. There is no

The Ranger mine gets under way *(N.T. News)*.

These tactics have all been used, it seems, at one time or another. They combine to damage considerably the Aboriginal ability to negotiate a fair agreement. They are divisive. They are calculated to minimise a company's costs, and minimise the return to the Aboriginal community.

Footnotes

1. This association is now known as 'Enterprise Australia'. For further details see article by its Director, published by Australian Mining Industry Council, March 1979.
2. Reported in the *Age*, 20 August 1976.
3. *Northern Territory News*, November 1976.
4. *Age*, 18 February 1978.
5. *Age*, editorial, 20 February 1978.
6. AMIC document on Aboriginal land rights, March 1979.
7. Interview by Nina Gladitz, 15 May 1978, privately communicated to author.
8. *Daily News*, 28 March 1980.
9. Newman Mines public relations officer in interview by the author, Newman, September 1979.

harm offering, as without such an offer, there is no hope of Aboriginal agreement (e.g. Esso at Beagle Bay; CRA on Noonkanbah). Employ an Aboriginal Elder, otherwise you will not know where the sites are. This gives the opportunity to try to influence a key Elder. Maybe you can get him to agree (as at Nabarlek) by offering his clan group particular benefits and saying other Aboriginal Elders want to take these from him, thus splitting the community.

7. Employ four or five other Aborigines as labourers with surveying teams. This gives some Aborigines a vested interest while cutting company costs. If mining starts, offer to employ 'employable' Aborigines. This does not tie company hands and is interpreted differently by different companies. Thus BHP on Groote Eylandt trains local Aborigines to take skilled workers' jobs, but at Newman an official dismissed having an Aboriginal training scheme as 'racist'.[9]

8. If valuable minerals are found in sacred areas, deny it is sacred in the full meaning of the word and dispute it as if Aborigines were not reliable experts on Aboriginal religion (Amax at Noonkanbah). Or, declare ignorance. If you suspect a site is sacred, get nothing in writing on this from the Aborigines, do not hire an Aboriginal adviser, make oral, nor written promises (as CRA at Argyle).

9. Do not give Aborigines an environmental impact statement describing likely impact if mining should follow exploration (as at Jigalong, Noonkanbah, etc).

28 THE WAY FORWARD

There are two principal requirements for the ending of the strife between Aboriginal and White in Australia. The first is more an Aboriginal responsibility and is one which Aboriginal people have put much work into. It is the building up of self-reliance and pride among their own people despite all the efforts of the whites to keep them dependent and weak. Examples of this are given below.

The second requirement for the ending of strife between whites and blacks in Australia is a white responsibility. It is the return of Aboriginal land, with its mineral rights attached, to Aboriginal communities in need of land and to traditional owners, as well as restitution for the terrible wrongs inflicted on the Aboriginal race. This is simply a matter of justice. The second part of this chapter considers what such a recognition would mean in terms of conduct by miners and the call for a 'treaty'.

Noonkanbah: A people standing proud

Robert Bropho, an Aboriginal spokesman for the fringedwellers of Western Australia, wrote of what he saw at Noonkanbah:

As we pulled up in front of the homestead, it was a sight to see hundreds of full-blood Aboriginal women, children and old men, men with their big hats, check shirts, moleskin riding breeches and high heeled boots who approached us . . . They spoke freely of their surroundings there on Noonkanbah Station. They had their own school going there on the premises, own stores, huge workshops, huge stock-pens. Everyone seemed to be busy moving about especially the Aboriginal women. As we stood there in a group, talking, in the far distance in the direction where we came clouds of dust started to rise . . . It was a huge head of horses being brought in by the black stockmen . . . riders started to pass us sitting in the saddle tall and straight, purple-black Aboriginal men

and Aboriginal boys, sitting in the saddle like they were born to be there. It was a sight to see from an Aboriginal man's point of view that these proud black beings trying their bloody hardest to keep their own bloody surrounding and create employment for themselves.

Sitting in their saddles with their straight backs, with their heads held high and their chins stuck out, challenging the bloody white man and his government, saying:

'Put me down again and I'll get up and do exactly what I want to do. I'll prove to you once and for all that I'm capable of being master of my own destiny.'[1]

The Nomads of Strelley Station

One of the most powerful stories this century of Aboriginal self-reliance is that of the self-styled 'Nomads' of Strelley Station in the Pilbara of Western Australia. It is a story of Aboriginal people who struck for decent wages, who opened their own mines to purchase what they needed and bought their own cattle stations.

By 1905 the Aborigines of much of the Pilbara were virtual slaves on the cattle stations. Aborigines who escaped sometimes joined the local gold miners and made money from mining. However, the police were sent out periodically to round them up and return them in chains to the stations.

During the Second World War some Aborigines found themselves employed on more equal terms by the army. They were needed as wharfies in Port Hedland and got better wages there too. They began to demand equal wages on the stations. They organised themselves. In 1946 they simultaneously walked off on strike from over twenty cattle stations and from jobs in the main towns.

The police tried to break the strike. Two Aboriginal organisers, Dooley and Clancy, were jailed for the crime of 'enticing natives' away from lawful employment without Government permission. A white man, Don McLeod, who had been invited to join with the Aborigines by Elders to help them deal with whites, was also arrested for 'being within five chains of a native camp'. But he was freed by the police when hundred of Aborigines marched on the jail. Later more Aborigines were arrested but the police still failed to break the strike. After the strike had lasted several years, wages for Aborigines were forced up on the stations and the strike had succeeded.

But this was not the only aim of the strike. Many of the strikers determined to work together to open their own mines and to earn money both to support themselves and purchase their own stations.

By 1949 they had started the Pinden Movement which worked as a co-operative to build up self-reliant settlements while keeping up traditional culture. By 1951 they had 600 members living in several different camps, using miner's rights to set up their camps where they wished. They formed the Northern Development and Mining Company and were the largest mining enterprise in the Pilbara. They fulfilled one of their ambitions by buying Yandeyarra Station and three others from mining profits. Using explosives and hand-tools they mined tin, copper, gold, wolfram, manganese and other minerals.

Then hard times followed. The Government took over their stations and made them into an official Aboriginal reserve under Governmental control. This is now the only Aboriginal reserve in the heart of the Pilbara. But some of the Aborigines left Yandeyarra and formed Nomads Ltd. They continued to support themselves by mining, still with Don McLeod, and by some port work. Eventually they obtained Strelley Station, where they now live.

This station community has today a model Aboriginal school where both Aboriginal culture and European skills are taught. They make their own books in their own language as well as in English. It is a thriving community.

In 1979, when the author visited, they were host to a great gathering of the people of their nation. They are the people of the Western Desert. They are now helping financially with the establishment of other bi-cultural schools. One of these is on Noonkanbah Station. Great emphasis is put on strengthening their culture by making it an essential part of their children's education.

These people are still standing strong and united with their Aboriginal brothers and sisters on other stations and camps. Their story shows that mining need not be opposed by Aboriginal people, that it can be done with respect to Aboriginal law and sacred places and the land. Aboriginal people need not always be used and exploited by mining as has happened again and again in Australia.

The Aboriginal outstation movement

The outstation movement throughout northern and central Australia is a sign of Aboriginal determination to once more be independent of white supervision and to live on their traditional lands.

The mass killings had stopped, the epidemics were less severe, there was no longer as much need to keep close to mission stations. Their tribal lands were often empty, open to being settled by whites without any Elders to protect the sacred places. The longer they stayed in the mission settlements away from their lands, supervised by whites, the greater was the danger for their culture.

For all these reasons, in the 1970s Aboriginal people started moving out of the settlements and back to their tribal lands. They won some support from the Whitlam Government for this move. This support continued under the Fraser Government. In some places airstrips were put in to allow emergency medical assistance and regular visits from teachers. This was in great contrast to the attitude of the previous Federal Governments, and of the current Queensland State Government which opposed such outstations as a hindrance to 'assimilation'.

The Elders began the move back, followed by the younger people, determined to live by their law in settlements and lands controlled by themselves. The authority of the Elders was being re-established.

Today the population of many of the mission stations has been halved. For example, by 1980, Hermannsburg Mission had lost 77% of its former population of 700. Over twenty outstations were established by people once resident at Oenpelli. The people of Yirrkala established sixty outstations, thus escaping from the influence of the Gove mining town.

The numbers on an outstation vary from perhaps seven to about sixty-five. Many live a modified traditional life. There is often not enough of their traditional foods because of the cattle. They may keep cattle themselves and make regular trips to the main settlement for supplies.

Many of these settlements still remain dependent on Government social services for a cash income, a situation that could change completely if they were to receive just compensation for their lost lands, damaged economy and disrupted way of life.

The outstation movement is today one of the most important developments right across northern and central Australia. The people are reclaiming their land, and the supervising institutions, from missions to Government welfare departments, are losing their control.

Health and legal Services

In the cities over the last ten years, Aborigines have started and built up under their own initiative a national network of free medical and legal aid services. These still continue to operate despite losing some of the support from Federal funds they won from the Whitlam Government. The Federal Government persists in giving much of the health funds for Aborigines to much less cost-effective State Health Departments forcing the Aboriginal Health Services, which treat many more Aborigines in the regions and cities where they operate than do the State services, to fight for their

Aboriginal vigil in Melbourne in support of Noonkanbah, 1980. A mock drilling rig was erected in the cathedral grounds (Jan Roberts).

survival. They are more than just a medical health service. They are centres of community life.

The Aboriginal Legal Services have been very active in supporting the land rights struggles. For example, the Sydney Legal Service supported the Paul Coe challenge to the denial of Aboriginal land ownership rights; Melbourne Aboriginal Legal Aid has been very active in supporting the Mara people of Portland in their fight against Alcoa.

The land councils

Most importantly, Aborigines outside the Northern Territory are now organising their resistance by setting up regional land councils similar to those of the Northern Territory. These councils unite the widely scattered Aboriginal communities and aid their struggles to protect their land.

Outside the Northern Territory and the north-west parts of South Australia, these land councils are not recognised by or financed by the Government. They are all very poor, but are increasingly effective. They are all democratic organisations with executives appointed by the communities.

The officially recognised land councils in January 1981 were the Northern, the Tiwi (which split from the Northern), the Central and the Pitjantjatjara. These all have the legal power to force mining companies to negotiate for the use of that land that is recognised as Aboriginal.

The first to be established without governmental help were the North Queensland and the Kimberley Land Councils. There is now a very active South-Eastern Land Council. Land councils are being organised in many other parts of Australia.

All of these land councils have as primary goals the protection of the lands of the Aboriginal people and the regaining of Aboriginal control over these lands.

When the Noonkanbah people had their sacred place desecrated by the oil-drilling rig in August 1980, they called a meeting of all the land councils at Noonkanbah. Six land councils attended. At this meeting they decided to form a national federation of land councils to give their people a stronger national and international voice. This federation will strengthen the growing international recognition of Australian Aborigines as a colonised people with the right to control their own affairs.

The Aboriginal Mining Information Centre

The Noonkanbah meeting of land councils in September 1980 also gave general approval to a proposal to establish a national Aboriginal Mining Information Centre.[2]

The North Queensland Land Council decided, with the agreement of the Kimberley and South-Eastern Land Councils, that the centre should start work immediately and operate nationally and internationally from a Melbourne base. (Melbourne is the centre for much of the Australian mining industry.) The centre will come under the National Federation when the Federation is fully formed.

The centre serves as the Aboriginal people's own information service on the mining industry. Too often Aboriginal communities are left in complete ignorance as to the plans of mining companies for their land.

Its other major role is to act as a counter to the influence of the Australian Mining Industry Council. It works nationally and internationally for the adoption of policies that respect Aboriginal rights both to their land and to their culture.

Recognition of Aboriginal land and mineral rights

This book paints a dismal picture of the colonisation of Australia. Some might say, what about all those non-Aborigines who tried to stop the killing, to improve Aboriginal health, who gave themselves unselfishly for their brothers and sisters who were Aborigines and oppressed?

There have always been a few white people who oppose the continued exploitation of Aboriginal people. Sadly, they have always been a small minority in Australia and have never succeeded in ending the offical denial of Aboriginal rights. There are far fewer who support Aboriginal people in a non-paternalistic way. Most presume eventual Aboriginal assimilation into a white way of life.

After all, a country which only gave the first Australians citizenship in 1964 probably has little to be proud of.

There are many people working for mining companies who are puzzled by the level of Aboriginal opposition to their operations and who adamantly deny they are racist.

This book is written in the hope that if people learn more of what the history of Australia has been for Aboriginal people, they may understand better how Aboriginal people feel today as they lose still more of their land to white people. It is written in the hope that people will listen more to what Aboriginal people have to say for themselves and seek to learn from Aboriginal culture rather than hold it in contempt.

Perhaps there is a way forward based on mutual respect and justice and not of continued exploitation. Seeking such a way forward, the Pitjantjatjara Land Council on September 29th, 1980 decided to:

Call for a national meeting of all land councils and of traditional owners with the Australian Mining Industry Council and the Australian Petroleum Industry Council as soon as possible to agree to a statement of principles dealing with mining on Aboriginal land and the protection of Aboriginal culture, communities and environment. [3]

Early in 1981 a set of guidelines for the mining industry and others was prepared by the Aboriginal Mining Information Centre. At the time of writing these are being submitted to the land councils for discussion and possible ratification. They have already been approved by the South Eastern Land Council.

These guidelines are included here as an indication of a possible way forward.

A code of behaviour for mining companies and other developers, local authorities, State and Federal Governments.

1. When planning operations of any nature, including archaeological surveys, for any bush areas, including on pastoral properties and farms, notify the local Aboriginal communities and their nominated representatives. Failing this, contact the regional land council or other representative Aboriginal organisation. (Note that areas near towns can be of importance to Aborigines.)

2. Tell them precisely what operations are planned and where. Detail the full environmental consequences utilising maps, diagrams and/or photographs. Include the infrastructure needs—roads, camps, dams, wells, etc., for your operation.

3. Tell them what may happen if your operation is successful—e.g., if you discover the mineral you are seeking in commercial quantities. Illustrate this with photographs or maps of similar developments elsewhere, and include probable infrastructre requirements.

4. Contribute to the cost of negotiations for the Aborigines so that they are able to negotiate as equals. This should include the cost of community meetings. (Some communites have gone hungry and neglected vital works because of the need for all to take part in continual meetings.)

5. Recognise the Aboriginal right to select their own advisers.

6. Do not request a map of all Aboriginal sacred sites. This information is often confidential in nature and is only produced through fear of losing these places. Instead produce your own plans and request permission to use the area designated. Accept Aboriginal decision as to what access is permissable. (This is the method used under the South Australian Pitjantjatjara Land Rights Bill. It is much prefered by the Elders as it minimises the need to give religious secrets to outsiders.)

7. Do not press for a fast decision. Time must be allowed for Aboriginal people to follow their law which may call for extensive consultations and discussions.

8. Offer fair compensation and financial return for minerals extracted and for other uses of their land, based on internationally recognised levels and the company's expected profits, with provision for inflation.

9. Accept the Aboriginal right to determine conditions and to veto. Note that the final decisions on these matters in Aboriginal law rests completely with the people responsible

for this land in their tradition. These people may not all be living in the same community. They must collectively agree. A land council cannot validly give permission without the collective agreement of these 'owners'.

The conditions set may :

a) Forbid access to certain areas.

b) Limit access to other areas.

c) Minimise the area to be disturbed.

d) Allow Aborigines to continuously monitor the environmental impact of your operations, adjusting conditions if agreed limits prove excessive and obtaining compensation for environmental damage.

e) Ask for regular financial reports on the project.

f) Ask for restoration costs to Aboriginal requirements.

g) Include classes for workers in appropriate Aboriginal law and culture (as laid down at Ranger).

h) Control the use of alcohol and the access of the company's staff to the Aboriginal community.

Such conditions are imposed by sovereign peoples on mines and other developments around the world. Aboriginal people in Australia have a right to similar conditions since they have never ceded their sovereignty. Without recognition of their rights to negotiate the use of their land and minerals, they remain a colonised people.

Some sections of the mining industry are beginning to accept some Aboriginal land rights, some are strongly resisting. But gradually Australian laws are being re-shaped and, despite the resistance of some States, it is hoped that it will not be long before there is a just settlement in all parts of Australia.

This is only a hope. It will not come about easily. It would be naive to expect this to happen without a backlash from those white Australians who feel their interests threatened. They are already financing campaigns to prevent such a just settlement. This can be seen from the public relations programme of such companies as the CRA-dominated Argyle consortium (described in Chapter 23, pp. 160-1).

But, despite this, Aboriginal people have expressed their hope that a just settlement can be achieved with good will. The increasing ability of Aboriginal people to get their voices heard nationally and internationally is increasing public pressure for such a settlement and countering mining company opposition with remarkable effectiveness.

If not only a just share in the revenues but also the adoption of a code of practice based on respect for Aboriginal law, such as that outlined above, can be achieved, then the conflict between miners and Aborigines will be over.

The call for a treaty and bill of rights

Finally, Aboriginal people have been calling for a treaty drawn up between themselves and the Australian Government as between two sovereign peoples. This treaty should include a bill of rights. It should be legally enforcable and embodied in the Australian constitution.

Kevin Gilbert, a well-known Aboriginal writer and campaigner, wrote powerfully of this in an article published in the Aboriginal newspaper *AIM* in 1980. He was critical of what he saw as a watered down and useless version of a treaty being discussed by the National Aboriginal Conference, a consultative representative body set up by the Federal Government. He said that this proposed 'Makarrata' agreement would be 'a deal between white government and men with no status.'

He wrote:

We, the Aboriginal people, have owned all of this country from the Dreamtime, from the time before time began. We are the owners of this land. We are ruler, king, of our country and we must make white government talk to us as kings of our own country.

He said that a treaty requires the prior recognition of Aboriginal people as a nation. It could not be negotiated by a body with only consultative status and dependent on the white Government for its existence. But if such a recognition were made and a representative body set up by Aboriginal people, then perhaps a real treaty could be negotiated.

But before this could happen, much educational and political work has to be done to make Australians ready for such a treaty. This may take a long time. The various smaller Aboriginal nations, or tribes, would need to approve and work over the details for themselves so that the treaty is in accordance with their own law. But the signing of such a treaty may well be the only way to finally set Australia's black-white relations on a foundation of justice.

Before such a treaty is finalised, white Australians must start returning land needed by Aboriginal people back to the original owners with its mineral rights attached. This is only just.

Aboriginal people are not going to die out

The following words of Robert Bropho's seem an appropriate conclusion to this book. Robert Bropho is from Western Australia which in 1979 'celebrated' its 150th Anniversary.

It's been 150 years now since the coming of the white man. The white man and the off-spring of the white man have come a long way in 150 years, and how far has the full-blood Aboriginal moved? He's still sitting on the fringes of any town in the continent of Australia. He's still sitting under the tree staring into space wondering in his own mind is there a place for him on this continent which he once owned? Looking around him at the pace of greediness and lust for power that the white man's human rat-race has set . . .

Aboriginal people are not going to die out. The full-blood Aboriginal will be around 'till the end of time, so it's no good the white man thinking and guessing and saying that the full-blood's going to die out. He may not be an educated gift-of-the-gab man but he knows that he's got the stamina and the will-power within him to suffer. He knows that the day will come when the white man and his government cannot ignore him any longer as a third-class full-blood citizen.

The Aboriginal problem will always be on the conscience of the white man. The white man came. He did not conquer. He invaded. He broke all the ten commandments in the bible. He stole, he committed adultery, he killed, he raped and plundered. He destroyed Aboriginal people. He used him up. And he made him what he is today, a fringedweller on the fringes of town. He's turned him into a dole-bludger by kicking him off stations and shutting down reserves. He's forcing him to be something that he doesn't want to be. He's trying to brainwash him with white ideas. The only thing he hasn't done yet and that is to get a can of white paint and paint him white. Aboriginal people are a race of people without a country. They have no freedom of choice. They are not masters of their own destiny from a white man's point of view.

Aboriginal people and all Ministers concerned in the welfare of the Aboriginal people are in a position now to solve the Aboriginal problem, only if the white man was to listen to the black man's ideas and let him be master of his own destiny, and that destiny is land.[4]

Footnotes
1. Robert Bropho, *Fringedweller* (Alternative Publishing Co-operative, Sydney, 1980, p. 134.
2. The author has been working as Research Officer for the Aboriginal Mining Information Centre.
3. Pitjantjatjara Land Council statement sent to other land councils, 29 September 1980.
4. Robert Bropho, p. 153.

An update to the 2008 Edition

An astonishingly hopeful event happened on February 07, 2008. The new Australian Prime Minister Kevin Rudd said in Parliament: 'There comes a time in the history of nations when their peoples must become fully reconciled to their past if they are to go forward with confidence to embrace their future. Our nation, Australia, has reached such a time. That is why the parliament is today here assembled: to deal with this unfinished business of the nation, to remove a great stain from the nation's soul and, in a true spirit of reconciliation, to open a new chapter in the history of this great land, Australia.'

'Last year I made a commitment to the Australian people that if we formed the next government … we would in parliament say sorry to the stolen generations. Today I honour that commitment … But, should there still be doubts as to why we must now act, let the parliament reflect for a moment on the following facts: that, between 1910 and 1970, between 10 and 30 per cent of Indigenous children were forcibly taken from their mothers and fathers; that, as a result, up to 50,000 children were forcibly taken from their families; that this was the product of the deliberate, calculated policies of the state as reflected in the explicit powers given to them under statute; that this policy was taken to such extremes by some in administrative authority that the forced extractions of children of so-called 'mixed lineage' were seen as part of a broader policy of dealing with 'the problem of the Aboriginal population.'

'One of the most notorious examples of this approach was from the Northern Territory Protector of Natives, who stated: "Generally by the fifth and invariably by the sixth generation, all native characteristics of the Australian aborigine are eradicated. The problem of our half-castes' to quote the 'protector', 'will quickly be eliminated by the complete disappearance of the black race, and the swift submergence of their progeny in the white...'

'It is for the nation to bring the first two centuries of our settled history to a close, as we begin a new chapter. We embrace with pride, admiration and awe these great and ancient cultures we are truly blessed to have among us, cultures that provide a unique, uninterrupted human thread linking our Australian continent to the most ancient prehistory of our planet.

'Growing from this new respect, we see our Indigenous brothers and sisters with fresh eyes, with new eyes, and we have our minds wide open as to how we might tackle, together, the great practical challenges that Indigenous Australia faces in the future.'[1]

What he said reminded me of a woman I met while making a film with Aboriginal Elder Robert Bropho in 1984.[2] She wept as she told how, as a child of mixed race, she was hunted down by the police. 'I shivered with fright when I saw the officer riding up. My mother put me in the sugar bag, and made as if to sit on me. The officer asked 'What is in that bag?' and she replied, 'Only my tucker.' 'But finally they got me and took me away and I could only see my mother at the gate.' 'As for the 'full-bloods' like my brother, they said they were useless and

---

[1] http://www.alp.org.au/media/0208/spepm130.php More is quoted in the new foreword.

[2] The film was coproduced by the author with Aboriginal elder Robert Bropho, and was entitled 'Munda Nyuringu: He has taken the land, he believes it is his, he will not give it back.' It won a unanimous Best Documentary nomination in the AFI Awards – and it is available from the publishers of this book. See www.janineroberts.com for details.

threw them away.'

The Canberra Times reported on February 25th 2008 that Aborigines still typically have a life expectancy of 15 years less than white Australians. Many are still extremely poor. In 2007 a 5-year study of 45 mining contracts with Aboriginal communities found half were 'basket cases that should never have been entered into' and half delivered few cultural and monetary benefits.[3] (From my experience as a mining consultant with the Aboriginal Land Councils, this was because Aboriginal communities were often told that is all that is possible.) Australia's wealthiest mining regions had the worst records. 'Many Aboriginal groups were no better off, or even worse off, than they would be in the absence of any agreement between the two parties.'[4]

In 2006 the cancer rates among Aboriginal people living near Australia's biggest uranium mine, the Ranger owned now by RTZ, were found to be almost double the expected rate. There had been no monitoring of Aboriginal health during the 20 years this mine has been in operation – yet 'since 1981 there were over 120 spillage and leaks of contaminated water at this mine located in the World Heritage-listed Kakadu National Park.'[5] This park is home to 2.5 million water birds, 900 plant species, 50 species of mammals and 100 species of amphibians and reptiles – and contains many brilliant displays of ancient Aboriginal rock art.

These same Aborigines in 2006-7 were told by the Federal government that it would recognise that Jabiru, the mining town set up on their traditional lands, was on their land if, and only if they agreed to a new RTZ uranium mine. The Mirarr indignantly refused.[6]

Earlier I mentioned the Aboriginal opposition to another prospective uranium mine, that of Yeelirrie (p134). Today this is in the hands of BHP Billiton and Aboriginal approval is still not yet given. Around this area live some 2,500 Martu Aborigines, Martu meaning 'One of Us.' The majority of these people are at least trilingual, with English as one of their languages.

In a recent land claim judgement in their favour, it was stated: 'The claimants are among a number of Western Desert peoples who maintain a very strong cultural base in their traditional laws and customs, and … close connections to their lands despite many decades of change stemming from the advent of Whites and the powerful impacts of governmental policies and practices. Because the frontier of contact between Whites and Aborigines continued in their lands until as recently as the 1960s, these groups are able to describe and demonstrate in great detail their laws and customs. Their religiously based traditions are embedded in a wealth of cultural elements: mythology, story, song, ritual, the features of the landscape, and secret-sacred paraphernalia – all of which contribute to a vibrant religious life that connects them to their creators and their homelands.'

Some moved from their lands as Europeans arrived, 'But this resulted in only a brief period of physical absence of the claimants from their traditional territories. Through the cultural mechanism of dream-spirit journeys, they kept contact with and responsibility for their countries while physically elsewhere. That is what they had always done in the desert where such absences were sometimes forced by lack of water and/or food resources in their core territories. Their hunter gathering activities continued and they went back into the desert from time to time so they did not lose contact. There was no serious cultural break with their traditional roots.

---

[3] Report by Griffith University academic Ciaran O'Faircheallaigh.

[4] Reported in The Australian by Victoria Laurie on 30 January 2007.

[5] Sydney Morning Herald 23 November 2006

[6] The Age, 6th March 2006

The return of people to live on the country has supported the maintenance of law and custom among them. They remain one of the most strongly "tradition-oriented" groups of Aboriginal people in Australia today partly because of the protection that their physical environment gave them against non-Aboriginal intruders. It is not a welcoming environment for those who do not know how to locate and use its resources for survival. Of great importance is the continuing strength of their belief in the Dreaming.'

'Prior to the arrival of Europeans, the huge Western Desert region, in which this claim lies, would have had the lowest population densities and the highest levels of Aboriginal mobility in the continent. These adaptations were necessary to live in this extremely marginal area, described by Gould as "the harshest physical environment on earth ever inhabited by man before the Industrial Revolution".'

The Aboriginal claimants came to the Hearing bearing a 'piti', or traditional wooden dish containing 'sand from their country' as a symbol of their claim. They presented this to the Tribunal - and it was returned to them with the legal decision that they had 'the right to possess, occupy, use and enjoy the land and waters of the determination area to the exclusion of all others' – and to mine ochre.

However the Tribunal decided it did not have the authority to return to them that part of their lands that is now the Rudall River National Park, with its important Aboriginal camping sites and permanent water holes. This, it ruled, had been legally removed from them by the decision to make it a national park. This is extraordinary given that Aboriginal rights to Uluru and Kakadu National Parks are recognized, and given that the Aborigines owned this land for millennia.

In this book I have not told of what travelling throughout the Outback with Aboriginal people has meant to me. It has given me the ability to see this richly varied land with new eyes. It has immeasurably enriched my life. I feel immensely privileged to have shared so much with them – and to have helped a little in their fight for justice. The carved 'piti' mentioned above – Aboriginal people also used such a dish to launch this book. They took it on a bed of sand in a 'piti' to give it to RTZ, thus endorsing the words of this book as of their land.

I have been to many of the places mentioned in this book. I have slept under the night sky in the desert, on sand warmed by a fire that was moved away, with a hip-hollow dug so I might be comfortable. I have enjoyed goanna and file snake. I have been shown how to gather roots from which one can pour water, and how to cut bark – although I often made a mess of the latter!

I had a game I played with their children when in the Outback. I would point to a tree or a bush and say: 'That is a rubbish plant. We can burn that one. ' The children would always chorus, 'No, Jani - not that one.' They delighted to tell me how it was used for medicine or food, sometimes with complex preparation. I could not find a plant that a 12-year old did not know of a use for it. This is their literacy. I remember one child in far north Queensland being puzzled about 'fields'. For him it was like clearing the shelves of a supermarket and leaving only wheat.

Their elders have told me how to interpret the night sky and spoken to me of their Gods, telling me what I can say of them to others. They have told me of the Dreaming tracks that weave this continent from side to side, with songs and dances and trading tracks, through the lands of many nations and languages, uniting a vast land in a non-violent way few peoples elsewhere have achieved.

I hope others now come to work with them to protect the land. The names of many Aboriginal people come to me, too many to recount, some of these my aunts and uncles that looked after me on my travels, some the senior men or women called 'Dreamers' with whom I camped. Thank you, and strength to you. I hope this book helps in some small way.

INDEX

Printed in the United Kingdom by
Lightning Source UK Ltd., Milton Keynes
137398UK00001BA/2/P